THEOLOGY AT THE
END OF MODERNITY

ESSAYS IN HONOR OF GORDON D. KAUFMAN

THEOLOGY AT THE END OF MODERNITY

Edited by
SHEILA GREEVE DAVANEY

TRINITY PRESS INTERNATIONAL
Philadelphia

First Published 1991

Trinity Press International
3725 Chestnut Street
Philadelphia, PA 19104

Interior design and production management by Publishers' WorkGroup
Cover design by Brian Preuss

Library of Congress Cataloging-in-Publication Data

Theology at the end of modernity : essays in honor of Gordon D.
Kaufman / edited by Sheila Greeve Davaney.
    p.   cm.
Includes index.
    ISBN 1–56338–011–0 (hard) : — ISBN 1–56338–017–X (paper)
    1. Theology. 2. Theology—20th century. I. Kaufman, Gordon D.
II. Davaney, Sheila Greeve.
BR50.T44 1991
230′.09′049—dc20   91–13306
                                           CIP

Contents

Acknowledgments

Many persons have contributed to this volume, most especially the theologians whose essays not only honor Gordon D. Kaufman but further the contemporary theological discussion. Others have also made this volume possible. Prominent among them is Harold W. Rast, director of Trinity Press International, whose enthusiastic commitment to the project has nurtured it to a successful conclusion. The excellent work done by Stephanie Egnotovich and Publishers' Work-Group added to the quality of the essays while remaining true to the intentions of each author. I would also like to express appreciation to my secretary, Gene Crytzer, and my student assistant, Joe Gorman, for all the work they put in on the volume.

Foreword

The title of this volume, *Theology at the End of Modernity*, is not one that would have immediately occurred to me in reflecting on my own theological work over the past thirty-five years. It seems to suggest an acceptance of the claim, quite fashionable today, that the "modern period" of Western cultural history has run its course and that we are now moving rapidly into something called "postmodernity"—a brave new world that will leave behind many of the foolish and destructive moves of the human spirit over the past three hundred years. Because this volume of essays has been put together in my honor, the title may seem to imply that the theological standpoint on which I have been working claims to be somehow poised to carry us forward into this new age. In my opinion, however, no one is in a position to make momentous historical judgments of this sort, however much we might wish we could peer into the future. We are much too close to the events of our own time to be able to distinguish the sort of patterns into which those events may today be falling.

Judgments on the question of modernity's end depend heavily, of course, on one's own interpretation of what has been most important about the modern period—its early understanding of itself as the beginning of a new age in which a universal, ahistorical rationality would overcome the superstitions of tradition and bring lasting peace and order into human life; the rise of the modern state and the modern sciences, together with the enormous growth of technology; the gradually growing critical consciousness which led, in the nineteenth and twentieth centuries, to the discovery of our radical historicity, the historical embeddedness and relativity of every dimension of human existence including our rationality; or perhaps something else. For my part, I am inclined to see and to judge "modernity" more in light of the emergence of the third of these themes during this period than in terms of the first two, though they also, of course, have been very important. What we are today witnessing may be the final dying away of certain mistaken but widely heralded early emphases of "the modern period," while other insights and understandings are gaining in influence and strength. Given this sort of continuity/discontinuity with the present, it would seem to be a debatable point (at best) whether we are really entering a genuinely new historical era.

I am pleased to point out (in view of these observations) that what is actually claimed by the title of this volume is more modest than I suggested above. The title does not in fact announce some "new age" into which we are entering but limits itself to suggesting that we are moving toward the end of what we have heretofore thought of as "modernity." Since what modernity is and means has become quite problematic, it now seems important to many, as Sheila Davaney puts it in the opening words of her introductory chapter, to undertake "the profound reevaluation of [its] assumptions and projects"—that is, to engage in a thorough questioning and reassessment of it. There would seem to be no reason to disagree with that judgment or to discount the importance of theologians participating actively in that task. The contributors to this volume are obviously all engaged in such fresh rethinking, and I am deeply touched that these colleagues and former students—all of them good friends—have brought their essays together here and published them in my honor.

In my teaching and writing I have always been concerned to ascertain and to conserve the major insights to which theological reflection in the modern age has come, especially as it has sought to appropriate newer understandings of the natural world, of human historicity, and of the importance of critical consciousness. I have regarded my own theological project—to develop an understanding of human existence that was thoroughly historical but avoided the sharp bifurcation between history and nature so characteristic of much German philosophical and theological reflection—as essentially an extension of earlier modern thinking on such issues. It took me a good many years and some rather involved experimentation (cf. *Systematic Theology: A Historicist Perspective* [1968] and *God the Problem* [1972]) before I realized how radical were the implications of these concerns for the understanding of what theology is and can contribute to human life. Not until the writing of my *Essay on Theological Method* (first edition published in 1975) did I feel I was really beginning to grasp what was at stake. Though I felt I was moving into new theological territory with the publication of the *Essay*, I regarded it as essentially a straightforward attempt to set out for theology (and for human religious life and self-understanding) the significance of the penetrating insights into human historicity that had emerged in the modern period, an issue much discussed when I was a graduate student at Yale and which I took up in my dissertation, *The Problem of Relativism and the Possibility of Metaphysics* (1955). The facts of human historicity have always seemed to me to undermine completely the grandiose Enlightenment claims about the universality of human reason. Whether consciousness of this should be said to involve movement to a new "postmodern" perspective depends, I suppose, largely on one's views about the difficult issue of historical periodization; in my opinion, I might say, our human tendency to reify our own historical judgments on such matters leads us all too often into arguments on issues like this that generate a good deal more heat than light.

In the writing project on which I am presently engaged, I attempt to reconceive into a more fully integrated pattern our modern ideas of nature, history, and God. What I call a "biohistorical" understanding of human existence can, I believe, overcome the bifurcation of nature and history so troubling in much modern reflection. And thus the central issues for the theological agenda today become such matters as the pluralistic character of all human life, culture, and religion; the ecological and nuclear crises we confront; and the necessity for us to take full responsibility not only for human social and cultural existence but above all for the overarching patterns of symbolism (religious and secular) which humankind has created during its long history—the symbolic contexts within which all our experiencing, thinking, and worshiping occur. This program moves us beyond certain emphases characteristic of the so-called modern period, but at the same time it involves working out (more fully, perhaps, than had been done before) the profound import, for theology and for ongoing human life, of modern understandings of our human biological and historical situatedness in the world.

If we are indeed living at the end of what has been thought of as "modernity," we can hardly do better to prepare ourselves for the unknown future we face than to gather together and develop further the best thinking of the modern age, along with other insights and understandings from a range of religious and cultural traditions. It is with this intention in mind that I carry on my own work, and it is this spirit that I see in the work of my colleagues represented in this volume. Instead of retreating into a fideistic confessionalism strongly reminiscent in its main bearings of the neo-orthodoxy of the mid-twentieth century—as do many of today's self-proclaimed "post-liberal" critics of theological modernism and liberalism—we are attempting to develop theological positions that, precisely because of their profound appreciation of human historicity, understand that they must strive to be thoroughly critical (and self-critical!) at every point. Thus we are all working together—each in our own ways—on "theology at the end of modernity."

I wish to express my deep-felt thanks to each of the good friends who has contributed to this collection of essays, and particularly to Sheila Davaney, who initiated this project and carried it through so successfully.

Gordon D. Kaufman
Harvard Divinity School

Introduction

SHEILA GREEVE DAVANEY

It is widely acknowledged that we are witnessing the profound reevaluation of the assumptions and projects of modernity and that such challenges carry enormous significance for theology at the end of the twentieth century. Theology in this century has been forged within the stream of intellectual and historical developments that commenced with the Enlightenment, were transmuted in the nineteenth and early twentieth centuries, and have now come to a point of crisis that indicates a transition to different historical projects and presuppositions. There is little consensus about the multifaceted nature of modernity itself and whether we should hasten its demise or bemoan its faltering presence; nor is it clear what prospects remain for theology at this juncture in history. There is, however, a widespread sense that this is a moment to reconsider the nature and tasks of theology and what kind of cultural role theology might play in our current context.

This volume offers such an appraisal of the contemporary situation and articulates a variety of proposals for theology's future direction. Although not advancing a monomythic interpretation of modernity or of what does or should prevail in its place, these essays do engage a series of interconnecting issues that are setting the parameters of contemporary theological debate. Moreover, they suggest, for all their diversity, a very definite trajectory for future theological construction, which stands in powerful contrast to other proposals on the present scene.

The essays in this book have been written in honor of Gordon D. Kaufman, Edward Mallinckrodt, Jr., Professor of Divinity at Harvard Divinity School. One of the most prominent contemporary theologians, Kaufman has been a central shaper of the current agenda of American theology through his articulation of a radical historicist perspective and a view of theology as imaginative construction. According to Kaufman, human life is fundamentally historical in nature, emergent from, sustained within, and dependent upon dynamic matrices of biological and cultural life. There are no human beings possessing a static human nature, untouched by temporal or historical location. There are only historical women and men, conditioned by and, in turn, shaping the various cultural and, indeed, natural contexts within which they exist.

In Kaufman's view, the historicity of human life finds definitive expression in the role language and culture play in human existence, because it is primarily through the interpretive processes of language that humans engage their world, explicating its meaning and the human place within it. By means of language and, in particular, comprehensive interpretive schemas, human life is given order and purpose.

For Kaufman theology's central task is to be about the construction and reconstruction of these interpretive systems and, most importantly, with the critical analysis and reconstrual of the symbols that focus such encompassing frameworks of meaning. Theology, when viewed in this manner, is a thoroughly human enterprise carried out for human purposes. It seeks, through the critical and creative capacities of the human imagination, to contribute to the construction of interpretive worlds through which human beings can gain orientation in life and thereby pursue sustainable and humane forms of existence.

Not only is theology carried out for such practical purposes, but its various efforts must, according to Kaufman, be assessed also in terms of pragmatic considerations. The central criterion for evaluating competing theological visions is thus not which one gives the apodictic rendering of the nature of reality and humanity's place within it—the ascertainment of which is impossible—but what modes of human life such visions inhibit or make possible. Theology, in its critical and constructive modes, is finally judged by its contribution to life's sustenance and enhancement, that is, to its ongoing humanization.

Kaufman is quite clear that no consensus exists about what constitutes such humanization. The various religious traditions and their secular analogues have, through time, developed alternative construals of the nature of existence and human life. Moreover, as our historical sensibilities deepen, these varied interpretations of reality appear increasingly distinct from one another. For many contemporary thinkers this recognition of radical historicity has produced a retreat to their particular traditions and a model of theology that is focused on conversations within traditions and on the appropriation and adaptation of historical interpretations, whose adequacy is assumed, for the contemporary context. For Kaufman such historicity suggests a very different direction for theology; precisely because theological reflection and religious discourse are historical products, which cannot lay claim to any sure or absolute truth but only to contextually defined adequacy, theologians must engage in the broadest forms of critical conversations. These conversations must take place not only within the traditions but across religious communities and secular movements and with representatives of the widest variety of other intellectual disciplines. Theology, if it is not to give up all hope of cultural relevancy, must then become fully public and critical, informed by multiple sources, and willing to contend for its proposals within the arena of common life and discourse. Hence insights into our human historicity lead Kaufman to a view of theology as imaginative construction, whose criteria are primarily pragmatic and whose mode is critical engagement of diverse perspectives in a pluralistic world.

The thinkers contributing to this volume represent a number of different perspectives, ranging from liberationist to process to deconstructivist positions. At times their assumptions and commitments diverge from both those of Kaufman and of one another. Yet they share with Kaufman and one another the basic assumption of the radical historicity of human life. The implications of such historicity are developed in a number of directions in these essays, but each essay begins with the conviction that recognition of the historical character of human life entails the abandonment or revision of many of the theological and philosophical projects of the modern period.

One of the strands of modern thought that these essays portray as having been irrevocably undermined is that of the Enlightenment-inspired search for certitude and truth, with its predication of an ahistorical and universal reason. As the Enlightenment challenged the appeals to ecclesial authority and tradition, so the radical historical consciousness of the present moment repudiates the atemporal character of the modern quest for sure foundations. With this challenge to the Enlightenment's understanding of reason have come an increased questioning of science's elevation within modernity as the embodiment of disinterested, rationally derived truth and a call for reconsideration of the relation between science and other forms of inquiry and discourse. A central motif of these essays is the exploration of the possibility for a rapprochement between science and theology in light of this reappraisal.

If the Enlightenment ideal of unencumbered reason appears untenable to these thinkers, so also does the turn to human subjectivity that is characteristic of a good deal of theology from Friedrich Schleiermacher onward. While science gained ascendancy as the model for truth and the traditional arguments for God's existence were eclipsed, theologians increasingly turned to the depths of human subjectivity as the source of religious experience and belief. This move, as Wayne Proudfoot argues in "*Regulae fidei* and Regulative Idea: Two Contemporary Theological Strategies," was an attempt to gain for religious experience and belief, as well as for their theological interpretations, an autonomous and protected location in a modern world where science reigned and religious claims had lost their rational force. Schleiermacher and a long line of successors claimed such protection by positing that religious experience was a unique dimension of experience, differentiated by its unmediated and nonlinguistically interpreted character and hence not accountable to the canons of scientific inquiry and explanation. Thus religious and theological spheres, without legitimacy or security in the arena of scientifically controlled discourse, appeared to have found a new and unassailable place in the modern world.

From the historicist perspective that is widely articulated in this volume, the theological turn to human subjectivity, as it was propounded by Schleiermacher and others, has become as problematic as the ahistorical quest of the Enlightenment, because as Proudfoot and Francis Schüssler Fiorenza argue, there are no forms of human experience utterly unmediated or unconditioned by their particular location in space and time. In "The Crisis of Hermeneutics and Christian

Theology" Fiorenza contends that precisely this failure to give a full account of the situated and interpreted character of human existence renders the modern liberal theological project also inadequate for today. Modern theological hermeneutics, focused on an ahistorical human subjectivity, severely misconstrued its subject matter and committed a mistake parallel to that of earlier hermeneutics of authority; it missed the radically historical character of human life.

Moreover, these essays testify that if religion and theology, by emphasizing an ahistorical human subjectivity, seemed to find an autonomous sphere protected from the challenge of other forms of inquiry, then the cost of such independence was the removal of both theology and religion from the public sphere. In "Resisting the Postmodern Turn: Theology and Contextualization" Linell Cady points to the growing separation between religion, understood as private and subjective, and the more communal arenas of societal life. Even though religion and theology appeared to gain a refuge, they also became more and more culturally extraneous, continuing to influence society but without a clearly defined or publicly legitimated role. Moreover, for Proudfoot such "protective strategies" have meant that theology is now not only culturally irrelevant but intellectually suspect, relegated to the province of the unargued and the arbitrary. Thus for Cady, Fiorenza, and Proudfoot the turn to human subjectivity in theology since the nineteenth century was grounded in a fundamental failure to be cognizant of the located and mediated nature of both experience and thought and has eventuated in the relegation of religion to the context of personal life and the dismissal of theology as subjective and unargued proclamation.

Accordingly, for many of the thinkers writing in this volume neither the pursuit of secure foundations and incontestable claims to truth nor the search for a unique and irreducible dimension of human experience is feasible today. They are not alone in this assessment of two of the central trajectories of modernity; indeed, there is a widespread consensus within theology today that new directions must be ventured. One of the major responses to the current appraisal has been the aforementioned return to traditions. Proponents of narrative theology and certain cultural linguistic perspectives have argued forcefully that the recognition of radical historicity leads to an understanding of humans as traditioned people, fundamentally shaped through the language, belief systems, and rituals of their distinctive historical lineages. From this understanding theologians such as George Lindbeck contend that theology is not properly about ascertaining indubitable truth claims about God or reality, nor about fathoming the depths of human subjectivity; rather, the task is to analyze and explicate the fundamental claims about reality and human life that have emerged within a specific tradition, so that believers might more fully appropriate and live out of their tradition's vision of reality. Theology's focus, therefore, is on a self-enclosed historical community; its method is interpretive, not critical; and its goal is to aid in the internalization of central claims, not the critique or reconstruction of that which we have inherited.

For all their diversity, the essays collected here represent a repudiation of this alternative to the projects of modernity. Acknowledgement of our historicity leads not to the refuge of insulated communities but to the opportunity to open places of conversation and debate that have long been closed and to engage voices that have heretofore been absent in the shaping of theological visions. In these pages there emerges a vision of theology as pluralistic, public, and critical.

One conversation partner that has excluded and been excluded by theology in the last several hundred years is science. From the Enlightenment on, science and theology have traveled separate paths, each staking out different spheres of analysis and offering disparate assertions. As the recognition that all claims to truth are historical, including those of science, and the acknowledgement that there are no uniquely privileged realms of human experience, including those of religion, have gained support, the possibility has emerged of a renewed engagement between theology and science.

Such an engagement is imperative today, according to Sallie McFague, William Dean, and James Gustafson. In "Cosmology and Christianity: Implications of the Common Creation Story for Theology" McFague states that contemporary theology has become more aware of its contextual nature and has recognized, with the inclusion of diverse voices, that theology is not a neutral enterprise but a form of advocacy. She contends, however, that one voice has continued to be absent and without significant advocates: the voice of nature. For McFague it is precisely this neglected natural context, upon which all human and nonhuman life depends and which has been profoundly damaged by our negligence, that must now have a central place in theological interpretations. Moreover, science, itself leaving behind outmoded construals of reality, is now developing a picture of a cosmic context that is organic, dynamic, and open-ended and within which all human and nonhuman forms of reality are interrelated and dependent upon one another for their very existence. Such a picture not only supports many insights of contemporary theology but also indicates the direction that theology's reconstructive efforts must take if our ideas of God, the world, and the self are to contribute to the now-imperiled continuance of life on this planet.

Dean's essay, "Humanistic Historicism and Naturalistic Historicism," supports McFague's proposals and challenges modes of contemporary historicism that focus exclusively on the human realm. Dean suggests that many forms of historicism reject the tenets of modernity but continue—often unaware that they do so—to presuppose the dualism of history and nature that has characterized modernity. Eschewing such a dualism, Dean calls for a "naturalistic-humanistic historicism" that includes the testimony of both human and natural history and that no longer sees the discourses of science as irrelevant to the theological interpretation of the human self. For Dean the results of such inclusion would be a renewed understanding of the continuity of humanity with nature and a new set of data in terms of which theological proposals would need to be tested.

Gustafson, too, calls for an open conversation between the various sciences and the theological disciplines. In the essay "Theological Anthropology and the Human Sciences" Gustafson argues that often theologians and ethicists set forth normative interpretations of the human that are predicated upon but fail to examine or defend particular descriptive "facts" about human nature. Scientists, for their part, often extend so-called descriptive positions into normative notions of human life, equally without argumentation. Gustafson therefore calls for a more self-conscious engagement of science and theology, through which foundational premises and normative implications might be fruitfully examined in aid of developing more adequate notions of human selfhood for today.

Although McFague, Dean, and Gustafson strongly espouse a reopening of the conversation between theology and science, they do not suggest that science be understood as providing a new sure foundation upon which theological claims can or should rest. Indeed, it is precisely the demise of science's hegemony and new insight into science's historical and constructive character that provide an opening for such

7

a conversation. Without privileging scientific claims, these theologians do argue, however, that theology has ignored science to its peril, thereby truncating notions of both the human and nature, and that it is time such neglect ended.

If science and nature have been perspectives missing in the theological discussion, there have also been other absent voices that these essays contend must now contribute to the shaping of theology's future. One such set of voices is that of the various religious traditions other than Christianity. The narrative and cultural-linguistic perspectives that advocate intratradition conversation are doing so at the very time that we are most aware of the multiplicity of traditions and of the fact that humans exist in pluralistic contexts that impinge upon us, not in insulated communities with monolithic pasts. The essays in this volume assert that this pluralism requires not only theological explanation but also a theological interpretation that makes dialogue among the world's religious communities a real possibility. M. Thomas Thangaraj writes, in "Toward a Dialogical Theology of Mission," that the context for theological discussion must be wider than any particular religious or ecclesial circle. He therefore seeks a basis upon which interreligious dialogue can proceed and suggests that such ground might be found in what he terms the *missio humanitatis*. This mission of humanity as self-conscious, historical, and ecological beings is to meet one another responsibly and in solidarity and mutuality. Only when humans encounter one another, forgoing claims to superiority and assuming there is something to be learned from one another, can we involve ourselves in the common task of creating a liveable world for all persons.

Fiorenza and Simon Maimela echo the concern for solidarity in their essays. Fiorenza critically analyzes both traditional theology—what he terms a hermeneutics of authority—and modern theology—titled a hermeneutics of human subjectivity—and faults each for its lack of understanding of human historicity. Fiorenza's own analysis of human historicity indicates that we are indeed traditioned beings but that such shaping traditions have always been pluralistic and the carriers of both explicit and hidden social and political interests. Moreover, the interpretive stance of contemporary persons as they engage their pasts is also value-laden. Fiorenza concludes from this neither that theologians should give up the hermeneutical task nor that all interpretive perspectives are equally valid for today. Instead, he contends that the interests that permeate the hermeneutical process must be made public; that is, he calls for a political hermeneutics. Moreover, Fiorenza argues that there are particular values that should be given priority today. For him the immensity of the suffering that has occurred in history and continues in the present, and the recognition that theology's exclusion of many peoples and perspectives often has rendered that suffering invisible, demand that an adequate hermeneutical stance today embody solidarity with the suffering of our world and allow the self-testimony of those voices, perspectives, and discourses, heretofore excluded. Only such inclusion and solidarity will break theology's ongoing participation in oppressive systems and yield the possibility of critically interpreting our own and others' histories, in the service of constructing more liberating visions for today.

In "Black Theology and the Quest for a God of Liberation" Maimela specifies what solidarity means for blacks and other persons of color in a racist world. For Maimela the growing insights of historical consciousness lead to an acknowledgment not only of the thoroughly constructed character of theological claims but also of their political nature. In particular, Maimela asserts that much Christian theology has been the expression of racist interests and has thereby contributed to ongoing oppression through this unholy alliance. With this analysis, Maimela is in agreement with many other liberation and black theologians. His essay, however, also articulates a significant departure from many of those theologies. In contrast to those efforts, he argues that the almost universal attempt by black and other liberation theologians to ground their assertions in the Bible, assuming that to do so will give them legitimacy, is a failure to carry through the dictates of historical consciousness. Instead, he proposes that black theology should claim its status as an alternative human construction whose validity is not predicated upon whether it is biblical but upon whether it offers a liberating vision for the oppressed. Thus Maimela calls for a more thorough acknowledgment of human responsibility for our theological constructions and insists that, finally, it is only the pragmatic outcome of our theological efforts that yields them any legitimacy.

The historicist perspective, evident in the call for a renewed conversation with science as enunciated by McFague, Dean, and Gustafson; in the assertion of the political, critical, and constructive character of theology as set forth by Fiorenza and Maimela; and in Thangaraj's summons to an interreligious, not intra-ecclesial, dialogue, also finds expression in the essays of Cady and Proudfoot. Both caution against the dangers of modes of theology that appear to embrace historicist insights but are really retreats into forms of fideism or "protective strategies" that seek ways of interpreting theological discourse so as to preserve its unique status. In contrast, Cady and Proudfoot assert the need for theology to return to the sphere of public and critical inquiry.

Cady in particular makes specific proposals concerning what this would entail. For her the recognition of the historical character of religious beliefs and theological claims not only involves undermining the authority of the past or of some basal experience but also suggests that theology's long-practiced focus on texts—especially the Bible—and inclination to debate theological ideas in abstraction from their embodiment in concrete religious communities and practices is fundamentally misguided. If Thangaraj proposes a move from ecclesial to interreligious dialogue, Cady argues for a shift from intratextual debates to cultural analysis in which the primary interest would be in concrete, lived religion. Theology's disciplinary conversation partners would be altered as well by this change of direction away from textual critics and philosophers and toward historians of religion, ethnographers, and sociologists. Theology, in short, would be far less theology of the word(s) than a theology of culture.

Although these essays suggest that thinking through radical historicity leads to a new direction in theology, they also indicate that there are significant areas that theology shaped strongly by a sense that historicity has yet to account for with much adequacy. John Cobb's essay, "In Defense of Realism," focuses upon one central example of this: the failure thus far of perspectives that stress the constructive character of human thought to explicate the role of the body and of the external world in shaping those constructions. Theology today must, according to Cobb, find a way to understand historicity in terms of not only the conditioned and creative character of language and ideas but also the embodied and concrete nature of human life. Without so doing, historicist thought risks being only a form of idealism, which ignores the reality that we not only are influenced by and influence ideas but also engage our world primarily through our bodies and that the world within which we exist, even though mediated, is not just a world of thought.

In "Communities of Collaboration: Shared Commitments/Common Tasks" George Rupp addresses an area that will also require reconsideration in our new context: that is, the meaning of communal identity. It is not only that we now know that humans exist and have always existed in plural communities but also that, as Rupp argues, today we are faced with the fact that there has been a steady erosion for several centuries of many traditional forms of communal life. The question Rupp poses is how humans, situated in pluralistic contexts, participating in different and often disparate segments of society, gain a sense of shared community. Rupp proposes that, in light of the reality of pluralism and the fact that we are not merely traditioned but multitraditioned, we should consider work or labor as a possible site for the forging of communal identity. Representing neither a return to the supposedly homogeneous communities of the past nor an acceptance of a view of labor as the product of "impersonal processes of markets and bureaucracies," Rupp's call is for a form of work shaped by shared commitments and goals, characterized by nonhierarchical and cooperative organization, and inclusive of diverse ethnic, religious, racial, and sexual groups. Such a location for communal identity is uniquely appropriate, in Rupp's view, in a world where the boundaries of group identity are less clear and traditional appeals to blood and land are no longer appropriate and, indeed, are dangerous.

For the most part, the essays in this book complement one another, announcing a general opposition to theological confessionalism and offering constructive proposals that resonate with one another. It would be a mistake, however, to read these articles as a happily, albeit accidentally, achieved mosaic of theoretical and political agreement, because running through them as through all of contemporary theology, are deep and divisive differences whose resolutions continue to elude us.

One point of tension between essays and even of ambivalence within several pieces concerns the varying assessments of modernity. Although all these essays repudiate the foundationalism of the Enlightenment and the turn to an ahistorical subjectivity characteristic of the nineteenth century, they do so in the name of a historical consciousness upon whose lineage and nature there is not full agreement. For some, such as Mark C. Taylor, radical historicity marks the move into a postmodernism that is not simply an extension of nineteenth-century historical consciousness. For others, such as Cady and Maimela, modernity itself produced the very insights into historicity that shape these essays. Hence the essays in this volume suggest that there remains the task of deeper exploration into the nature of radical historicity, its presuppositions, and its historical sources, and with it an ongoing appraisal of modernity, its failures, and its continuing promise.

A second place of divergence revolves around the historically shaped issue of idealism and realism, raised by John Cobb and, indirectly, by William Dean. The problem, Cobb and Dean suggest, is not simply that the body and nature continue to be left out of our historical consciousness. We also must ask if the current historicism can, in fact, genuinely include the body and nature in its understanding of those contexts within which thought and experience are formed; that is, we must ask if contemporary historicism has an epistemology that can point not only to the agential character of knowing and the role that language plays in mediating experience but also to the embodied nature of human life. For Dean and Cobb contemporary historicism remains too dualistic, with an epistemology that can account for the linguisticality of human existence but not for its physicality. It therefore stands in need of a new epistemology that neither commits anew the faults of older realisms nor leaves the human self disembodied and isolated in a world of language.

Another area of possible conflict concerns the tension between those thinkers who espouse a political reading of the theological enterprise and those who articulate a view of theology as public conversation. Maimela clearly sees theology as a conflictual process, whereby groups with competing social and political agendas contend for the symbolic universes through which communities interpret themselves and their world. In a just and inclusive community in which all persons were treated equitably and had full access to the various forms of power, theology might look like a broad, publicly based conversation. In our unjust world, however, it is not nearly so polite an activity but one fraught with dissension, the outcomes of which, as Maimela's essay testifies, carry profound human consequences. Both Maimela and Fiorenza suggest that "open" and "public" inquiry is not a neutral, objective activity and that if theology is to be an arena in which multiple voices have a say, then theologians must self-consciously engage in the struggle to include those historically absent voices and, indeed, to prioritize them. Without such struggle, Fiorenza and

Maimela suggest, the tension between public and partisan theology will remain.

This tension also points to the ongoing question of how theological assessments should, in a historicist perspective, be adjudicated. It is clear in these essays that conformity to the past should not be the central norm for evaluating claims to adequacy or contemporary validity; nor can older appeals to universal reason and unique experience be resuscitated. In contrast to these norms, the prevalent suggestion of these essays is that the primary criteria of evaluation and adjudication should be pragmatic ones—for example, what the repercussions are of different theological visions. These essays, however, do not solve the dilemma of whose pragmatic judgments, in a pluralistic context marked by deep conflict, should have priority. Although all call for a broader, more inclusive conversation and many suggest that those voices traditionally left out—be they voices of the oppressed or of nature—should carry a certain weight, there is less consensus or, indeed, clarity about how particular judgments should be made.

There is one final area in which clearly divergent perspectives are at play in this volume: the question of talk about God. It is not surprising that the idea of God should remain so problematic at the end of a century that has spoken of God both as definitively revealed in radical faith and as definitively dead, culturally and morally. Although the essays presented here share a strong historicism, they do not offer a consensus about what that means for the nature and status of God-talk or its future prospects.

For Maurice Wiles the collapse of foundationalism has meant that the traditional theoretical arguments for God's existence can be no more compelling today than they were at the dawn of the modern period. On this a modernity that sought sure grounds for belief and a contemporary moment that contends such a search is misguided are in full agreement. Wiles argues, however, that relinquishing the quest for unassailable theoretical arguments about God does not leave the theologian only the options of giving up talk about God or retreat to fideistic and arbitrary proclamation. Instead, he proposes that a number of contemporary theologians are making other kinds of arguments predicated upon their analysis of what it means to be human. These anthropological arguments, although not indubitable, do suggest that the idea of God can be interpreted as making sense of human experience and, for Wiles, offer a legitimate alternative to fideism and foundation-alism.

Taylor, in "The End(s) of Theology," presents a quite different pro-posal. Taylor comments that for many thinkers during the last several centuries, modernity was equated with the eclipse of religion and with the assumed and hoped-for demise of all religion historically represented. Nevertheless, Taylor states, religion has not disappeared; indeed, at the end of modernity it is flourishing more strongly than ever, as it rebels—especially in its fundamentalist versions—against the very modernity that sought to dismantle it. In such fundamental-ism and its theological analogues Taylor discerns a desire to return to premodern times, to "the peace and security of a world in which truth seemed knowable and morality doable." For Taylor such a return is impossible; therefore, the task is, as it was for Wiles, to find an alterna-tive to modernity that is not a retreat to a premodern world. For Tay-lor that alternative lies in the acceptance of radical uncertainty, in openness to the other, and, finally, in the death of God in and through which the sacred might be glimpsed.

By way of developing his proposal, Taylor juxtaposes his position to that of Thomas J. J. Altizer, who declared the death of the transcen-dent Barthian God and the advent of the utterly immanent divine in the finite world. For Taylor, Altizer's reversal of the Barthian God is finally inadequate because it ultimately denies the reality of the other and proclaims an immanence that absorbs all that is different. In con-trast, Taylor proposes that we learn to think beyond transcendence and immanence to a radically historical moment in which the other remains and the task is to remain open to difference without the totali-tarian urge to control. Thus beyond Barth's transcendent God and Altizer's immanent divine lies the sacred who is other and in whom difference is given play.

Van Harvey's essay, "Feuerbach on Religion as Construction," revisits that earlier thinker's projection theory as a means of exploring the constructed character of the idea of God and, by so doing, raises anew questions concerning the status of religious language in general and language about the divine in particular. Harvey argues that inter-preters of Feuerbach have focused too much attention on his early theories of religion as the projection of humanity's species nature and of the alienation that results from the failure to understand this pro-cess. These theories, Harvey argues, now appear too essentialist, too

Hegelian even in their inversion of Hegel's position, and too theistic to account with any adequacy for the diversity of religious forms. According to Harvey, however, this was not the only projection theory Feuerbach developed; in his later work Feuerbach outlined a more sophisticated theory of religion, in which religion was interpreted as a response to nature and a reaction to human dependency upon that which gives life and takes it. Moreover, religion is rooted not in a fundamental alienation but in an affirmation of life in the face of this mysterious other. For Harvey this theory has the advantages of portraying human life as part of nature and of seeing religion as a response to the broader world, at the same time maintaining a central emphasis upon the constructive activity of the imagination, which issues forth in symbolic universes endowed with human meaning. Harvey's essay implies that, as such, it is suggestive for the contemporary effort to rethink the nature and status of religions and theological language, in a time when they are no longer isolated from critical scrutiny.

Wiles, Taylor, and Harvey all eschew any return to foundationalisms, be they of reason, revelation, or religious experience. With Wayne Proudfoot they reject special pleading for God-talk that implies it by definition could be safeguarded from the challenges of our day. They also all are cognizant of the constructive dimensions of both theological and religious symbols. Nonetheless, there is considerable distance between Wiles's God, who is the intellectually legitimate correlate of the human experiences of hope, meaning, and freedom; Taylor's sacred, who is revealed in the demise of the God who failed; and Harvey's projected God, who symbolizes the human attempt to contend with that which eludes its control. Moreover, this diversity is further heightened when the relation between power and religious symbolism comes to the fore, as it does in Maimela's work. Thus although a certain sense of the historicity of human life and its implications can be discerned throughout these essays, the result is not a consensus about God-talk and its nature, legitimacy, or viability but, if anything, a growing diversity of proposals offering competing assessments and different constructive alternatives. These essays suggest that the question of God remains fundamentally open and that a central theological agenda for the future is what talk about God can mean when reason, faith, and experience have all lost their privileged positions and have been replaced by insights into the historical, interest-laden, and constructive nature of the idea of God.

15

From these essays a picture emerges of a theology that acknowledges its historical and relative character, embraces this historicity not
as an excuse to turn inward but as the impetus for entering broad and
diverse conversations, and understands its tasks to be primarily critical and constructive ones. Moreover, these essays suggest that carrying through the implications of historical consciousness entails, not the
loss of the possibility of espousing normative visions, but the necessity
of contending for them in the public realm. By so doing, they argue for
a form of theology that is critical, constructive, public, and shaped by
the interplay of multiple perspectives. Such a theology will be characterized not by uniformity but by diversity, indeed, conflict, as the
connection between political and social interests and theological proposals becomes clearer; nor will the idea of God find any safe or
protected refuge in this mode of theology. This concept, perhaps
above all others, demands critical scrutiny and radical reconstruction
in our day. The kind of theology envisioned in these pages stands at a
great distance from both traditional and modern theologies, as well as
from other contemporary alternatives; but in its departure from these
other forms of theology lies its promise that theology might play a
revitalized role in personal, communal, and public life at the end of
modernity. Such is the hope of Gordon Kaufman and so, too, the hope
of these essays written in his honor.

PART I

THEOLOGY, SCIENCE, AND NATURE

1

Cosmology and Christianity: Implications of the Common Creation Story for Theology

SALLIE McFAGUE

Liberation theologies are theologies that advocate: they speak in support of the oppressed. They do not pretend to be objective or neutral, or merely interpreting the tradition in contemporary terms. They are destabilizing, engaging in deconstruction and reconstruction of the central doctrines of Christian faith.[1] They are, I believe, the kind of theology needed in our time. The issues facing us are burning ones: oppression of people due to gender, race, class, or sexual orientation, as well as the increasingly pressing concern for ecological deterioration. Liberation theologies have taught us that all theology is contextual, but one context has not been considered with the seriousness it deserves: that is, the context of human beings as a species among species in a home we all share. Although it is by no means the only

1. Gordon D. Kaufman, in his 1982 Presidential Address for the American Academy of Religion, called on theologians and students of religion to turn attention as scholars to the human nuclear capability to annihilate ourselves and most of the rest of the living creatures. The times are such, he insisted, that, whether we like it or not, we have thrust upon us the responsibility to turn our research programs toward the deconstruction and reconstruction of the central symbols of the Judeo-Christian tradition—God, Christ, and torah—so that they will help divert rather than court disaster. See the published speech, "Nuclear Eschatology and the Study of Religion," *Journal of the American Academy of Religion* 51, no. 1 (1983):3–14, and his *Theology for a Nuclear Age* (Philadelphia: Westminster Press; and Manchester, Eng.: Manchester University Press, 1985). Although the nuclear issue appears less pressing at present, others have increased in urgency, esp. ecological deterioration with the two issues related as "bang" vs. "whimper": quick kill vs. slow death.

context, it is surely the broadest one, the one in which other contexts, those of race, class, gender, sexual orientation, and so forth, exist and qualify what we say about ourselves as a species.

The ecological context has not received the attention of the others, in part because the integrity of the planet has often been seen to be in competition with the needs for food, raw materials, energy, and so forth of the oppressed, especially the poor; or ecology has been viewed as a pastime of the leisured class—nature lovers and animal-rights enthusiasts of the so-called First World. Both of these positions are seriously at fault. A sound ecosystem is a necessity if the poor are to be fed: bread cannot be shared if wheat cannot be grown. A sound ecosystem is not the business of a self-chosen few; it is probably the most important subject for every human being to learn about, although responsibility for making the most drastic changes in life-style certainly rests with the First World, because we have created most of the problems and are, per capita, the greatest consumers of scarce goods, including energy. We are becoming aware that ecology and human oppression belong to the same system. The World Council of Churches has revised its rallying cry from "peace and justice" to "justice, peace, and the integrity of creation." We are being called to do something unprecedented: to think about "everything that is," to think holistically about the oppressions facing us, because the issues are intimately interrelated.

If theology is to advocate, to speak in support of the oppressed, one critical issue it must address is the most basic one of the health of the planet, because we depend on that good health profoundly and totally in ways we are only dimly beginning to realize. In spite of continuing political tensions among nations, the most dangerous threat to the world's well-being is not war but the closing down of the earth's most basic systems, which support us and all other forms of life. A nuclear holocaust would be the most extreme consequence of the modern posture toward the natural world, a posture of control and destruction, with little sense of who we really are in the scheme of things and what, therefore, we can and cannot do in and to it if we and other species are to survive and prosper. Whether consciously or in blissful ignorance, we are perpetrators and accomplices in "crimes against creation" on a massive scale. The threat of a nuclear holocaust and ecological deterioration are symptoms manifesting how out-of-touch with reality we are, the reality—or "house rules," if you will—of our one and only home, planet Earth.[2] Advocacy theology—theology on the side of life and its fulfillment—must be based in contemporary reality: not the reality of the scriptural world nor of the medieval or Reformation world nor of Isaac Newton's or René Descartes's world but reality as understood by postmodern science.[3] Theology cannot "plead the case" for a different way of looking at things, a cosmocentric rather than the current anthropocentric point of view, unless it can show that the different view is mandated by reality as understood in our time.

This is the theme of my essay: advocational theology, the kind of theology needed in our time, cannot be either merely heuristic, playing with different imaginative possibilities, or merely utilitarian, insisting that God and nature be seen as benefiting human existence. Rather, this theology—as is true of all theology—must, I believe, be rooted in the sense of reality current in our time. But what is the "sense of reality current in our time" and what is it based upon? As in Descartes's world or Galileo's, our sense of reality derives from the view of the universe, its inner workings, and postulated origins that the scientific, philosophical, and theological discourses of the period are developing. In our world the scientific advances are especially important and have too often been ignored by some philosophers and many theologians.

2. David Tracy and Nicholas Lash, speaking of the "omnicide" that faces us, call for a "deprivatizing" of theology, which involves a return not only to real history (and not merely historicity) but also to nature. "The questions of cosmology are not properly understood as *only* concerned with the origin and natural structure of the world. Those cosmological questions include the destiny of human beings, indeed of history itself—as 'inextricably bound up' with the destiny of the cosmos" (in *Cosmology and Theology*, ed. Tracy and Lash [New York: Seabury Press; and Edinburgh: T. & T. Clark, 1983], 89).

3. Some currently are voicing this concern. Wolfhart Pannenberg, bemoaning Barth's decision "in principle" that a theological doctrine of creation should not concern itself with scientific descriptions of the world, concludes, "If theologians want to conceive of God as the creator of the real world, they cannot possibly bypass the scientific description of that world" ("The Doctrine of Creation and Modern Science," in *Cosmos as Creation: Theology and Science in Consonance*, ed. Ted Peters [Nashville: Abingdon Press, 1989], 156–57). Physicist and theologian Arthur Peacocke states: "Any affirmation about God's relation to the world, any doctrine of creation if it is not to be vacuous and sterile must be about the relation of God to the creation, and this creation is the world that the natural sciences describe. Theology really has no other choice unless it wants to retreat to a ghetto where people just talk to themselves and not to the rest of the world" ("Theology and Science Today," in *Cosmos as Creation*, ed. Peters, 30). Physicist Hanbury Brown writes: "When religious beliefs lose touch with reality they are likely to turn *inwards* and present a picture of the world which is no more than a mirror of ourselves, and such a picture . . . is potentially dangerous. If our system of religious beliefs is to form a coherent world-view, as it did in the Medieval Model, it must look *outwards* to what contemporary science is telling us about the world around us" (*The Wisdom of Science: Its Relevance to Culture and Religion* [Cambridge: Cambridge University Press, 1986], 172).

What, then, does the current scientific worldview suggest for advocational theology?

Perhaps the first and most important question to ask in light of the view of reality coming to us from the sciences is not who God is but who we are. Traditionally, theological anthropology, by constructing the human image after the divine image, as a reflection of it, has separated human existence from its empirical, cosmic setting. To take this starting place does not mean that a theological anthropology should be dictated to by science, either in general or in its particulars; rather, it means taking that setting seriously as one very important element, although by no means the only one, in a Christian statement about who we are. We are "of the earth, earthy," whatever more and else Christian theologies want to say about human existence. It is precisely our setting on planet Earth that is the focus of this essay.

To insist that theology take the scientific view of reality seriously, so seriously that it use it as a resource for reconstructing its central doctrines, is contrary to the practice of modernity. For the past two hundred years at least, and perhaps as far back as Martin Luther's retreat to the self as the locus of contact between God and the world, theology and science have gone their separate ways. Only history, and only human history, has been seen as the place where God touches our reality; hence the natural world has been considered irrelevant to theology. Since the Reformation, redemption of human beings has been the focus of divine activity, with creation similarly focused on human existence. Thus Luther could say, "I believe that God created *me*," or John Calvin could see nature as the stage of salvation history, or Friedrich Schleiermacher could deal with creation as merely an extension of the feeling of absolute dependence. This tradition continued into our century, with Karl Barth's insistence that the reality of creation is known in the person of Jesus Christ and Bultmann's claim that to believe in creation means confessing oneself to be a creature. In every case the emphasis is on the individual human being and usually on human existence existentially understood. Even the liberation theologies, with the exception of some feminist theologies, although broadening redemption in political ways by insisting on physical and economic liberation of the masses rather than the inner freedom of anguished sinners, still limit their concern to human well-being. The fate of the natural world is seldom considered; God the liberator does not appear to be the Creator of the universe.

The contemporary conversation between theology and the sciences is little known by many, even though the picture of reality coming to us from the sciences is not only one that we must take seriously if our planet is to survive and flourish but also probably the most attractive picture for theology since the medieval synthesis. I suspect this conversation is seen by some as erudite and irrelevant, at best material for academic conferences between the elite few theologians who can understand the complexities of quantum physics and the equally few scientists who find religious questions interesting if not necessarily important.[4]

Nothing, I believe, could be further from the truth. For the first time in several hundred years we have the possibility of thinking holistically about God and the world, and this possibility is being given to us by the "common creation story" coming from the sciences, from cosmology, astrophysics, and biology.[5] This possibility has nothing to

4. The conversation is a lively and animated one, with an increasing number of books and essays attempting to interpret the importance of postmodern science to theology. See, e.g., Ian G. Barbour, *Religion in an Age of Science*, vol. 1 (New York: Harper & Row, 1990); Thomas Berry, *The Dream of the Earth* (San Francisco: Sierra Club Books, 1988); Charles Birch and John Cobb, Jr., *The Liberation of Life: From the Cell to the Community* (Cambridge: Cambridge University Press, 1981); Hanbury Brown, *The Wisdom of Science*; David Ray Griffin, *God and Religion in the Postmodern World* (New York: SUNY Press, 1989); idem, ed., *The Reenchantment of Science: Postmodern Proposals* (New York: SUNY Press, 1988); James M. Gustafson, *Ethics from a Theocentric Perspective* (Chicago: University of Chicago Press, 1981); John E. Haught, *The Cosmic Adventure: Science, Religion and the Quest for Purpose* (New York: Paulist Press, 1984); Conrad Hyers, *The Meaning of Creation: Genesis and Modern Science* (Atlanta: John Knox Press, 1984); Jay McDaniel, *Of God and Pelicans: A Theology of Reverence for Life* (Louisville, Ky.: Westminster/John Knox Press, 1989); Ernan McMullin, ed., *Evolution and Creation* (Notre Dame, Ind.: University of Notre Dame Press, 1985); John M. Mangum, ed., *The New Faith–Science Debate: Probing Cosmology, Technology, and Theology* (Minneapolis: Fortress Press, 1989); Jurgen Moltmann, *God in Creation: A New Theology of Creation and the Spirit of God* (San Francisco: Harper & Row, 1985); A. R. Peacocke, *Creation and the World of Science* (Oxford: Clarendon Press, 1979); idem, ed., *The Sciences and Theology in the Twentieth Century* (Notre Dame, Ind.: University of Notre Dame Press, 1981); Ted Peters, ed., *Cosmos as Creation*; John Polkinghorne, *Science and Creation* (London: SPCK, 1988); Holmes Rolston III, *Science and Religion: A Critical Survey* (New York: Random House, 1987); Robert John Russell et al., eds., *Physics, Philosophy and Theology: A Common Quest for Understanding* (Notre Dame, Ind.: University of Notre Dame Press; and Rome: Vatican Observatory, 1988); David Schindler, ed., *Beyond Mechanism: The Universe in Recent Physics and Catholic Thought* (New York: University Press of America, 1986); Stephen Toulmin, *The Return to Cosmology: Postmodern Science and the Theology of Nature* (Berkeley: University of California Press, 1982); David Tracy and Nicholas Lash, eds., *Cosmology and Theology*.

5. Over the past decade or so a large number of books written for the educated layperson, giving various aspects of this story, have appeared. See, e.g., Robert K. Adair, *The Great Design: Particles, Fields, and Creation* (New York and Oxford: Oxford University Press, 1987); John D. Barrow and Joseph Silk, *The Left Hand of Creation: The Origin and Evolution of the Expanding Universe* (New York: Basic Books, 1983); Paul Davies, *The Cosmic Blueprint: New Discoveries in Nature's Ability to Order the Universe*

do with integrating science and religion or finding proofs from the sciences for the existence of God, such as one sees in the unfortunate remark by Pope Pius XII in 1951 that the singularity billions of years ago, called the Big Bang, provides evidence for a creator and hence for God.[6] Such a God-of-the-gaps, a deistic God who starts the show going, is certainly not the concern here. What is of interest to theology is the picture of reality from postmodern science, painted in broad strokes. Theological reconstruction is not interested in fringe issues relating science and religion or in supporting cosmetic changes in theology to avoid clashes with science, such as interpreting Genesis as a myth rather than history or giving psychoanalytic interpretations of miracles. It is the broad features of the postmodern scientific view of reality that are exciting and fruitful for reformulating the essentials, not the minutiae, of the faith.

Moreover, the relation between science and theology that I am suggesting is not so much a dialogue as an "eavesdropping": theologians should listen to what the scientists are telling us about reality, and use it as an important resource for reformulating doctrines concerning God and the world. There are many other issues in the relationship between science and religion—issues of method, of epistemology, of the uses of technology, of the ethical implications of research, and so on—which are dialogical and from which scientists have much to learn from theologians. The one I am concerned with, however, is different: scientists do not become better scientists by incorporating religion into their research (in fact, such work becomes suspect), but theologians cannot interpret the God/world relationship in credible,

---

(New York: Simon & Schuster, 1988); Freeman Dyson, *Infinite in All Directions* (New York: Harper & Row, 1988); George B. Field and Eric J. Chaisson, *The Invisible Universe: Probing the Frontiers of Astrophysics* (Boston: Birkhauser, 1985); Edward Harrison, *Cosmology: The Science of the Universe* (Cambridge: Cambridge University Press, 1981); Stephen Hawking, *A Brief History of Time: From the Big Bang to Black Holes* (New York: Bantam Books, 1980); Carl Sagan, *Cosmos* (New York: Random House, 1980); James S. Trefil, *The Moment of Creation: Big Bang Physics from before the First Millisecond to the Present Universe* (New York: Charles Scribner, 1983).

6. See his address to the Pontifical Academy of Sciences, November 22, 1951, "The Proofs of the Existence of God in Light of Modern Natural Science": "Thus with that concreteness which is characteristic of physical proofs, it [science] has confirmed the contingency of the universe and also the well-founded deduction of the epoch [some fifteen billion years ago] when the cosmos came forth from the hands of the Creator. Hence, creation took place in time. Therefore, there is a Creator! Therefore, God exists!" (quoted in Stanley Jaki, *Cosmos and Creator* [Edinburgh: Scottish Academic Press, 1980], 19).

holistic, persuasive ways unless they take the scientific picture of the world seriously.

It is understandable why there have been hundreds of years of stalemate on this issue. Modern science—that is, the science of Bacon, Descartes, and Newton—painted a mechanistic, static view of reality in which separate individuals (most basically, atoms) were central and interacted only externally with others. Theologically, it was not an attractive picture, with little for God to do but wind up the clock of the world. During the early years of our century, with the rise of positivism, the picture became even bleaker. It is, therefore, no mystery why theologians have seen the only meeting place with God to be human history and especially the inner, hidden heart and mind of the human being as the place of last resort, a place presumably beyond the reductionism of science.

Postmodern science, however, presents a very different picture of reality. The picture it provides of reality is organic, dynamic, and open, one in which relations are more central than individuals and internal relations pertain among all its constituent parts. The universe is a whole: it has a common history dating back fifteen billion years, gradually emerging through transformations of enormous complexity into the billions of galaxies of the present observable universe, including our own tiny planet Earth. All that make up our planet, from bacteria to coal, robins, water, iron, wildflowers, oak trees, deer, and human beings, have a common origin and are, at some stage, related. We are distant cousins with everything else that exists in the universe and close cousins with everything that exists on our planet. I will say more about this picture and its implications for theological anthropology presently, but its theological attractiveness is immediately evident. For a religious tradition such as the Christian one, which, at least in its classic forms, has emphasized God as the Creator of all that is as well as being in some sense incarnationally present in and to that creation, the new creation story from the sciences offers very rich possibilities.

Before continuing with features of this picture, especially as they impinge on theological anthropology, three issues must be addressed. The first concerns the suspicion that reformulating the God/world relationship in light of postmodern science might be a sneaky attempt at a new foundationalism, yet another effort to ground theology in the shifting sands that, over the last two hundred years, have destroyed all the sure supports of Scripture, history, and the self. But foundational-ism, I believe, is not at issue here. I am not suggesting that science grounds theological formulations by giving them a firm purchase on reality. This would be the case only in a positivistic, absolutistic view of scientific truth as the one and only truth. Postmodern science is far more modest, aware that all theories are partial, tentative, and incomplete and, given the basic character of the universe as changing and evolving, present theories will undoubtedly change also. The work of Thomas Kuhn and others on the paradigm-dependency of scientific theories has meant that scientific interpretations of reality, like all others, are partial, relative, and changing. Moreover, it is well known that scientists use particular metaphors, such as particle and wave, but many also see the scientific picture of reality itself as a metaphor describing a complex and perhaps incomprehensible reality in terms that we can grasp and use.[7] It is, at any given time, the best picture we have; that is the important point. It is not the only one or the permanent one, but the best we have at the present time.

Theologies that are credible and persuasive, that make sense to people living at a particular time, are ones that take seriously the public portrayal of reality current in their day. Augustine's success was due to his doctrinal reformulations in Neoplatonic terms; Thomas Aquinas created the medieval synthesis with the help of Aristotle; the Deists of the eighteenth century worked with the picture of Newtonian science. In our day, process theology has taken postmodern science seriously and many feminist theologies are informed by an ecological, evolutionary sensibility—reasons why, I believe, both of these movements

---

7. E.g., Hanbury Brown, speaking of the whole scientific picture of the physical world as a metaphor, says, "This picture is limited, not only by our understanding, but also by our tools of observation, so that it is always incomplete, always unfolding and always provisional" (*The Wisdom of Science*, 140). Elsewhere he adds, "*All* our non-trivial interpretations of the world, religious and scientific, are more or less uncertain, they are working hypotheses, and like metaphors must be discarded when they no longer work" (180). Philosopher of science Mary Hesse, speaking of the fact that scientific theories are dependent upon frameworks and paradigms used by concrete scientific communities, sums up the present consensus: "It has been sufficiently demonstrated that data are not detachable from theory, and that their expression is permeated by theoretical categories; that the language of theoretical science is irreducibly metaphorical and unformalizable, and that the logic of science is circular: interpretation, reinterpretation, and self-correction of data in terms of theory, and theory in terms of data" ("In Defence of Objectivity," *Proceedings of the Aristotelian Society* [1973]:9).

strike many as the most viable current theological options.[8] At any rate, the point at issue is that when the picture of reality undergoes a paradigm shift, theology must attend to it. Reformulating doctrine in light of a new picture is not a form of foundationalism, for the so-called foundation itself can and will change and the reformulated doctrines will have to be reformulated again.

A second issue that doctrinal reformulation poses, in light of the scientific picture of reality, is whether this reformulation is a form of essentialism or universalism; that is, if this reformulation is the privileging of one voice, the scientific one, which in popular culture at least is widely viewed as the objective truth about things. At the very time that deconstruction and feminist hermeneutics are insisting on decentering the dominant discourse, is my thesis restoring privilege to scientific discourse, which, as several feminist scientists have pointed out, has been not only masculinist but also often sexist, racist, homophobic, and militaristic in many of its technological projects and products?[9] In our time science has presented us with so-called objective studies showing that certain races are inferior to others, with "cures" for homosexuality, and with a wide variety of contraceptives for women (and few for men), many with unknown side effects. Science, especially in its practical, technological side, has also created dangerous chemicals that deteriorate the environment; it gave us the nuclear bomb and pumps consumer goods into an already consumer-glutted economy. Science has indeed conquered nature as Francis

8. Feminist theologies emphasizing relationality and ecological issues range widely from reformist to radical, including goddess and witchcraft perspectives. See, e.g., Rita Nakashima Brock, *Journeys by Heart: A Christology of Erotic Power* (New York: Crossroad, 1988); Carol P. Christ, *Laughter of Aphrodite: Reflections on the Journey to the Goddess* (San Francisco: Harper & Row, 1987); Mary Daly, *Pure Lust: Elemental Feminist Philosophy* (Boston: Beacon Press, 1984); Elizabeth Dodson Gray, *Green Paradise Lost* (Wellesley, Mass.: Roundtable Press, 1981); Carter Heyward, *The Redemption of God* (New York: University Press of America, 1982); Catherine Keller, *From a Broken Web: Separation, Sexism and the Self* (Boston: Beacon Press, 1986); Mercy Amba Oduyoye, *Hearing and Knowing: Theological Reflections on Christianity in Africa* (Maryknoll, N.Y.: Orbis Books, 1986); Rosemary Radford Ruether, *Sexism and God-Talk: Toward a Feminist Theology* (Boston: Beacon Press, 1983); Starhawk, *The Spiral Dance: The Rebirth of the Ancient Religion of the Goddess* (New York: Harper & Row, 1979); idem, *Dreaming the Dark: Magic, Sex and Politics* (Boston: Beacon Press, 1982); Dorothee Soelle, *To Work and to Love: A Theology of Creation* (Philadelphia: Fortress Press, 1984); Alice Walker, *The Color Purple* (New York: Washington Square Press, 1983).

9. See esp. Sandra Harding, *The Science Question in Feminism* (Ithaca, N.Y.: Cornell University Press, 1986), which makes the point with power and at length. For similar perspectives, see Sandra Harding and Merrill Hintikka, eds., *Discovering Reality: Feminist Perspectives on Epistemology, Metaphysics, Methodology and Philosophy of Science* (Dordrecht, Neth.: D. Reidel, 1983).

Bacon told it to do several centuries ago, with never a thought for the consequences to human beings, other creatures, or the earth.

Is this the voice we should privilege? Scarcely. I would make two points, both much too briefly. The scientific picture of reality can be distinguished from the uses, both good and bad, of scientific technology. The former is concerned with how the various components of the physical universe, from the microscopic to the macroscopic and everything in between, are related and differentiated: everything that is, is both different from everything else and at the same time related to everything else in complex and astounding ways. As physicist and theologian Ian Barbour puts it, "Cosmology joins evolutionary biology, molecular biology, and ecology in showing the interdependence of all things."[10] Scientific technology, in contrast, does not intend to give us a picture of how all creation is related but puts some of that knowledge to use in order to provide society with goods needed or desired. The uses may be ethical or unethical, as judged by the moral standards of a society. Unfortunately, in many minds scientific technology and scientific theory are conflated, with the latter often reduced to its usefulness to human beings. The feminist critique of science is oriented mainly toward the abuses of scientific technology, whereas the picture of reality coming to us from the sciences overlaps significantly with many features characteristic of feminist visions of reality.

The second point I would underscore is that the postmodern scientific picture of reality is not a monolithic, absolutistic, objective ideology, masking a new essentialism or universalism, in part because many of the characteristics of this picture actually attack the bases of any monolithic objectivity. The characteristics of this picture, which have been emerging gradually over the last hundred years or so, beginning with Darwin and taking great leaps forward with the insights of Einstein and quantum physics as well as the cosmology and biology of the last forty years, have been pieced together by many hands. Moreover, at least some feminist scientists stress difference as one of the critical features of postmodern science. Because two of the most significant characteristics of the picture are individuality and interrelatedness, difference as well as interdependence is underscored. Evelyn Fox Keller, writing about Barbara McClintock, a Nobel laureate

10. Ian G. Barbour, "Creation and Cosmology," in *Cosmos as Creation*, ed. Peters, 147.

plant biologist, claims that McClintock's epistemological stance in relation to her plants is not the usual subject/object one of masculinist science based on the Baconian paradigm of male scientists dominating female nature but one which respects difference. It is a form of empathetic attention to the otherness of the other, even the otherness of a corn plant.[11] The scientific picture of reality supports this epistemology, which I would claim is not a distinctively feminist epistemology (although many feminists would affirm it) but a way beyond gender (as well as beyond other dualistic hierarchies and beyond essentialism) to what Keller calls "a world of difference"—one world, in which all are interconnected and interrelated and, at the same time, in which each thing, in its own self, is wonderfully, intricately, radically different.

The third issue that doctrinal reformulation in the context of postmodern science raises is the complex one of criteria. In this enterprise, does science dictate to theology? What is the role of Christian identity and faith in the reformulation of doctrine? To which science and which scientists does one pay attention? In my brief comments here I cannot adequately address these difficult questions. It is certainly the case that, although agreement on many broad features of physical reality can be found in the scientific community, disagreement on many issues exists as well. Theologians must choose their sciences and scientists, with the proviso that the selection be of central issues and figures, not idiosyncratic ones, as it is, after all, the "sense of reality current in our time" that needs to ground a persuasive, advocational theology. As to the issues of science dictating to theology and the role of Christian identity and faith, it is certainly not the case that science tells theology anything. Recall that I used the metaphor of "eavesdropping" for the relationship: theology listens to what science is telling the world, not theology, about itself and takes what it finds pertinent. What it will find pertinent will be both what fits with as well as what illuminates and transforms its understanding of Christian faith. This understanding is an interpretation, indeed, a construction of Christian faith in dialogue with the tradition, but also one deeply informed by the particular contexts out of which the theologian reflects, the contexts of race, class, gender, and so forth, as well as by the pressing issues of our day. I have written extensively on this elsewhere and can

11. See Evelyn Fox Keller, *Reflections on Gender and Science* (New Haven: Yale University Press, 1985), 158–76.

only give here my one-sentence version of Christian faith, as a white, middle-class woman from a mainstream Christian background. Christian faith is, it seems to me, most basically a claim that the universe is neither indifferent nor malevolent but that there is a power that is on the side of life and its fulfillment. Moreover, the Christian believes that we have some clues for fleshing out this claim in the paradigmatic life and death of Jesus of Nazareth, especially in his destabilizing, inclusive, nonhierarchical vision of fulfillment, which is open to all—particularly to the poor and oppressed—and which we need to extend as well to the entire planet and all its living creatures.[12] As I, one Christian theologian speaking out of a particular context, listen to the scientific story of the cosmos, I take what I find consonant with the main features of this version of Christian faith, at the same time remaining open to novel and fruitful ways in which that story can transform, reconstruct, and illuminate Christian faith, ways that will help make Christian faith credible, persuasive, and valuable in dealing with the threats to our planet's well-being. It is obvious that no one thing is serving as the foundation here. A diversity of criteria, I believe, is at work in a theological construction that is making a claim to be meaningful and true for our time. Among these criteria are a hermeneutical reconstruction of Christian identity and faith, that is, of what, most basically, Christianity is about; the need for such a reconstruction to be illuminated and transformed by insights from other areas of learning, including the sciences; an awareness of a variety of theological positions, given different social contexts, including those of race, gender, class, and sexual orientation; recognition of the tentativeness and partiality of all positions, including theological ones, or, to phrase it differently, recognition of the metaphorical character of all nontrivial interpretations of reality; and, finally, awareness of the praxis of and value-laden nature of theological reflection. Is this construction good for the polis and the cosmos?[13]

12. See Sallie McFague, *Models of God: Theology for a Nuclear, Ecological Age* (Philadelphia: Fortress Press, 1987), chap. 2.

13. My position on theological methodology has changed from that in *Models of God*, where I subscribed to a form of the "method of correlation," to one closer to that of Gordon Kaufman in his *The Theological Imagination: Constructing the Concept of God* (Philadelphia: Westminster Press, 1981); to the American pragmatic tradition (e.g., William Dean, *American Religious Empiricism* [Albany, N.Y.: SUNY Press, 1986]; Nancy Frankenberry, *Religion and Radical Empiricism* [Albany, N.Y.: SUNY Press, 1987]; and Rebecca Chopp, "Feminism's Theological Pragmatics: A Social Naturalism of Women's Experience," in *Journal of Religion* 67 [1987]:239–56); and to the critique of foundational theology and substitution of a "political broad reflective equilibrium" in the work of Francis Schüssler Fiorenza (*Foundational Theology: Jesus and the Church* [New York:

We turn now to some central features of the postmodern scientific view of reality. At its heart is the common creation story. In broad strokes, the story emerging from the various sciences claims that some fifteen billion years ago the universe began from a big bang, exploding matter, which was infinitely hot and infinitely concentrated outward to create some hundred billion galaxies, including our galaxy, the Milky Way, itself containing billions of stars and housing our sun and its planets. From this beginning came all that followed, so that everything that is, is related, woven into a seamless web, with life gradually emerging after billions of years on our planet (and probably on others as well) and evolving into the marvelously complex and beautiful forms we see about us. All things living and all things not living are the products of the same primal explosion and evolutionary history and hence are interrelated in an internal way right from the beginning. We are cousins to the stars, to the rocks and oceans, and to all living creatures.

From this story several features need to be highlighted as we consider how it might help reformulate a postmodern theological anthropology, that is, an understanding of "who we are" in terms of this story. First, the scales of space and time in this story are immense,

---

Crossroad, 1984]). Although these perspectives vary considerably, they lend support for the following points: (1) the impossibility of grounding thought (including theology) in the past or in any one foundation; (2) the centrality of contemporary experience, esp. concrete experience (including that of the oppressed and, by implication, the "experience" of the voiceless oppressed of our planet, the nonhuman animals and the plants); (3) the recognition that all experience is already contextualized and interpreted; (4) the insistence on the continuity between nature and history; (5) the need for constructive, imaginative, projective possibilities, rather than mere interpretations of a tradition; (6) the metaphorical character of all nontrivial interpretations of reality; (7) the importance of the comprehensibility, coherence, and meaningfulness of a construct, rather than its correspondence to some presumed reality; (8) the centrality of communities of discourse, to which various interpretations and constructions are accountable; and (9) the significance of value as a criterion—the well-being of the polis, although in our time this must mean the well-being of the cosmos.

What these thinkers insist upon is the multifaceted character of the judgments we make of constructs that we consider meaningful or true. A summary of many of these points is given by Mary Hesse when she writes: "We need a quite different theory of truth which will be characterized by *consensus* and *coherence* rather than by correspondence, by *holism* of meanings rather than atomism, by *metaphor* and *symbol* rather than by literalism and univocity, by intrinsic judgments of *value* as well as of fact" ("Cosmology as Myth," in *Cosmology and Theology*, ed. Tracy and Lash, 54). Criteria range from what one finds empirically and concretely to be "true to" one's experience and that of one's community, to what is fruitful, illuminating, and provocative, and to providing a holistic vision and bettering life in its many dimensions and forms. Rather than saying a theory or construct or interpretation is "true," it might be better to say it makes sense in terms of my experience (and that of the community to which I belong), provides me with a way of seeing the world as a whole, and will be good for the world and its inhabitants. Needless to say, many constructs will be "true" in these ways.

practically infinite. The observable universe contains some hundred billion galaxies, but beyond what can be observed may be billions more. The age of the universe, fifteen billion years, is equally difficult for the human imagination to conceive. The common example used for the age of the universe is a twenty-four-hour day: on that clock, human existence appears a few seconds before midnight. This suggests, surely, that the whole show could scarcely have been put on for our benefit; our natural anthropocentrism is sobered, to put it mildly. Nevertheless, because it took fifteen billion years to evolve creatures as complex as human beings, the question arises of our peculiar role in this story, especially in relation to our own planet.

A second feature of the postmodern picture is its story character: it is a historical narrative with a beginning, middle, and presumed end, unlike the Newtonian universe, which was static and deterministic. In our new cosmic story time is irreversible, genuine novelty results through the interplay of chance and necessity, and the future is open. This is an unfinished universe, a dynamic universe, still in process. Other cosmologies, including mythic ones such as Genesis and even earlier scientific ones, have not been historical, for in them creation was "finished." At the very least this suggests that in our current picture, God would be understood as a continuing creator; but of equal importance, we human beings might be seen as co-creators, as the self-conscious, reflexive part of the creation that could participate in furthering the process.

A third characteristic of the common creation story is precisely its common character: it is one story, so that everything that is traces its ancestral roots within it. All things have a common origin and hence are interrelated and interdependent. The organic character of the universe in no sense, however, supports a leveling or simplifying direction, that is, a lack of individuation. Precisely the opposite is the case. Whether one turns to the macrocosm or the microcosm, what one sees is an incredibly complex, highly individuated variety of "things," both living and nonliving. No two things, whether they be two exploding stars or the veins on two maple leaves, are the same; individuality is not just a human phenomenon, it is a cosmic one. At the same time, however, the exploding stars and the veins on the leaves are related through their common origin. The implications of this feature of the universe for theological anthropology are immense. The common character of the story undercuts notions of human existence as separate from the natural, physical world, or of human individuality as the only form of individuality, or of human individuals existing apart from radical interdependency and interrelatedness with others of our own species, with other species, and the ecosystem. As physicist Brian Swimme puts it, "No tribal myth, no matter how wild, ever imagined a more profound relationship connecting all things in an internal way right from the beginning of time. All thinking must begin with this cosmic genetic relatedness."[14] Were this feature of the scientific picture to become a permanent and deep aspect of our sensibility, it would be the beginning of an evolutionary, ecological, theological anthropology that could have immense significance in transforming how we think about ourselves and our relations and responsibilities toward other human beings, other species, and our home, planet Earth.

A fourth feature is the multileveled or, if you will, hierarchical character of the universe, from the flow of energy in subatomic reality to the incredibly complex sets of levels that comprise a human being. One critical aspect of this complexification is increasing subjectivity or the ability to experience and feel. Whatever one might or might not want to say about subjectivity in atoms or rocks, it surely increases as one progresses to animals and to its present culmination in human self-consciousness. This means, among other things, that there is no absolute distinction between living and nonliving things, because life is a type of organization, not an entity or substance. Thus, as Barbour puts it, "the chemical elements in your hand and in your brain were forged in the furnaces of the stars."[15] In contrast, the higher levels cannot be reduced to or understood entirely in terms of the lower levels, although the debate on this issue rages among the biologists, some of whom insist they can be so reduced.[16] What is significant here for theological anthropology is not only the continuity from the simplest events in the universe to the most complex but the inverse dependency as well, which undercuts any sense of absolute superiority in the

14. Brian Swimme, "Science: A Partner in Creating the Vision" in *Thomas Berry and the New Cosmology*, ed. Anne Lonergan and Caroline Richards (Mystic, Conn.: Twenty-third Publications, 1987), 87.

15. Barbour, "Creation and Cosmology," 147.

16. For a description and analysis of the "new biology" (molecular biology, sociobiology)—the biology of F. Crick, Jacques Monad, and E. O. Wilson, in which living organisms are "nothing but" atoms and molecules—see Arthur Peacocke, *God and the New Biology* (London: J. M. Dent & Sons, 1986). Peacocke claims that, as a philosophy, sociobiology is deterministic, reductionistic, and implicitly antitheistic (chap. 8).

hierarchical levels; that is, the so-called higher levels depend on the lower ones rather than vice-versa. This is obviously the case with human beings and plants—the plants can do very nicely without us (in fact, better), but we would quickly perish without them—but it is also the case with aspects of our earth that we have until recently taken for granted, such as clean air and water. The higher and more complex the level, the more vulnerable and dependent it is upon the levels which support it. For theological anthropology this is a very sobering thought, especially for a tradition that has been accused of advising human beings to "subdue" and "have dominion" over all the other created things.

Finally, the common creation story is a public one, available to all who wish to learn about it. Other creation stories, the cosmogonies of the various world religions, are sectarian, limited to the adherents of different religions. Our present one is not so limited; any person on the planet has potential access to it and, simply as a human being, is included in it. This common story is available to be remythologized by any and every religious tradition and hence is a place of meeting for the religions, whose conflicts in the past and present have often been the cause of immense suffering and bloodshed as belief is pitted against belief. What this common story suggests is that our primary loyalty should be not to nation or religion but to the earth and its Creator (albeit that Creator may be understood in different ways). We are members of the universe and citizens of planet Earth. Again, were that reality to sink into human consciousness all over the world, not only war among human beings but also ecological destruction would have little support in "reality," which is not to say that they would disappear but that those who continued in such practices would be living a lie, that is, living in a way that is out of keeping with reality as currently understood.

Who are we, then, according to the common creation story? According to the major characteristics of that story, human beings are radically other than what either the Christian tradition, especially since the Reformation, claims we are or what secular, modern culture allows. The two pictures differ in critical ways, with the religious picture focusing on the centrality of human beings, especially those who accept Jesus Christ as Savior, and the secular picture elevating individualism, consumerism, and technology. In both cases, however, the focus is on human beings, especially in terms of individual well-being.

Both God and the modern economic state appear to agree that the flourishing of human individuals is the center of all things.[17] In light of the common creation story this is a narrow vision indeed; yet it is so profoundly a part of the post-Enlightenment consciousness that we, for the most part, accept it as "natural," as the proper order of things. Immanuel Kant epitomizes the sacred-secular agreement on the position of the human, especially rational man: "As the single being on earth that possesses understanding, he is certainly titular lord of nature, and, supposing that we regard nature as a teleological system, he is born to be its ultimate end."[18] One has to ask here, What of women, slaves, primitive peoples, or the retarded, not to mention other animals who have their own kinds of reason and their own scale of values? The narrowness of modern, Western anthropology, whether religious or secular, is further underlined when its "human being," according to the cultural hegemony, is unmasked and shown to be male, white, educated, straight, healthy, and relatively affluent.

According to postmodern science, however, the religious/secular/modern picture of human reality is a lie, a very large and very

17. Various cultural historians find rampant individualism to be both a major characteristic and curse of modernity. Thomas Berry contrasts the individualistic, consumer-oriented story of modernity with "courtesy" and gratitude toward the earth found, e.g., in an eleventh-century Chinese administrative official who wrote: "Heaven is my father and earth is my mother and even such a small creature as I finds an intimate place in its midst. That which extends throughout the universe, I regard as my nature. All people are my brothers and sisters and all things are my companions" (quoted in *The Dream of the Earth*, 14–15). British philosopher and ethicist Mary Midgley sees our most critical problem to be "unbridled, exaggerated individualism, taken for granted as much by the left as the right—an unrealistic acceptance of competitiveness as central to human nature" (*Evolution as a Religion: Strange Hopes and Stranger Fears* [London: Methuen & Co., 1985], 140). The central thesis of the study of American religion, past and present, by Robert Bellah et al. is its radical individualism, which appears to cut across white middle-class denominations and sects (*Habits of the Heart: Individualism and Commitment in American Life* [New York: Harper & Row, 1985]). The issue of individualism in feminist hermeneutics is complex, as manifested in the varying responses to Carol Gilligan's study of the formation of female relatedness vs. male individualism in our culture (*In a Different Voice: Psychological Theory and Women's Development* [Cambridge: Harvard University Press, 1982]). "Individuality," the search for a sense of self, is not the same as "individualism," an ideology privileging the individual (human being) before all else. As our analysis of postmodern science revealed, individuality or "difference" is a mark of all existence. Moreover, it is ironic—and perhaps not entirely coincidental—that at the very time when women and other oppressed minorities who have not been allowed to speak their individuality are emerging, deconstruction insists that the self is an illusion and must be decentered. Could it be that as the one (male, white, Western) voice is losing its hegemony, it insists that no speakers exist, or is this not yet another masquerade to ensure its continued (although now hidden) control as the one who sets the rules of discourse?

18. Quoted in Mary Midgley, *Beast and Man: The Roots of Human Nature* (Ithaca, N.Y.: Cornell University Press, 1978), 219.

dangerous lie. According to the common creation story, we are not the center of things by any stretch of the imagination, although in a curious reversal we are, increasingly, very important. Even as our sense of our insignificance deepens when we see our place in an unimaginably old and immense universe, on our tiny planet, because of the wedding of science and technology we are in a critically important position. We have the knowledge and power to destroy ourselves as well as many other species; but we also have the knowledge and the power to help the process of the ongoing creation continue. This means, in a way unprecedented in the past, we are profoundly responsible. We have powers of destruction no other species has ever had, as our deteriorating ecosystem clearly illustrates. The ongoing history of our planet will necessarily involve our partnership and our participation for its well-being. This does not mean assuming an attitude of control toward the planet, hoping we can come up with a quick technological fix. Responsible partnership means adjusting to the rules and rhythms of the earth, adapting to its reality. Listening to the earth, not telling it what it must do, is a major aspect of our responsibility.

It is obvious that the model of the human being as seeking its own individual salvation, whether through spiritual or material means, is not only anachronistic to the postmodern sense of reality but also dangerous. We must think holistically, not just in terms of the well-being of humans. We must move beyond democracy to biocracy, seeing ourselves as one species among thousands of other species on a planet that is our common home.[19] Albert Schweitzer once wrote, "I am life desirous of living in the midst of life which also desires to live."[20] Our loyalty must move beyond family, nation, and even our own species to identify, in the broadest possible horizon, with all life: we are citizens of planet Earth.

Such identification is neither sentimental nor romantic; it does not emerge from a "love of nature" or fondness for charming panda bears or baby seals. It is simply the truth about who we are according to the contemporary picture of reality. We are profoundly interrelated and

19. Thomas Berry speaks of our need to reinvent the human as a species among species, rather than as nations or as ethnic peoples. "We need a constitution for the North American Continent. We need a United Species, not simply a United Nations" (The Dream of the Earth, 161).

20. Quoted in Gunter Altner, "Theology and Natural Science: The Debate Today," in Science and the Theology of Creation, Church and Society Documents (Bossey, Switzerland: World Council of Churches, 1988), 15.

interdependent with everything living and nonliving in the universe and especially on our planet, and our peculiar position here is that we are radically dependent on all that is, so to speak, "beneath us" (the plants on land and the microorganisms in the ocean as well as the air, water, and earth). At the same time, we have become, like it or not, the guardians, the protectors, the gardeners of our tiny planet. In a universe characterized by complex individuality beyond our comprehension, as well as by interrelations and interdependencies also beyond our comprehension, our peculiar form of individuality and interdependency has eventuated into a special role for us. We are the responsible ones, responsible for all the rest upon whom we are so profoundly dependent. No longer can we speak of ourselves as children, especially in a religious context: the passive, needy children of a loving, all-powerful father who will take care of us and our planet. We cannot continue to act like willful, brash adolescents out of control, as we have been doing in the modern story of scientism, militarism, individualism, and consumerism. We must become who we really are, neither the possessors nor principal tenants of planet Earth but self-reflexive "adults," the only species on the planet that knows the common creation story and can assume responsibility as partners to and with it. We no longer have the excuse of ignorance, because the story unfolding before our eyes over the last hundred years has revealed our "place" in the whole. This proper place has decentered and recentered us: we are no longer the point of the whole show, as Kant and the Christian tradition both thought, but have emerged as bearing heavy responsibilities for the well-being of the whole, responsibilities that will be difficult and painful to carry out, such as limiting both our population and its insatiable appetite for material goods.

Theological anthropologies emerging out of this understanding of human being can and will vary greatly, given the tradition, social context, and kinds of oppression experienced by different communities and individuals. For instance, nothing is said here about the critical issues of gender, race, and class. The context with which we are dealing is the broadest one possible—the human being as species. This allows, of course, enormous latitude for different theologies. Nonetheless, there would be some common notes as well: a focus on gratitude for the gift of life rather than a longing for eternal life; an end to all dualistic hierarchies, including human beings over nature; an appreciation for the individuality of all things rather than the glorification of human individualism; a sense of radical interrelatedness and inter-dependence with all that exists; the acceptance of responsibility for other forms of life and for the ecosystem, as guardians and partners of the planet; the acknowledgement that salvation is physical as well as spiritual and hence that sharing the basics of existence is a necessity; and, finally, the recognition that sin is the refusal to stay in our proper place—sin is, as it always has been understood in the Jewish and Christian traditions, living a lie.

We began our theological anthropology with the place of human beings as seen in the common creation story, rather than as a reflection of divine reality understood either from revelation or from fundamental theology. My thesis has been that whatever more one wants to say about who we are, to be credible and persuasive, as well as on the side of life and its fulfillment for our planet, it must be in keeping with the broad parameters of the view of reality coming from postmodern science.

It is important to underscore that this is a modest thesis, not directly concerned with the redemption and liberation of the outcast and the oppressed; in other words, with the heart of Christian faith, as I understand it. My focus has been on our empirical, cosmic setting as earthlings, even though that setting has significant implications for understanding redemption in our time, as we have seen. This setting has been, for the most part, neglected in recent theology and needs to be recalled and reinterpreted. Christian theologians will want to say "more" and "other" things about who we are, but we need to begin with our planetary citizenship.

It is a modest thesis but, given the great differences between the understanding of our proper place in post-Reformation Christianity and the common creation story, theological reflection conducted in terms of the new story would have revolutionary results. Once one accepts this view of who we are in the scheme of things there can be no return to anthropocentrism. Once the scales have fallen from our eyes, once we have seen and believed that reality is put together in such a fashion that we are profoundly united to and interdependent with all other beings, everything is changed. One sees the world differently: not anthropocentrically, not in a utilitarian way, not in terms of dualistic hierarchies, not in parochial terms. One has a sense of belonging to the earth, of having a place in it, and of loving it more than one ever thought possible.

In conclusion, it is precisely this sense of belonging, of being at home, that is the heart of the matter. It is the heart of the matter because it is the case—we do belong. As philosopher Mary Midgley writes: "We are not tourists here. . . . We are at home in this world because we were made for it. We have developed here, on this planet, and we are adapted to life here. . . . We are not fit to live anywhere else."[21] Postmodern science allows us to regain what late medieval culture lost at the Reformation and during the rise of dualistic mechanisms in the seventeenth century—a sense of the whole and where we fit in it. Medieval culture was organic, at least to the extent that it saw human beings, although central, as embedded in nature and dependent upon God. For the last several centuries, for a variety of complex reasons, we have lost that sense of belonging. Protestant focus on the individual and otherworldly salvation as well as Cartesian dualism of mind and body divided what we are now trying to bring back together and what must be reintegrated if we and other beings are to survive and prosper. But now, once again, we know that we belong to the earth, and we know it more deeply and thoroughly than any other human beings have ever known it.[22] The common creation story is more than a scientific affair; it is, implicitly, deeply moral, because it raises the question of the place of human beings in nature and calls for a kind of praxis in which we see ourselves in proportion, in harmony, and in a fitting manner relating to all others that live and all the systems that support life.[23]

21. Midgley, *Beast and Man*, 194–95.

22. It might be more accurate to say that for the last five thousand years, during the period of patriarchy, our primitive and ecologically correct sense of our place in the scheme of things has been lost. As contemporary research into early matriarchal, goddess religions shows, human awareness of belonging to the earth is very old. The literature on goddess religion and spirituality is vast and growing. For titles through 1986, see Anne Carson, *Feminist Spirituality and the Feminine Divine: An Annotated Bibliography* (Trumansburg, N.Y.: Crossing Press, 1986). Other religions, including, e.g., Native American ones, also attest to the awareness of human embeddedness in nature that comes "naturally" to people who live in close contact with the natural world.

23. In addition to Mary Midgley, other philosophers and theologians currently are exploring these themes. Stephen Toulmin speaks of living in the world as "home" rather than as "hotel"; the former way "means making sense of the relations that human beings and other living things have toward the overall patterns of nature in ways that give us some sense of their proper relations to one another, to ourselves, and to the whole" (*Return to Cosmology*, 272). James Gustafson, writing, as Toulmin does, in the context of postmodern science, says that God requires "consent to being, to what is right and good for human beings as they confront their awesome possibilities and their inexorable limitations" (*Ethics from a Theocentric Perspective*, vol. 1, 96–97). He also writes, "We are to conduct life so as to relate to all things in a manner appropriate to their relations to God" (113).

To feel that we belong to the earth and to accept our proper place within it is the beginning of a natural piety, what Jonathan Edwards called "consent to being," consent to what is. It is the sense that we and all others belong together in a cosmos, related in an orderly fashion, one to the other. It is the sense that each and every being is valuable in and for itself, and that the whole forms a unity in which each being, including oneself, has a place. It involves an ethical response, for the sense of belonging, of being at home, only comes when we accept our proper place and live in a fitting, appropriate way with all other beings. It is, finally, at a deep level, an aesthetic and religious sense, a response of wonder at and appreciation for the unbelievably vast, old, rich, diverse, and surprising cosmos, of which one's self is an infinitesimal but conscious part, the part able to sing its praises.

2

Humanistic Historicism and Naturalistic Historicism

WILLIAM DEAN

Ironically, most postmodern theologies have become so pluralistic, relativistic, and communally bound that they have reintro-
duced just those problems that initiated the modern study of theology.
Modern theology began with the attempt to become nonauthoritarian,
not to dismiss but to take account of and often to incorporate the full
scope of contemporary human opinion. Postmodern theologies seldom espouse premodern notions, but, I contend, they have lost most
grounds for rejecting premodern authoritarianism and its supernaturalistic, biblically literal theological teachings; and sooner or later,
using postmodern methods, these theologies are likely to reintroduce
such notions into academic theology. George Lindbeck's insinuation
of an apparently supernaturalistic eschatology into a sophisticated
postmodern theory of doctrine may be an early sign of just this.[1]
Therefore, although academic theology is robust today, there is on its
cheeks a disturbing color.

If postmodern theologies are to be remembered as the beginning of
a series of positive developments, rather than as a passing
phenomenon, then they need to avoid premodern eventualities
without reverting to modernism. Postmodern modes of religious
thought must find a way to honor the spirit of modern theology

1. See George A. Lindbeck, *The Nature of Doctrine: Religion and Theology in a Post-*
liberal Age (Philadelphia: Westminster Press, 1984), 57–63.

through refusing authoritarianism, supernaturalism, and biblical literalism, but they must not accomplish this with the modern sledge-hammer of foundationalism.

My claim is that one way to do this, quite appropriate to the history of American religious thought, is to develop a naturalistic historicism. Postmodern theologies practice a new historicism already, where the deepest ground of truth is historical interpretations of human culture and where the objects of these interpretations are still earlier interpretations of human culture, in an endless chain of cultural interpretations. In all this it is acknowledged that the range of plausible interpretations is not unlimited but is limited by (as well as capable of surpassing) the history of earlier interpretations. A naturalistic historicism introduces interpretations of nature, particularly scientific interpretations and the partial limitations of earlier scientific interpretations, and shows by contrast the humanistic focus of prevailing historicisms. A naturalistic-humanistic historicism includes and integrates both historicisms, and adds new historical data as well as new restrictions on what is plausible.

Recent postmodern theology and philosophy of religion are usually humanistic. They are new historicisms in principle, refusing to leave history through either premodern authoritarianism or modern foundationalism, but they are humanistic when they limit historical data to interpretations of human culture, thus omitting scientific interpretations. This restriction finally allows postmodern theology to become unnecessarily restricted to whatever is communally preferred—and, where it is communally satisfying, to accept premodern authoritarianism. Including scientific interpretations, I argue, would diminish such communalism or group subjectivism and its openness to premodern authoritarianism.

Such a naturalistic new historicism can appear oxymoronic. Naturalism, particularly scientific naturalism, typically has accepted varieties of determinism and objectivism and has denied the new historicism's contingency (its dependence on the accidents of interpretation). Similarly, most theologies of nature deny historicism in the new historicist sense. Although they have avoided determinism, they have retained a kind of objectivism, a belief that the evidence will allow them to see nature's laws as they are and as they will be. Some process and empirical theologians adopt, then, a theology of nature incompatible with new historicism.

Equally, most recent postmodern theologians (narrative, deconstructionist, and neopragmatic theologians) make a naturalistic new historicism oxymoronic by denying naturalism or by reducing it to human culture. In citing a chain of philosophers from Immanuel Kant to G.W.F. Hegel, from Martin Heidegger to Jacques Derrida, they abandon any simple foundationalism, any correspondence theory of truth, and offer a new and constructive historicist paradigm. Sometimes this leads them as historicists simply to diminish science's historicity, viewing science as Kant did, as a body of necessary and noncontingent truths. More recently they have reduced science to human culture, ostensibly following Thomas Kuhn in treating science as just one more communal expression. Accordingly, Lindbeck can say:

> The sharp division between the natural sciences and humanistic studies is breaking down. One hears exacting scholars, as I did at a recent Smithsonian consultation, casually remark with the authority of the commonplace that the epistemological grounding of a physicist's quarks and a Homer's gods is exactly the same. It is rhetorical force rooted in forms of life which gives them different cognitive status.[2]

This hegemonic caricature reduces the sciences to a branch of the humanities or of culture for which, as Paul Feyerabend has said, "anything goes."[3] Either way, whether by ignoring or reducing science's history, postmodern theologians avoid naive objectivism; but, also either way, they avoid the critique of theology that might come from science or from a religious naturalism and open themselves to a kind of group subjectivism. Thus in theology, while the American naturalists lack a Continental self (that is, a self important enough to affect basically everything it interprets), the Continental tradition even in America lacks a natural world (that is, a nature included in the theological world).

Continentally oriented, postmodern theologians appear to be in the ascendancy in American theology, and so it is to them rather than to the naturalistic theologians that I turn. They have so excluded any distinct testimony of nature from their considerations, I contend, that they are unwittingly open to a supernaturalistic and premodern authoritarianism. For them religious truths live in human history, and

2. George A. Lindbeck, "The Church's Mission to a Postmodern Culture," in *Postmodern Theology: Christian Faith in a Pluralistic World*, ed. Frederic B. Burnham (New York: Harper & Row, 1989), 51.
3. See Paul Feyerabend, *Against Method: Outline of an Anarchistic Theory of Knowledge* (London: Verso, 1984), chap. 1.

the history of nature (if nature is thought really to have a history) is religiously unimportant. Consequently, the scientific tradition about nature, interpretive as it itself might be, loses the capacity to raise any veto to what might be proposed theologically. These theological historicists trap religion within a nonnatural, human, even linguistic history, and thus flirt with a kind of group subjectivism. All this diminishes, I believe, these otherwise profoundly valuable efforts to develop a new and sustainable theological paradigm, making it less persuasive to our still-scientific age.

What is needed, I argue, is to include scientific naturalism within a theological historicism. Most generally stated, this new naturalistic-humanistic historicism would include not only the testimony about human history but testimony about natural history, thus replacing the old theological jargon of nature and history with a new theological jargon of nature as (one form of) history. Nature, this assumes, is not a determined state of affairs but a chain of interpretations with its own topic that provides its own limits on language. Now testimony about natural history would broaden the data but add new limits to the ways in which historicist claims could be pragmatically argued—eliminating, for example, the supernaturalistic claims so typical of human cultures. Such a naturalistic-humanistic historicism would remain parochial, provincial, and in that sense relative in its imaginative formulations, because even the scientific community's testimony is itself interpretive and biased. A theological naturalism would not introduce a new foundationalism or a new objectivism; but a naturalistic-humanistic historicism would include a new range of testimonies and be open to stricter pragmatic tests than those provided by a humanistic historicism alone.

Most of all, a naturalistic-humanistic historicism would be likely to escape authoritarianism and reinvoke the spirit of modern theology by incorporating the full scope of human opinion—including, that is, scientific opinion. Unlike a humanistic historicism, it would effectively require historicist theology to justify itself not only before the bar of an interpreted human history but also before the bar of an interpreted natural history. This allows theological historicism effectively to criticize, for example, yesterday's Nazi pseudo-science about Aryan racial superiority or today's pseudo-science of Christian supernaturalism (including creationism, literalist eschatology, and objectivist stands on the ordination of women and birth control), and to do so without going metaphysical. Also, it makes possible a historicist mandate for a responsible religious environmentalism.

To illustrate that theological postmodernists do not quite avoid group subjectivism and to argue that they could benefit by a naturalistic dimension added to their historicism, I turn first to the narrative theologians of the Yale School. Second, I return to the foregoing general encomium for a naturalistic dimension by noting that to omit a naturalistic historicism is to flirt with two kinds of inconsistencies.

Before this two-part investigation I will more completely define the "new historicism" in theology. For theological "new historicists" history is prior to everything and is shaped by a chain of interpretations, a chain itself shaped by the interaction between how the theologian wants to interpret the past and how a tradition appears to limit the theologian's range of possible interpretations. By contrast, "old historicists" allow nonhistorical forces to contribute to the shaping of history. Old historicists are materialists, sometimes in the mode of Karl Marx's dialectical materialism, or idealists, sometimes adopting a rationalistic version of Hegelianism or the sort of vestigial absolutism found even in Ernst Troeltsch's historicism. With the "old historicisms" something beyond history sets the tune by which history dances, rather than the other way around. For the old historicism a material law or an ideal condition precedes and thus to some extent determines historical existence. By contrast, the new historicism means to include no such nonhistorical conditions. I am proposing that this theological new historicism[4] could be strengthened and could avoid reversion to premodernism if it included in its notions about history the testimony of scientists about natural history.

There are today three widely recognized schools of theological new historicists: the neopragmatists, the deconstructionists, and the narra-

4. I work from the standpoint of a specifically American new historicism; see William Dean, *American Religious Empiricism* (Albany, N.Y.: SUNY Press, 1986); and idem, *History Making History: The New Historicism in American Religious Thought* (Albany, N.Y.: SUNY Press, 1988). Although I recognize that there are important differences between Gordon D. Kaufman and myself, I very much support Kaufman's work toward combining what I call a humanistic historicism and a naturalistic historicism. Specifically, in *An Essay on Theological Method* (Missoula, Mont.: Scholars Press, 1975; 1979), chap. 3, Kaufman argues that his use of theological imagination does not treat God as a subjective fantasy but as "a sort of logical structure" beyond imagination; in his *The Theological Imagination* (Philadelphia: Westminster Press, 1981), chap. 1, Kaufman characterizes God as a "cosmic movement" in nature; and in his *Theology for a Nuclear Age* (Philadelphia: Westminster Press, 1985), 39–43. Kaufman views God as a "hidden creativity" in nature.

tive theologians of the Yale School. The neopragmatists have reached their historicism on a route extending from eighteenth-century British empiricism, to positivism, to language analysis, to the neopragmatism traceable from Willard Quine to Richard Rorty. The deconstructionists have reached their historicism by way of a historicist reading of Hegel, through phenomenology and semiotics, to structuralism, to Jacques Derrida's deconstructionism. The narrative theologians of the Yale School have reached their historicism through an explicitly theological route, depending heavily on neo-orthodox theologians, especially Karl Barth and H. Richard Niebuhr. Admittedly, the narrativists are a broad lot in religious studies, containing people of a number of persuasions. I will discuss only those Gary Comstock calls "pure narrative theologians,"[5] and here I think primarily of the Yale School theologians George Lindbeck (*The Nature of Doctrine*), Hans Frei (*The Eclipse of Biblical Narrative*), and Ronald Thiemann (*Revelation and Theology*).[6]

I focus on the Yale theologians because I believe that, among the three historicist schools, they may be most conscious of avoiding just the group subjectivism I criticize above.[7] I accept Lindbeck's claim[8] that Frei, and implicitly Lindbeck himself and Thiemann, are coming closer to meeting Jeffrey Stout's and Alasdair MacIntyre's criterion that theology must "respond to modernity without becoming either incomprehensible to it or so much like it as to sacrifice the claim to distinctiveness."[9] Although the narrative theologians have enough group

5. The variety of narrative theologians is demonstrated by Comstock, who lists Paul Ricoeur, Hans Frei, David Tracy, George Lindbeck, Stanley Hauerwas, Julian Hartt, Sallie McFague, Johann Baptist Metz, Carol Christ, Brian Wicker, David Burrell, James McClendon, Sam Keen, and Harvey Cox. These are supported by people outside Christian theology: Michael Goldberg, Elie Wiesel, Robert Bellah, Arthur Danto, Alasdair MacIntyre, Jean-Françoise Lyotard, Richard Rorty, Amos Wilder, and Nathan A. Scott (Gary L. Comstock, "Two Types of Narrative Theology," *Journal of the American Academy of Religion* 55 [Winter 1987]:687).

6. See the reference to Lindbeck in n. 1, above; Hans W. Frei, *The Eclipse of Biblical Narrative: A Study in Eighteenth- and Nineteenth-Century Hermeneutics* (New Haven: Yale University Press, 1974); and Ronald F. Thiemann, *Revelation and Theology: The Gospel as Narrated Promise* (Notre Dame, Ind.: University of Notre Dame Press, 1985).

7. I also select the narrative theologians because I have dealt elsewhere and somewhat in this light with neopragmatists and deconstructionists; see esp. chap. 5 of *History Making History*, where I discuss two deconstructionists, Mark C. Taylor and Jacques Derrida, and two neopragmatists, Jeffrey Stout and Cornel West.

8. In a revised but unpublished manuscript of an important lecture delivered in Chicago on November 7, 1988, titled "Hans W. Frei and the Future of Theology in America."

9. Jeffrey Stout, *The Flight from Authority: Religion, Morality, and the Quest for Autonomy* (Notre Dame, Ind.: University of Notre Dame Press, 1981), 97.

integrity to ignore apologetic efforts to establish their modernity meta-physically, they are interested in avoiding incomprehensibility, at least to the extent, Stout says, that they would undertake "fruitful conversa-tion and collaboration with nonbelievers on specific issues of common concern."[10] For moral purposes, at least, they would hope to retain the capacity to respond comprehensibly to modern culture.

Nevertheless, I urge a naturalistic historicism because it might best add to theology what the novelist John Updike calls artistry—in addi-tion to the merely critical. "An artist," Updike says, "mediates between the world and minds: a critic merely between minds. An artist therefore must even at the price of uncouthness and alienation from the contemporary cultural scene maintain allegiance to the world and a fervent relation with it."[11] Updike is worried that critics will shrink the world to talk about merely human talk, and he wants to retain talk about a larger world. Similarly, I am worried that humanis-tic historicists will shrink the religious world to language about human communities, and I want to retain in that world language about natural communities.

NATURE IN NARRATIVE THEOLOGY

At the opening of *The Nature of Doctrine* Lindbeck asks himself the practical question, How do we account for the fact that there is a new reconciliation in ecumenical discussions, even though the participants continue to hold theological beliefs that once caused apparently irrec-oncilable differences? How, in short, can it now be possible to have reconciliation without capitulation? The question nags because tradi-tional "cognitive propositionalists" and liberal "experiential expres-sivists" cannot answer it; they find reconciliation only through the capitulation of all parties but one: the party that has the right cognitive belief or the right generic religious experience. Lindbeck, however, believes his "cultural-linguistic" notion of doctrine and theology can account for this development, thus showing its pragmatic superiority. According to the cultural-linguistic approach, beliefs of first-order language (claims to truth in particular religious groups) are incom-mensurable, remain incommensurable, and should capitulate to no

10. Jeffrey Stout, *Ethics after Babel: The Languages of Morals and Their Discontents* (Boston: Beacon Press, 1988), 186.
11. John Updike, *Hugging the Shore: Essays and Criticisms* (New York: Vintage Books, 1983), xviii.

one. Reconciliation is based not on such first-order beliefs but on doctrines, which pertain not to truth but to grammar, the systematic framework, the language at the second order, in terms of which first-order truth-claims are organized. Although doctrine may not give truth, it reconciles Christians as Christians, giving them the basis for constancy through time and for unity across Christian denominations.

The distinguishing characteristic of doctrines is that they are based on the biblical narrative, so that Christians are those people who see their lives in the world of that narrative. This notion of biblical narrative was given a startling rendition by Frei. It is not enough to say that he protected the sui generis status of the narrative by the *via negativa*, refusing to allow it to be reduced to anything else, such as the facts of history, generic human experience, general ideas, or arguments. Frei's claim centered on an account of narrative's positive role. In his words, "the meaning of the narrative is the narrative structure itself"; "the meaning emerges from the story form, rather than being merely illustrated by it," so that one can appreciate "the narrative features of the biblical stories in their own right."[12] The consequence is that the biblical stories should be read as the realistic English novel is read, where "the meaning of the realistic stories was taken to be the realistic, fact-like depictions themselves, regardless of their reference, of the question of their factual truth or falsity, or of the 'spirit' pervading the writing."[13] Hence the distinguishing characteristic of narrative and of doctrine is not that they refer to anything but that they provide a framework of meaning that is real in, of, and by itself.

Following Frei, Lindbeck says, "just as an individual becomes human by learning a language, so he or she begins to become a new creature through hearing and interiorizing the language that speaks of Christ."[14] In other words, "meaning is *constituted by* the uses of a specific language rather than being distinguishable from it."[15] This is the converse of the position of "experiential-expressive" liberals, for whom meaning is constituted by experience so that language is based on experience, not experience on language. It rejects also "cognitive propositionalists," for whom meaning is constituted by cognitive argument so that language is based on argument, not the other way

12. Frei, *The Eclipse of Biblical Narrative*, 310, 280, 220.
13. Ibid., 218.
14. Lindbeck, *The Nature of Doctrine*, 62.
15. Ibid., 114. Emphasis mine.

around. Narrative theology, by contrast, uses language in the form of narrative and doctrine to give logic and meaning to a particular religious group's theological formulations, practices, and moralities as they operate at the first order in a particular culture. It is precisely this narrativist approach that allows Lindbeck to argue both for "the permanence and unity of doctrines" (the second-order language) and for the relativity, plurality, and shifting of the theological formulations that relate doctrines to particular cultures in particular times (the first-order language).[16] Consequently, there can be reconciliation without capitulation.

This would seem to enable Lindbeck to be historicist without being either a group subjectivist or implicitly premodernist. He is a historicist in that he concedes that one's theological truth is correlative to one's specific theological community. He intends to avoid group subjectivism by contending that the group's common grammar is set by the broad, ecumenical Christian world. Accordingly, Lindbeck's theology would be local and yet avoid group subjectivism.

The second-order language, in short, would save the Yale School narrative theologian from group subjectivism. Lindbeck insists that doctrine (and, presumably, all second-order language) is as neutral as grammar is and makes no truth claim. It is precisely its truth-neutral, grammatical, rules-only mode of speaking that allows it to serve as a clearing house for and a reconciler among diverse Christian truth claims, thus preventing, presumably, a destructive relativism and irrelevance to a larger world. This language of ecumenism keeps any theology "realistic" in the sense that it brings the utterly parochial into contact with a larger world.

One might ask, however, is not this second-order bridge between narrow communities also a product of narrow communities? Does the second-order language of narrative escape the group subjectivism of first-order language? Are not grammar and formal rules always already loaded with specific, local views of the world, and thus implicit claims to truth? It was the claim that doctrine grows out of a real and shared biblical narrative, not out of particular forms of human experience, that allowed the Yale narrativists to distinguish themselves from the old liberals. But is not the formal language of narrative and doctrine itself a function of a chain of particular and local human

16. Ibid., 84.

experiences? Is not Lindbeck inflating a relative narrative into an ostensibly irrelative metalanguage, making the metalanguage a function of a particular language after all?

Within three pages of *The Nature of Doctrine* Lindbeck speaks of Scripture's "own domain of meaning"; of "the text," which absorbs the world; and of Scripture functioning as "the lens." These all are accounts of ostensibly second-order functions.[17] It must be remembered, however, that access to Scripture's "own" meaning or to "the" text or to "the" lens comes only through particular historical circumstances. This would appear to reduce Scripture's "own meaning" to merely "our" meaning or make "the" text and "the" lens merely "our" text and lens.[18] The truth-empty character of second-order language can be challenged by noting that its purportedly formal grammar of faith is, after all, a claim born of a particular twentieth-century, academic, and neo-neo-orthodox faith. The second-order language can be seen, then, as the product of a particular historic community's commonsensical view of the world. To the extent that that view is specific and uninformed by positions beyond the group's natural interests, it omits unintentionally and unnecessarily just those interests that do not accord with its own, such as particular scientific interpretations of nature. Accordingly, the most dangerous of blindnesses may be allowed: the unrecognized blindness.

Lindbeck appears to have tied his second-order Christian narrative to a local cultural matrix, reducing what Updike called "the allegiance to the world" to an allegiance to local minds. This, in turn, jeopardizes Lindbeck's claim that doctrine speaks for a world distinct from what is merely local. If Lindbeck fails to defend the translocal character of second-order language (language that would span denominations), then he is caught in mere group subjectivism—a subjectivism open, in principle, to premodern thought.

A variation of this charge has been advanced by Timothy Jackson in a review of Lindbeck's *Nature of Doctrine*. Jackson argues that the book fails as foundational realism because of what it concedes to relativity. It fails as pragmatic relativism because of what it claims for unity of

---

17. Ibid., 117–19.
18. For an important statement of this and similar criticisms, see Terrence W. Tilley, "Incommensurability, Intratextuality, and Fideism," *Modern Theology* 5 (January 1989): 87–111.

doctrine across time and denominations. This leaves Lindbeck's theology in an untenable position, says Jackson, for beyond these two options "there is no third alternative."[19]

Jackson, however, assumes that all realism must be objectivizing and metaphysical and that all relativism must be dominated by something like the linguistic turn in philosophy. His "no third alternative" assertion neglects that a third alternative has been strongly defended in the past, and that now even Lindbeck himself seems to be seeking some such an alternative. That Lindbeck seeks a third option is suggested in Jackson's own claim that *The Nature of Doctrine* is an incoherent mixture of realism and relativism. Lindbeck may not spell out his position, but he does leave place markers for a kind of pragmatism and a kind of reference to experience. Pragmatically, Lindbeck says that the truth of religious utterances is known only as "a function of their role in constituting a form of life"; and he goes on to discuss J. L. Austin's notion of the performatory use of language.[20] Qualifying his dismissal of experience, Lindbeck says: "Turning now in more detail to the relation of religion and experience, it may be noted that this is not unilateral but dialectical. It is simplistic to say (as I earlier did) merely that religions produce experiences, for the causality is reciprocal. Patterns of experience alien to a given religion can profoundly influence it."[21] Pragmatism offers a way of relating local, first-order claims to the larger world of "the Ultimately Real" (to use Lindbeck's language) without introducing correspondence tests of truth and objectivism. Experience offers a way of relating formal, second-order claims to a world beyond those formal systems. The stark dichotomy between pure linguistic formality and pure communal relativity might be circumvented by the pragmatic and experiential referentiality Lindbeck suggests.

Moreover, in his confidence that there is no third alternative, Jackson, like most scholars today, ignores classical American philosophy

19. Timothy P. Jackson, "Against Grammar," *Religious Studies Review* 2 (July 1985):244. Jackson argues that the true pragmatist would reject both the correspondence theory of truth implicit in Lindbeck's first-order propositional claims and the constancy across time and place in his second-order doctrinal claims. Further, he argues that the second-order claims seem to smuggle in ontological foundations. Here I criticize only the second-order claims, not because of hidden foundations but because of their constancy.

20. Lindbeck, *The Nature of Doctrine*, 65.

21. Ibid., 33.

and the theology that has used that philosophy.[22] Here I introduce not only the classical American philosophy and theology of yesteryear but also neopragmatism and much postmodern thought in America today, which, as Rorty, Cornel West, and Richard Bernstein[23] have shown, are in some respects extensions of the classical philosophy. This American, radically empirical, and pragmatic philosophy might augment Lindbeck's hints of a third position.

William James, writing eighty years before Lindbeck, faced a predicament similar to Lindbeck's. He was antagonized by the objectivists (the positivists) and ontological realists (the tender-minded absolutistic idealists) of his day. Also like Lindbeck, James was unwilling to give all moral and religious authority to a tough-minded relativism. Rather than treat these as simple incommensurables, he sought a third position.

James differed from Lindbeck in one major point: he included as referents for his world-affirming and faith-affirming language not only narrative testimonies about human culture but testimonies about nature. I am not contending that this permitted James to escape relativism and pluralism, for it did not; nor am I claiming that James saved the day for the old liberals or the Enlightenment cognitivists through identifying in a newly acceptable way the generic human experience or the right propositional arguments. My contention is that James's use of the naturalistic referent moves his thought partially out of a humanistic historicism onto a broader plain, but one that prohibited the use of premodern claims. James's world is larger because he pragmatically tests his claims by reference not just to words or cultures alone but also to scientific testimonies about nature. Even though James's naturalism is not objective and is relative, it does give scientific testimonies a veto capable of overriding what any particular theological claim might propose.

The introduction of the distinctiveness of scientific testimony is important even for Kuhn. He may argue that science is guided by the

22. Jackson also disregards the work of Maurice Merleau-Ponty, who sought a "middle way" beyond classical empiricism and idealism. See esp. Merleau-Ponty, *The Phenomenology of Perception* (London: Routledge & Kegan Paul, 1962).

23. See Richard Rorty, *Consequences of Pragmatism (Essays: 1972–1980)* (Minneapolis: University of Minnesota Press, 1982); Cornel West, *The American Evasion of Philosophy: A Genealogy of Pragmatism* (Madison: University of Wisconsin Press, 1989); Richard J. Bernstein, *Beyond Objectivism and Relativism: Science, Hermeneutics, and Praxis* (Philadelphia: University of Pennsylvania Press, 1983).

interpretive bias of the scientific community, but he also acknowledges that, for science, "observation and experience can and must drastically restrict the range of admissible scientific belief."[24] Science may be a cultural-linguistic construct but it is one guided or limited by the observation and experience distinctive to the sciences. Kuhn uses observation and experience of nature to avoid a group subjectivism (to restrict belief) without reverting to foundationalism. His distinction is comparable to Ludwig Wittgenstein's distinction between hard, riverbed empirical propositions and fluid, river water propositions: while the riverbed propositions (unlike absolutely immovable foundational truths) are slowly movable, they do limit the flow of the more fluid propositions. Analogously, we might say scientific observation and experience in some nonfoundational ways do limit scientific language.[25] This naturalistic limitation need not introduce a correspondence theory of truth or a naive realism, but—for the purposes of this discussion—only a pragmatic test of scientific hypotheses. This does give scientific language a distinctive testimony. Accordingly, when theology is asked to avoid supernaturalism by entering into conversation with scientific testimony, the request is not trivial.

Lindbeck does include language about nature in his narrative world but, unlike James and Kuhn, he incapacitates science's veto by making testimonies about nature an instrument of the narrative world of the Bible. He speaks of the religion's narrative world as "all-encompassing," as extended "over the whole of reality," as "able to absorb the universe," even the so-called "extrascriptural realities."[26] This religious captivity of science's language, then, allows Lindbeck in good conscience to advance what he calls a "prospective theory" of salvation, which appears to be a first-century supernaturalistic eschatology. Lindbeck allows that this will seem "mythological or unreal to those who think science or philosophy makes it impossible to affirm a temporally and objectively future eschaton."[27] He attempts to allay

---

24. Thomas S. Kuhn, *The Structure of Scientific Revolutions*, 2d ed. (Chicago: University of Chicago Press, 1974), 4.

25. See Ludwig Wittgenstein, *On Certainty*, ed. G.E.M. Anscombe and G. H. Von Wright (New York: Harper & Row, 1969), p. 15, pars. 96–99. For this use of Wittgenstein's river analogy I am indebted to Everett J. Tarbox's paper "Wittgenstein, James, and a Bridge to Radical Empiricism," given at the 1989 annual meeting of the Highlands Institute for American Religious Thought.

26. Lindbeck, *The Nature of Doctrine*, 115, 117.

27. Ibid., 62.

this concern by arguing that: (1) the liberal claims about prelinguistic religious experiences will seem just as unreal to those who accept the cultural-linguistic position—assuming, apparently, that one problem excuses the other; (2) "mythological elements (in the technical, non-pejorative sense of 'myth') are indispensable in any religion"; and (3) in any case, "what is real or unreal is in large part socially constructed."[28] It is the third point that most pointedly ignores the testimony of the sciences. Scientific language is, in large part, socially constructed, but Lindbeck never asks whether the constructions distinctive to science might have an indispensable voice in his own version of history, one that cannot simply be subsumed by the religious narrative; nor does he acknowledge that scientific language has a distinctively observational and experiential way of limiting language, leading it to confute the supernaturalism of eschatological language.

In contrast to the Yale narrativists, a group of theologians spawned by American classical philosophers gave to scientific testimony a distinctive voice. They included in theology the weight of scientific observations, or observations and experiences referring to nonhuman phenomena. Admittedly, today we would argue that those nonhuman realities never can be accessed except through human frames of interpretation, so that they never are known in their rawness. Ian Barbour, more than anyone else, has shown how this acknowledgement of the power of interpretation need not nullify a theology of nature informed by science.[29] Nevertheless, simply that scientific language refers to observations and experiences of a nonhuman world limits that language in distinctive ways. Specifically, it prohibits supernaturalistic language. Thus scientific language has a distinctive voice, one that must be included in the theological enterprise or else that enterprise is open to premodern ways of speaking.

Here, then, is that third option, which Jackson assumed did not exist and which I believe Lindbeck sought, no doubt in another form. It includes what Updike would call the artistic as well as the critical, because it refers to a world larger than the world internal to human cultures, and thereby it can criticize testimonies referring only to human phenomena.

28. Ibid., 62–63
29. For Barbour's current and best rendering of this point see his *Religion in an Age of Science: The Gifford Lectures 1989–1991*, vol. 1 (San Francisco: Harper & Row, 1990).

This third approach would build on the old "Chicago School" of theology (principally, the work of George Burman Foster, Gerald Birney Smith, Shailer Mathews, and Shirley Jackson Case) and empirical theology (principally, the work of D. C. Macintosh, Henry Nelson Wieman, Bernard Meland, and Bernard Loomer). These theologies are the natural antecedents for a naturalistic-humanistic historicism because they were not obsessed with metaphysics, sometimes took history very seriously, and sought to sustain along with their neonaturalism a distinctively Christian understanding of nature and of human fulfillment.

Such a theological undertaking would seek to escape the worst forms of group subjectivism by refusing to turn a blind eye to what is extrascriptural and extraecclesiastical. It would be able, thereby, to avoid premodern beliefs and to retain the spirit of modern theology without accepting the metaphysical content of that theology.

PROBLEMS OF INCONSISTENCY

Even if the theory of humanistic new historicism carried no potential for reintroducing premodern beliefs into postmodern theology, it would remain problematic in two ways. First, simply in the statement of their theory, new historicists concurrently affirm and deny that knowledge claims are historically contingent. On the one hand, affirming historical contingency, they claim that all theories speak only for particular peoples in particular locations in time and space; on the other hand, denying historical contingency, they claim that their own theory speaks for all peoples everywhere. In order vigorously to insist on historical contingency they deny historical contingency. Historicist theory is itself a claim and therefore must be historically contingent, but historicist theory must be noncontingent (universally and eternally applicable) because it intends to apply to all claims from all histories. Consequently the theory itself must be a noncontingent— even though as a theory itself it must be contingent.

Escapes from this inconsistency are possible if either of these two aspects were denied. That is, the new historicists could deny their claim's contingency by arguing that their theory claim is not really a historical claim and can be treated without inconsistency as historically noncontingent. By contrast, they could deny their theory's noncontingency by arguing that their theory is not really a nonhistorical claim and should be treated as historically contingent. However, neither denial successfully escapes the inconsistency:

1. Escape (a): *Denying historical contingency.* The new historicists could argue that their own theory claim is merely a formal statement, a metalanguage that merely sets rules for historical language and, as such, need not itself adhere to rules for historical language. This account ignores that metalanguages themselves are the products of particular groups in particular times and places. As historical languages, metalanguages are incapable of making historically noncontingent claims. To deny the historical contingency of metalanguages is to neglect that accumulation of studies, beginning at least with Kuhn's *The Nature of Scientific Revolutions*, according to which those ostensibly most metalinguistic of all statements (those of science) are in fact local, social, and particular.

2. Escape (b): *Denying historical noncontingency.* The new historicists could argue that their theory claim is just one more relative historical claim uttered by this group in this time and place and, as such, need not defend itself as presumably noncontingent. This account is unsustainable for two reasons. First, in insisting on the contingency of their own theory of contingency, historicists merely postpone the noncontingency of their claims by one step. The very assumption that theory claims about contingency must be itself contingent assumes that contingency is universal, that is, that contingency is noncontingent.[30] It assumes that even one's own theory claim is made contingent for only one reason: there is something about language that is universal and noncontingent, so that all claims in all times and places simply must be contingent. Second, even if scholars concede that historicism arose only contingently, they must acknowledge that historicist theory was designed to apply to all people in all histories; its genius

---

30. In his excellent *Relativism, Knowledge, and Faith* (Chicago: University of Chicago Press, 1960), Gordon Kaufman recognizes this type of problem. He seeks to deny the noncontingent status for his "internal history" historicism by acknowledging that as a theory it is not absolute but is made only "on the basis of our personal and communal history" (120). I question if this does not itself only postpone noncontingent status. By the mid-1970s Kaufman introduces into his theology a naturalistic dimension, thus laying the groundwork for alleviating this problem (see n. 4, above).

and notoriety lies in proposing a truth that is universally applicable. Thus it carries pretensions to noncontingency. The whole point of historicism is that the historicist shoe pinches everyone, even those nonhistoricists who don't want to wear it. This accusatory stance is intrinsic to the historicist argument; without it, the real thrust of the historicist claim is lost.

Admittedly, a historicism that includes a naturalistic dimension logically overcomes neither of these problems. Nevertheless, if the task is to advance a theory persuasively, a naturalistic-humanistic historicism has a pragmatic advantage over a humanistic historicism because of the breadth of its data; it includes the scientist in the historicist conversation. Although relative, historicist, or subjective in origin, a naturalistic-humanistic historicist's claims can be tested in a broader conversation—to function, thereby, with greater pragmatic success. The testimony of an evolutionary or paleontological theorist, for instance, may be just as communal and historically contingent in its derivation as a testimony about human history alone; it depends equally on the accidents of the scientist's social or cultural context (see, for example, Stephen Jay Gould's account of group dynamics among paleontologists in *Wonderful Life*).[31] Nevertheless, within a naturalistic-humanistic historicism the naturalists contribute that trustworthiness that comes from greater breadth, from reflection on natural communities as well as reflection on human communities. The language of naturalistic historicism introduces the limits, as well as possible openings, from observations and experiences of millions of biological species and the testimonies that are affected by those observations and experiences.

A second problem is found in those humanistic new historicists who relate their work to biblical religions. The Yale narrativists explicitly and the deconstructive and neopragmatic religious thinkers implicitly adopt the biblical narrative, yet they make little use of biblical naturalism. If religious historicism is to be consistent with its tradition, the neglect of this naturalistic element raises questions about the intratextual consistency of Christian humanistic historicisms.

31. Stephen Jay Gould, *Wonderful Life: The Burgess Shale and the Nature of History* (New York: W. W. Norton, 1989). He shows how in the last thirty years one group of paleontologists completely reinterpreted museum drawers of fossils that had been alternatively interpreted fifty years earlier.

For both Gerhard von Rad and H. Paul Santmire the Hebrew Bible is not naturalistic in the way Canaanitic religions were, but it appears, nevertheless, to have a naturalistic dimension. Although von Rad will acknowledge that it took Israel a very long time to connect the idea of creation with salvation history, he claims that eventually Isaiah and Deutero-Isaiah argued for "the theological derivation of Yahweh's power over history from his authority as Creator." Equally, the Yahwist and the Priestly writers made creation itself a soteriological act, so that creation provided, von Rad says, "a different foundation from the one which the old Credo could supply."[32] Additionally, for the wisdom literature "creation was in reality an absolute basis for faith, and was referred to for its own sake altogether."[33] For von Rad "this wisdom, which we have understood as the primeval world order, as the mystery behind the creation of the world, rules in similar fashion in the non-human creation as well as in the sphere of human society."[34] Apropos of those who would confine history to human history, von Rad contends, "The dualism, familiar to us, of rules for human society on the one hand and rules for nature on the other, was unknown to the ancients."[35]

Santmire advances a more deep-running biblical naturalism. He argues that even von Rad makes nature an adjunct to human salvation, so that his theology of nature is anthropocentric.[36] Advancing "an ecological hermeneutic," Santmire lays out an alternative reading of the Hebrew Bible, where the land itself plays a central role and where, from creation to eschaton, God is the lord of heaven and earth.[37] Equally, in the expectations of Paul a "new earth" plays a central role. Although Santmire acknowledges that the metaphor of "spiritual ascent" has been predominant in Christian theology and is well based on the Gospel of John, on Hebrews, and on Barthian and other theologies, he attempts to demonstrate the at least equal importance of the biblical metaphor of a "fecund earth."

32. Gerhard von Rad, *Old Testament Theology*, vol. 1 of *The Theology of Israel's Historical Traditions*, trans. D.M.G. Stalker (New York: Harper & Brothers, 1962), 138–39.

33. Ibid., 140.

34. Gerhard von Rad, *Wisdom in Israel*, trans. James D. Martin (Nashville and New York: Abingdon Press, 1977), 161.

35. Ibid., 159.

36. See H. Paul Santmire, *The Travail of Nature: The Ambiguous Ecological Promise of Christian Theology* (Philadelphia: Fortress Press, 1985), 192.

37. In *The Travail of Nature* Santmire convincingly argues from works by Walter Brueggemann and Claus Westermann. See also Santmire, "Toward a New Theology of Nature," *Dialog* 25 (Winter 1986): 43–50.

Nature, too, seems to belong in the biblical narrative. By omitting a naturalistic dimension, biblical, humanistic new historicists open themselves to questions about the internal consistency of their theologies. If the biblical narrative itself points to natural realities, where is the intratextual consistency in narrative theology's omission of natural history? John Hick makes a similar argument, although referring to realistic testimonies generally rather than to naturalistic testimonies particularly. He uses Wittgenstein to argue that an authentic description of religious language games shows that they refer beyond the world circumscribed by the language game. "To suppress this intention," Hick says, "is to do violence to religious speech and to empty the religious 'form of life' of its central and motivating conviction."[38]

An American naturalistic historicism offers, then, to postmodern historicist theology a way more clearly to avoid the arbitrariness of group subjectivism and its possibility of introducing premodern notions. Further, it provides a way pragmatically to diminish or to avoid problems of inconsistency. This American contribution would add the hermeneutics of nature to the hermeneutics of written texts, permitting both histories about nature and histories about human culture to contribute to traditions of religious interpretation. This would preserve communal traditions but carry them beyond words about human communities, even to words about nature.

38. John Hick, "Seeing-as and Religious Experience," in *Faith*, ed. Terence Penelhum (New York: Macmillan, 1989), 184.

3

Theological Anthropology and the Human Sciences

JAMES M. GUSTAFSON

Barry Schwartz of Swarthmore College several years ago published an interesting and provocative book titled *The Battle for Human Nature: Science, Morality and Modern Life*. He proposes that the book "is about a struggle between the language of science and the language of morality for hegemony in describing what it means to be a person."[1] The main line of his argument is clear: the languages of various sciences of human nature and action provide descriptions and explanations that have or can have corroding effects on morality. These languages seek comprehensive and determinative explanations that have implications for how life ought to be conducted and what ought to be valued about life. Such implications can run counter to our sense of moral responsibility and our duty to participate in achieving the common good.

Schwartz attends particularly to three disciplines: rational choice economics; evolutionary biology and, particularly, sociobiology; and behavioristic psychology. He sets each of these disciplines in its historical context and develops "parallels" among them, at the same time attending to their differences. All three, for example, view organisms as "moving in the direction of maximizing—of preference in economics, of reinforcement in behavior theory, and of inclusive fitness in

1. Barry Schwartz, *The Battle for Human Nature: Science, Morality and Modern Life* (New York: W. W. Norton, 1986), 18.

61

biology."[2] They issue in what he calls "a common vision of human nature."

> In essence, human beings are economic beings. They are out to pursue self-interest, to satisfy wants, to maximize utility, or preference, or profit, or reinforcement, or reproductive fitness. They are greedy, insatiable in the pursuit of want satisfaction. As soon as one want is satisfied, another takes its place. . . . Groups of people (societies) are just collections of individuals. The interests of society are the summed interests of its members. The wants of society are the agglomerated wants of its members. The good society is the successful society, and the successful society is one that allows its individual members to satisfy their wants.[3]

Schwartz notes that much in this vision is correct but that it "leaves out any consideration of morality, of how people *ought* to be as opposed to how they are. There is nothing accidental about this omission."[4]

The struggle, therefore, is between the language of science and the language of morality for hegemony in describing what it means to be a person. The battle is between descriptions and explanations of human being on the one hand and the moral criteria for being human on the other hand.

Schwartz's analysis shows, in effect, that these three very persuasive disciplines of contemporary academic life function in a way similar to Gordon Kaufman's view of the function of theology. They "create a framework of interpretation which can provide overall orientation for human life."[5] Kaufman gives us an argument about theology and God; theology is an activity of the imagination that seeks to reconstruct the image or concept of God. The image or concept of God, rather than Schwartz's three sciences, is to provide the interpretation and orientation for human life.[6] The Christian understanding of God has a relativizing and a humanizing function. The principal concern of contemporary theology "should be to construct a symbol which can function both thoroughly to relativize and thoroughly to humanize our contemporary existence, institutions and activities."[7]

---

2. Ibid., 147.
3. Ibid., 148.
4. Ibid., 149.
5. Gordon D. Kaufman, *Theology for a Nuclear Age* (Philadelphia: Westminster Press; and Manchester, Eng.: Manchester University Press, 1985), 26.
6. Ibid.
7. Ibid., 34.

I think it is correct to say that Kaufman's theological enterprise is basically a moral one, and that (to use Schwartz's polarization) its impact is to sustain the hegemony of the language of morality in describing what it means to be human. He uses the word "humanizing" in a profoundly moral sense; it refers to values of human life in the world that ought to be sustained and preserved against forces of technology, politics, social customs, economics, and other factors that threaten them. The image of God will relativize the claims for comprehensiveness and sufficiency that Schwartz finds in his three sciences. It will sustain humanization because "God is seen as ultimately a *humane* being."[8]

This essay explores some relations between descriptions and explanations of human being on the one hand and valuations involved in discussions of being human on the other hand. The fundamental focus of attention is as old as reflective thought and expressed in documents from various cultures; it takes different specific forms in contemporary writings because of the newer sciences of human life and activity. To remember how ancient the concern is, one need only recall the importance of the *Imago Dei* notion in Genesis and the ways in which this fundamentally descriptive term has been the basis for valuing human life and for directing its proper conduct. Kaufman's early article "The *Imago Dei* as Man's Historicity" is but one example of how an account of the descriptive significance of that notion has implications for how human life in the world is interpreted and valued.[9] Indeed, one of the interesting themes in the history of Christian and Jewish thought is how that notion has been delineated differently and therefore leads to different views of the human "essence" and of what is to be valued as an outcome of those views.[10] Parallel studies of the relations of the description and explanation to the valuation of the human can be made in the Western philosophical tradition and in other religious traditions.

Several things make this exploration interesting and important. Theologians and philosophers whose work fits Schwartz's hegemony of the language of morality have descriptive and explanatory premises

8. Ibid.
9. Gordon D. Kaufman, "The *Imago Dei* as Man's Historicity," *Journal of Religion* 36 (1956):157–68. See also idem, *Systematic Theology: A Historicist Perspective* (New York: Charles Scribner's Sons, 1968), 329–51.
10. See, e.g., Douglas John Hall, *Imaging God: Dominion as Stewardship* (Grand Rapids: Wm. B. Eerdmans, 1986). After a discussion of the biblical background of the *Imago Dei*, Hall analyzes two historical streams of thought about it, the "substantialistic" and the "relational" (88–112).

in their interpretations of human being and human action. For example, Reinhold Niebuhr's interpretation of the unique feature of the human to be "spirit" and thus freedom, although spirit is curiously compounded with nature, is a description on the basis of which he provides explanations of human action. Thus the critical analyst can explore what evidences are given to back the description, what sources are used to sustain its intelligibility and persuasiveness.[11]

Another example can be found in the work of moral philosopher Alan Gewirth, who develops his Principle of Generic Consistency (PGC) from a description of two interrelated generic features of action: "voluntariness or freedom and purposiveness or intentionality."

> By an action's being voluntary or free I mean that its performance is under the agent's control in that he unforcedly chooses to act as he does, knowing the relevant proximate circumstances of his action. By an action's being purposive or intentional I mean that the agent acts for some end or purpose that constitutes his reason for acting; this purpose may consist in the action itself or in something to be achieved by the action.[12]

From this description are derived certain generic obligations, for example, to refrain from coercing or harming the recipients of an action and to assist them to have freedom and well-being when they are deprived of necessary goods and the actor can help them "at no comparable cost to himself." The PGC then is: "Act in accord with the generic rights of your recipients as well as of yourself."[13] Humans are descriptively voluntary and purposive; prescriptively, we are obligated to respect our freedom and that of others and to aid others to fulfill their well-being.

Abraham Heschel in *Who Is Man?* writes that "there is an ontological connective between human being and being human."[14] The normative, who we are, "is inherent as a desideratum in human being," that is, in what constitutes our being. Nevertheless, he fences out certain approaches to human being when he writes, "We can attain adequate understanding of man only if we think of man in human terms . . . and abstain from employing categories developed in investigations of

---

11. See Reinhold Niebuhr, *The Nature and Destiny of Man*, 2 vols. (New York: Charles Scribner's Sons, 1941), 1:12–18, for a capsule summary of his view.

12. Alan Gewirth, *Reason and Morality* (Chicago: University of Chicago Press, 1978), 27.

13. Ibid., 135.

14. Abraham J. Heschel, *Who Is Man?* (Stanford, Calif.: Stanford University Press, 1965), 16.

lower forms of life." His description stresses our capacities for responsiveness to the realities of which we are aware, "to the being that *I* am, to the beings surrounding *me*, to the being that transcends *me*."[15] Therefore he postulates, "Who is man? *A being in travail* with God's dreams and designs."[16] Heschel's concern is that who we are ought to determine what we become; but, because there is an "ontological connective" between the two, the descriptive and the normative are tightly circular.

As in Niebuhr's case, in Gewirth's and Heschel's it is appropriate to inquire about the evidences for the descriptions on which their moral views rest. In all three examples the description is of the uniquely human, of that which distinguishes the human from other forms of life; and Heschel explicitly proscribes use of evidences from biology in attaining an "adequate understanding" of the human. In all three, I believe, the hegemony of the language of morality is sustained; but the account of the moral rests on descriptive premises, and it is these premises that investigators of the human in other disciplines might challenge. After all, the distinctively human can also be described and explained biologically.

Schwartz's argument that the three sciences he attends to provide a "vision of human nature" and thus predispose persons to certain interpretations and orientations toward life is in general true. He is clearly aware that there are differences among his three examples, and anyone acquainted with literature from the three fields knows that not all persons within these disciplines agree. Some investigators attempt to be more exhaustive of what can be explained by their work than others; that is, some are more reductionistic than others. Just as theologians and moral philosophers do not fully and articulately defend the descriptive grounds of their views of the human, scientists can draw moral visions of the world and make normative claims not fully backed by their descriptions. Some are more self-consciously critical in their moral extrapolations than others; but, regardless of the degree of care taken, there is evidence that various scientific descriptions and explanations predispose persons to preferential valuations of life in the world.

From the discipline of economics, Gary Becker is an important example of a scholar who extends the spheres to which principles of

15. Ibid., 3.
16. Ibid., 119.

market economy are applied. In a chapter titled "A Theory of Marriage" he offers what he assures the reader is "a simplified model of marriage," but he makes a great deal of it. It rests on "two basic assumptions":

> (1) each person tries to find a mate who maximizes his or her well-being, with well-being measured by the consumption of household-produced commodities; and (2) the "marriage market" is assumed to be in equilibrium, in the sense that no person could change mates and become better off. I have argued that the gain from marriage compared to remaining single for any two persons is positively related to their income, the relative difference in their wage rates, and the level of nonmarket-productivity-augmenting variables such as education or beauty. . . . [T]he gain to a man or a woman from marrying compared to remaining single is shown to depend positively on their incomes, human capital, and relative difference in wage rate.[17]

The appendix to the chapter works out this and other aspects of his interpretation of marriage in mathematical form.

Becker does not, to my knowledge, propose that his interpretation is the basis for how one ought to decide to marry or not to marry, and other social and behavioral sciences would argue reasons and motives for marriage that are much more complex than his account. He shows only a positive correlation; it is not a sufficient explanation. Nevertheless, implied in Becker's argument is a valuation of marriage; the economic description and analysis backs and sustains an economic valuation. We have here the hegemony of the language of a particular science.

A moral view of marriage would use very different language; it would show not only biologically grounded inclinations that lead to marriage but also the importance of a covenant between the partners in the presence of others, the duties and obligations as well as the fulfillment of aspects of well-being that are involved, and the responsibilities entailed in becoming parents. Some description and explanation of human life and activity, including the institution of marriage and its functions, would be implied if not explicit in a moral interpretation.

Even scholars who recognize the ambiguity of possible uses of their research cannot always restrain themselves from envisioning a moral

---

17. Gary S. Becker, *The Economic Approach to Human Behavior* (Chicago: University of Chicago Press, 1976), 232.

future, from functioning in much the same manner as Kaufman's interpretation of how theology functions. In *Physical Control of the Mind: Toward a Psychocivilized Society* José Delgado describes an experiment he performed during his investigations of the brain. He implanted electrodes into the brain of a bull and played the role of the toreador, holding an electrical transmitter. The bull was stimulated to charge the toreador by the normal means of that "sport." By transmitting an electrical impulse Delgado brought the bull in full charge to an abrupt stop. Aggression, in bulls or in human beings, can be controlled physically.

Although he acknowledges possible morally wrong uses of this knowledge, he also describes desirable future outcomes of it. He becomes a moralist when he writes, "We are now on the verge of a process of mental liberation and self-domination which is a continuation of our evolution . . . based on the investigation of the depth of the brain in behaving subjects." The integration of the results of his research with other sciences can lead

> to a more intelligent education, starting from the moment of birth and continuing throughout life, with the pre-conceived plan of escaping from the blind forces of chance and of influencing cerebral mechanisms and mental structure in order to create a future man with greater personal freedom and originality, a member of a psychocivilized society, happier, less destructive, and better balanced than present man.[18]

Some premises are elided between the results of Delgado's experiment in the ring and this vision of the future prospects of humankind. A paradox that is pointed to over and over seems to be present in this book as well: when we scientifically understand the determinants of behavior, we will have the freedom to control it. Delgado moves from his description and explanation to a vision of the future that could be an outcome of the knowledge he provides. He clearly favors this outcome. What he values about human life is extrapolated, with some gaps, from how he explains human behavior.

One can engage in a comparable account of many books from the various sciences of the human. The interpretations and orientations toward life are not all the same. Some are bleak, such as Jacques Monod's; he sees the human living "in a world that is deaf to his music and is as indifferent to his hopes as it is to his sufferings or his

18. José M. R. Delgado, *Physical Control of the Mind: Toward a Psychocivilized Society* (New York: Harper & Row, 1969), 223.

crimes."[19] Some argue from the evidences of their work to general views; Edward O. Wilson, for example, claims that "scientific materialism is the only mythology that can manufacture great goals from the sustained pursuit of pure knowledge." He, like others, cannot avoid the language of "spiritual," that is, the spiritual dilemma of a choice. "The human species can change its own nature. What will it choose?" We can remain "teetering on a jerrybuilt foundation of partly obsolete Ice-Age adaptations" or "press on toward still higher intelligence and creativity, accompanied by a greater—or lesser—capacity for emotional response." In his peroration Wilson writes, "The true Promethean spirit of science means to liberate man by giving him knowledge and some measure of dominion over the physical environment."[20] In these and other cases the focus of attention in the research on the human—on the contexts in which it comes to be and continues to exist—predisposes preferential interpretations of the meaning and value of human life. All such writings aspire to the hegemony of science, but something in the interests of the scientists evokes interpretations of the wider meanings of life and induces them to tell us how we ought to orient ourselves and our activities, individually and collectively.

Many other examples could be analyzed that have their centers of gravity in one or the other of the poles set by Schwartz. The basic general issue in focus in this essay is the same or very similar in all the materials. It can be reduced to abstract statements on which a great deal of philosophical literature has been written: the relations of facts to values or the relation of the "is" to the "ought." Philosophers and others have engaged in various ways either to defend a radical differentiation between the languages involved or to overcome the radical gulf between them.

The types of literature used in my examples are important for theologians to engage for two reasons. First, the "ises" and the "oughts"—the facts and the values—in both the scientific and the theological and ethical materials are particularized, and the particularizations are different for different writers. Even within the same general field of research the opinions among different investigators, theologians and scientists alike, lead to different outcomes: for example, on the capaci-

---

19. Jacques Monod, *Chance and Necessity* (London: Fontana, 1974), 160.
20. Edward O. Wilson, *On Human Nature* (Cambridge: Harvard University Press, 1978), 207, 208, 209.

ties for human self-determination, accountability of behavior, and values to be sustained. (I have not included examples from recent biopsychology. Various positions, from radical dualism through dual interactionism to eliminative materialism, all have some defenders, and each has different implications for explaining human activity and for what can and ought to be valued about the human.)[21] From the pole of theologians and moralists the values that are supported are backed, for example, by different premises about the significance of desires, inclinations, habits, and more persisting characteristics of persons, relative to the ends that they seek and their capacities to control behavior and thus be accountable for it. Classic theological debates between Pelagians and Augustinians, Arminians and Calvinists, as well as current discussions are in considerable part about the accuracy or adequacy of explanations of human nature. The general issues that can be abstracted are complex in their particularizations, and a general resolution of the abstraction does not necessarily resolve or fully illumine the issues in particular contexts.

Second, contemporary intellectual and academic life is the context in which theologians and moralists have to make their work intelligible and persuasive. The history of thought about these matters is important and interaction with that history and with contemporary philosophy is necessary. One might end up, generally, with issues that have been clearly formed by David Hume or Immanuel Kant, but the publics addressed in our time use different vocabularies, evidences, and theories than those that informed scholars of the past. The issue of free choice and determinism might be essentially and abstractly the same now as it has always been, but one now has to engage the research done by sociobiologists, neurophysiologists, and social and behavioral scientists, not only classic arguments. Representatives of these explanatory disciplines provide evidences and theories that are based upon research in genetics, neurology, bioanthropology, sociological data and principles of interpretation, and so forth. Evaluative and normative accounts of the human in our culture have to engage the materials that inform both students and a wider public in order to be intelligible and persuasive.

Schwartz uses the metaphor of "battle" in the title of his book; in the text he uses the word "struggle." Such metaphors prompted Mary

21. For an analysis of positions and an argument for eliminative materialism, see Paul M. Churchland, *Matter and Consciousness* (Cambridge: MIT Press, 1984).

Midgley to use the football match, in which one side must win and the other must lose, to shed light on this confrontational approach. She points to a polarity like Schwartz's when she comments on contemporary ethical writings: "The main dispute . . . these days lies between people who stress the *autonomy* of morals to avoid debasing them, and those who stress the *continuity of morals with other topics* in order to make them intelligible."[22] As she points out, once one makes distinct things out of science and morality, brain and mind, or biology and philosophy, it becomes remarkably hard to bring them into intelligible relation—even into dialectical relation—with each other, much less to produce some view to try to integrate them.

Midgley's own burden is to show that the metaphors of battle, struggle, or football matches do not exhaust the possibilities for relating explanations and valuations of the human. It is worth developing the range of choices that the disciplines of theology and ethics have in their responses to the current sciences of the human and noting some of the difficulties in each of them.

At one extreme is the option to undercut the credibility of these sciences on their scientific merits. Very few, if any, theologians have the technical knowledge to do this, and those who do have competence in one or two of the sciences at best. If the theologian chooses to do a competent critique of a relevant science, she or he can either examine fundamental assumptions that are made about reality or examine the evidence for the particular probability claims that are made in the research based on these assumptions.

The former is the more likely tack, and in pursuing it the work of philosophers and historians of science is of great assistance. The temptations in taking this tack are to overgeneralize about science and not to examine with care the differences between the claims of various sciences and of various investigators within each. It is all too easy for theologians to take a statement such as Wilson's "true Promethean spirit of science" to represent more scholars than it actually does. It is too easy to forget more modest claims, such as Melvin Konner makes by using a quotation from Bertold Brecht as the motto of his work: "The aim of science is not to open the door to everlasting wisdom, but to set a limit to everlasting error."[23] The difficulty of the second tack is

22. Mary Midgley, *Heart and Mind: The Varieties of Moral Experience* (Brighton, Eng.: Harvester Press, 1981), 132.
23. Melvin Konner, *The Tangled Wing: Biological Constraints on the Human Spirit* (New York: Harper & Row, 1982), xvi, quoting from Brecht's *Life of Galileo*.

twofold: the data and evidentiary proceedings in various sciences are esoteric for the theologian, and the arguments among investigators in a given field are often over highly technical matters couched in the precise terms of subspecializations.

At the opposite extreme is the option to base a theological or moral anthropology on relevant sciences, either by the strong claim of some logical entailment between the science and a theological or ethical view, by what are judged to be plausible inferences from the sciences, or by rationally defensible extrapolations from the sciences. The history of theology since the rise of modern science in the seventeenth century provides various examples of the use of this option, such as the development of Deistic doctrines of God on the basis of Newtonian physics and the various efforts, including those of Teilhard de Chardin,[24] to reformulate both theology and ethics on the basis of evolutionary theory since Darwin. Just as a theological critique of the sciences can focus either on broad generalizations that are already ways of viewing the world or on particular investigations of particular phenomena, so theologians who build from sciences can opt for general principles of interpretation developed in abstract metaphysics or use research such as that on the "split brain" to base anthropological and even theological claims. I take it that process theology is an instance of the first of these options. One finds discussions of examples of the second option in occasional articles in *Zygon*.

Between the extreme options is a continuum of types of critical engagement. One is a mutually critical analysis of the gaps in writings by scientists when they move to interpreting the world and orienting life and of the sufficiency of evidentiary claims about the human that are made in theology and ethics.[25]

Gaps occur in literature by scientists that moves beyond what is sustainable on the basis of current evidences. Wilson ends his book *On Human Nature* with a chapter titled "Hope." To be sure, the hope is in scientific materialism, but it is not clear that his sociobiological perspective gives us a persuasive explanation of hope. Konner ends his

24. See Teilhard de Chardin, *The Phenomenon of Man* (New York: Harper & Row, 1961). Many popular comprehensive "theological" and ethical theories based on the sciences are written by imaginative authors who have limited competence in any of the fields they draw upon.

25. See my lecture "Explaining and Valuing: An Exchange between Theology and the Human Sciences" (Department of Religious Studies, Arizona State University, Tempe), in which I compare in some depth Reinhold Niebuhr's *The Nature and Destiny of Man* and Melvin Konner's *The Tangled Wing*.

The Tangled Wing with a chapter on "The Dawn of Wonder," and recognizes that he is, in a nonpejorative sense, a moralist. He writes: "We must try once again to experience the human soul as soul, and not just a buzz of bioelectricity; the human will as will, and not just a surge of hormones; the human heart not as a fibrous, sticky pump, but as the metaphoric organ of understanding."[26] Like Wilson, he ends with a call to make a choice about the future.

Some authors from the human sciences are more self-aware than others about the existence of these gaps, and one can analyze the sources from which insights and metaphors have been drawn, for example, in Konner's case, from Western literature. Nevertheless, because the weight of such books is a synthetic argument drawn from the sciences, it is fair to examine whether the "theological" (in Kaufman's sense) conclusions necessarily follow or are utterly contradictory with what precedes them or are even "permissible." If hope and a sense of wonder are part of human experience, then is that experience fully explained by the scientific accounts that dominate such works? These are interesting, important, and fair questions and need to be explored in the particular accounts of human being and action.[27]

The sources used in theological and moral anthropologies, and what can be considered gaps from some scientific perspectives, are equally worthy of analysis. It is interesting to note, for example, that when Reinhold Niebuhr argues against a dualistic account of spirit and nature he draws upon Western religious texts. In contrast to "Greek philosophy," he says, the "Hebraic sense of the unity of body and soul is not destroyed while, on the other hand, spirit is conceived of as primarily a capacity for the affinity with the divine." Pauline texts are expounded to support this.[28] Thus he takes a position on the body–mind problem, and although debates continue to rage on that relation, one could examine Niebuhr's general point to determine

---

26. Konner, *The Tangled Wing*, 435.
27. Theodosius Dobzhansky was the most theologically literate American biologist of his generation. His *The Biology of Ultimate Concern* (New York: New American Library, 1967) is based on not only his career as a geneticist but also his reading of Paul Tillich, Teilhard de Chardin, and Arnold Toynbee, and closes with an ambivalent response to de Chardin. The book merits more attention than many written by scientists because of his study of theology. Mary Midgley has published an interesting account of extrapolations from science to moral and religious views in her *Evolution as a Religion: Strange Hopes and Stranger Fears* (London: Methuen, 1985).
28. See Niebuhr, *The Nature and Destiny of Man*, 1:152.

what scientific arguments would support it, at least for the sake of contemporary intelligibility. When Niebuhr writes that faith "illumines experience and is in turn validated by experience" he is making appeals to what can be, in some general sense at least, empirically tested.[29] The weight of the argument will be affected by such examination. There are points at which Niebuhr draws even more directly on biblical theology: for example, in his provision of an ultimate ground of hope beyond tragedy—the idea of the kingdom of God. The belief in the coming kingdom might be empirically, for some, a basis of hope, but it is authorized only by Christian revelation. His interpretation of anxiety and the ways in which it is overcome, however, is susceptible to psychological examinations and might find support from some authors in that field.[30]

The traditional Thomistic account of human activity, as being moved by our natural loves for what we correctly or falsely judge to be the good, uses concepts drawn from classical thought, which are reformulated for this theological purpose. The theological anthropology contains an analysis of human nature at both the level of natural appetites and other motivations and the level of the distinctively human—namely, our capacity to use reason and make choices. To an important extent, the ethics that follows is grounded in that anthropological analysis. Can contemporary investigations of biological anthropology reformulate the understanding of our "nature"? Stephen J. Pope of Boston College has argued well that they can, and that in so doing it is possible to move toward an ordering of our loves and relations that formally is similar to the Thomistic account. One effect of this proposal is to criticize recent Roman Catholic interpretations of love that draw heavily on phenomenology and have the effect of a radical separation of "personhood" from biological groundings of desires and relations.[31]

Other materials could be used to show the extent to which theological and ethical anthropologies rely upon descriptive premises and how these premises engage in explanations and evaluations of human activity. Descriptions and explanations of human nature in theological accounts ground valuations of the human just as they do in modern

29. Ibid., 2:63.
30. Ibid., 1:182, for the analysis of anxiety.
31. See Stephen J. Pope, "The Contributions of Contemporary Biological Anthropology to Recent Roman Catholic Interpretations of Love," (Ph.D. diss., University of Chicago, 1988).

scientific accounts. The common issue between the two poles is human nature, and on this ground it is appropriate at least to probe the adequacy and accuracy of those accounts in the light of the human sciences.

Because the scientific accounts are disputed, as Pope specifically recognizes in his study, it is not a case of simply inserting the "true" one into the theological interpretation, but it is still of value to examine the theological in the light of these accounts. It may be, as is likely in Heschel's *Who Is Man?* that a primarily evaluative purpose determines what evidences are adduced in the description. Surely such a view demands qualifications and revisions. If the theological account cannot be utterly falsified by scientific accounts, then it can be corrected by them through critical usage and careful argumentation.

The process of mutual criticism does not resolve the question of an appropriate relationship between the poles. If one chooses to reject the battle metaphor with its implication that one language must win, then two other options are possible and have been hinted at in the foregoing. One is a dialectical relationship between the two languages; the other is a synthetic one. In the dialectical relationship one can construe the possibility of changes in either the scientific or the moral language as various arguments are taken into account. A synthetic relationship seeks to include both languages in a larger whole.

To pursue this further the terminology will be changed, although I believe the fundamental issue is the same. Various philosophers, theologians, and others distinguish the radically conditioned or determined aspects of persons and their activities from the capacities of the human person for self-determination. Kant's distinction between the noumenal and phenomenal aspects of the human, George Herbert Mead's between the "I" and the "Me," and Karl Barth's between "real man" and "phenomenal man" are but some examples of how this distinction is conceptualized. Theories of action in recent philosophy have worked with great precision to formulate terms and arguments about whether actions can be caused, whether there are conditions for action, whether reasons for actions are the causes of actions, and similar issues. Writers who reject a radical dualism—for instance, the idea that the self is the "ghost" in the machine or that the "soul" exists somehow independent of the body—have not resolved to the satisfaction of all precisely the best way to formulate a nondualistic position. Nor will I.

Among those who opt for some kind of dialectical relationship, I believe that, at least in practical matters, the boundary has changed in some instances, and the degree of accountability for actions alters with the choice of boundary. The phenomenon of homosexuality and the varied responses to it would make an interesting and complicated case study. There have been shifts in moral judgments about it; it is not as widely condemned as it was. There are different explanations of homosexuality from the side of the hegemony of the language of morality—that is, the side of accountability for the condition and for overt actions—which lead to different judgments of its moral status. To those for whom it is a "natural" condition—explicable biologically or in a combination of biological and sociopsychological factors—homosexuality needs no excuses from accountability. The "natural" is the good. For some the recognition of dispositions grounded in various natural factors is separated from the capacities to restrain or redirect them in a morally approvable manner. Finally, there are those who affirm the capacities of choice and will to run counter to a natural tendency. Each response, as with responses to destructive aggression, implies a judgment about the relations of "fact" to "value," of "is" to "ought," of the phenomenal to the noumenal or "real" in humans, of the "Me" to the "I." My point is that the boundary shifts as a dialectical process between the language of science and the language of morality takes into account various current findings.

Public awareness of the limits of scientific claims, based on knowledge of errors in science, on consciousness that studies can be interpreted or designed to serve particular interests, and on even wider philosophical critiques of science as a method, makes use of the sciences in theological or moral anthropologies problematic. The relation of what is determinative to what persons can self-determine shifts with various studies; the skin between them is porous, permitting effects to go both ways. The unresolved issues are how porous it is and at what point the pores are blocked, for what reasons, and on the basis of what evidence. Most theological and moral anthropologies reject a radical dualism without agreement on how to state or defend a particular nondualistic position. Some dialectical relation seems to be necessary and accepted; that even authors of highly deterministic positions issue calls to responsible moral action—for example, Wilson, Delgado, and Konner—makes this clear. It is even clearer among theologians and moral philosophers.

What about the synthetic alternative? Is it feasible to think of a "more synthetic position," which reduces the parameters within which a choice that is finally dialectical is made? Midgley is one among a number of authors who shows "Why Neurology Cannot Replace Moral Philosophy," to quote one of her section headings. The argument essentially is that the concerns of ethics (and one can add theology) cannot be reduced to biological explanations. She states in her conclusion: "Philosophy and biology are not in competition; they are different aspects of one inquiry."[32] For Midgley, efforts to reduce the ethical to the biological are reductionistic, but not wholly in error; what is required is "philosophizing better." Her project has a double polemic: against reducing the moral to what can be stated in the language of science and against those views of the moral that refuse to be open to evidences and interpretations of the human that come from the sciences, for fear of denigrating "autonomy."

A move toward a synthetic position does not eliminate non-equivalence of the language of science and the languages of morality and theology; but the polarization is not as radical as it would be if eliminative scientific materialism and a "hypervoluntarism" were the only possibilities. It opens the possibility of specifying how our purposes and ends are grounded, although by no means exclusively, in our "natures" and how our capacities of self-determination not only depend on our natures but provide direction to our acts and activities grounded in those natures. The criteria of judgment about the moral worthiness of our purposes, the rightness of our conduct, will have independence from what is explained by the language of science, but the skin between languages is more porous than in some alternative views.

The discussions can become more precise as theologians and moralists locate the long-standing issues in current studies of the nature of the human. At stake is the theological and moral status of the natural. The human sciences provide us with a new prologue to a perennial issue. Engagement with them is important to render moral and theological anthropologies more intelligible in the context of, at least, the investigations of our colleagues in modern universities. Such engagement is also important in the process of justifying arguments for

32. Mary Midgley, *Beast and Man: The Roots of Human Nature* (Ithaca: N.Y.: Cornell University Press, 1978), 174.

human accountability that are made by theologians and philosophers. If synthesis of the languages is not possible, at least the evidences to be taken into account and the parameters within which discussions occur will be more particularized. For some of us these sciences have to inform quite deeply a theological and moral perspective that seeks "to create a framework of interpretation which can provide overall orientation for human life," as well as an orientation to specific occasions of human activity.

PART II

THEOLOGY
AND PUBLIC DISCOURSE

4

Resisting
the Postmodern Turn:
Theology and Contextualization

LINELL E. CADY

It should not be too surprising that theologians are attracted to postmodernism, the movement most often associated with the dismantling of modernity. Whatever its virtues, the modern epoch has not been hospitable to religion, let alone to theology, and consigned both to the private realm where opinion, not knowledge, reigns supreme. The increasing attacks upon modernity and its characteristic assumptions and sensibilities have emboldened theologians to seek a legitimacy and role denied to them in recent centuries. I share the general sentiment that the intellectual and social currents loosely associated with the movement of postmodernism create a more receptive context for theological reflection, but I also worry that this emergent clearing may be taken as space to carry on business as usual.

My sense is that many theologians are seizing upon the amorphous movement of postmodernism to legitimate their enterprise without aedquately confronting the need for basic changes in the genre of theology. Most troubling, perhaps, is the way in which elements of this movement are being appropriated, indeed, coopted by many theologians for confessional purposes, generating theologies with little resonance to postmodern sensibilities. Even those theologies with impeccable postmodern credentials, however, do not help chart a direction for theology if it is to gain a footing and, perhaps, a hearing in the contemporary world. This essay will explore some of the costs, whether hidden or acknowledged, associated with the turn to post-modernism. I shall argue that the future of academic theology depends upon resisting the initial but, I think, temporary legitimation that this orientation provides.

In this context, especially, Gordon Kaufman's work has much to contribute. The need to purge theology of its confessional and authoritarian impulses has been a recurring refrain in his writings. If my reading of contemporary theological currents is correct, then his attack on theologies that exhibit such tendencies has not lost its relevance. Just as importantly, in his constructive moves he suggests a model for theology that moves it beyond a modernist orientation without succumbing to the confessionalism or playful elitism of so much of the postmodern trajectory. In so doing he helps to chart a direction for theology that may help to reverse its growing intellectual and cultural isolation.[1]

The conception of theology that emerges in Kaufman's writings has ramifications for the genre, which, in my judgment, are not fully realized in his own work. The historicist dimensions of his theology remain undeveloped, abstractly noted but not yet controlling factors in his critical and constructive work. His model of theology suggests the need for more careful attention to the historical and cultural context within which theological reflection is located. Moving in this direction would align theology closely with the history of religions. The excessive preoccupation with the isolated texts or primary symbols of a tradition would be muted as theologians became more attentive to the analysis and evaluation of embodied religion. The skills of the sociologist and ethnographer would begin to shape theological expertise, providing important supplements to the prevailing exegeti-

---

1. It is difficult to be for or against postmodernism *tout court*, given the variety of candidates vying for the title. At this point one enters a confused and confusing definitional battle that seems hardly worth the effort. It is, however, interesting to speculate upon the motivations behind the competition. As I use the term, I do not intend to encompass everything that assiduously avoids "modernism" (construed as the attempt to escape historicity and establish secure foundations for knowledge). Although postmodernism, as I intend it, constitutes a rejection of modernism, it represents one trajectory beyond it, not all. From other vantage points my essay dwells upon the limitations of some forms of postmodern theology, leaving untouched other forms. Indeed, from some angles one might argue that Kaufman's theology is itself a version of postmodern theology, although I think expansive usage of the term dilutes it and makes it impossible to highlight the interesting features of a particular movement beyond modernism.

cal and philosophical orientations. My essay, then, has a twofold agenda: to articulate more fully the attractions and dangers of postmodernism for theology and to venture a recommendation for the future direction of theological reflection, taking Kaufman's model as a point of departure.

Two cautionary notes are in order. First, this essay is an exercise in prescription rather than prediction. Indeed, if I were to hazard a guess about the most likely future for theology, it would bear little resemblance to that which I am outlining. In this essay, then, I am not above the fray of theology, divining its future, but a participant in the struggle to shape its trajectory. Second, my concern is with the future of academic theology. Theological reflection occurs in a variety of institutional locations and is inevitably shaped by this fact. My interest is not in lambasting confessional forms of reflection in faith communities but in undermining their hegemony within the academic context.

SHIFTING CONFIGURATIONS: MODERNISM AND POSTMODERNISM

The tendency to identify the shifting intellectual and social configurations of our time in and through the contrast between modernism and postmodernism is as pervasive as it is problematic. These categories have become so trendy, polemically charged, and variously used that their heuristic value is questionable. Nevertheless, it is difficult to escape their use or some closely parallel contrast; the very currency of the labels makes them difficult to avoid. The theme of this volume, for instance, "theology at the end of modernity," implies some such contrast, albeit leaving open what comes next.

More importantly, there is a growing sentiment across a number of fields that the modern epoch, with its characteristic accents and prejudices, is waning in power and influence as an alternative paradigm gains ascendancy. On one level, the use of the categories of modernism and postmodernism reflects an attempt to take account of this intellectual and cultural shift. On another level, the use of the distinction between these categories goes beyond any purportedly neutral attempt to capture descriptively the current situation. Postmodernism is a label coined by critics of modernity who strive to move beyond its controlling assumptions and values. To speak of the end of modernity or the emergence of a postmodern world, then, is to engage in an interpretive strategy that seeks to legitimate and extend the incipient signs of a fundamental intellectual and cultural transformation. It is not value-neutral categorization but interested, engaged subversion and re-creation.

These categories do not facilitate historical precision about the various and conflicting strands that comprise intellectual developments of recent centuries. What they do is call attention through typological caricature to contrasting orientations, which are sufficiently complex and integrated to be construed as alternative gestalts or paradigms giving shape to distinctive epochs. Herein lie both their power and their limitations. Because the contrast between modernism and postmodernism is drawn by advocates of the latter, postmodernism is invariably made to look good at the expense of the former. Furthermore, the very use of the prefix "post" to designate an alternative to modernism plays upon a deeply rooted bias in favor of the new. Who would choose to remain a modern in a postmodern world? Recognizing these limitations helps to resist being limited to the options generated by the oppositional categories of modernism and postmodernism in any mapping of the contemporary scene.

With these caveats in mind, I will offer a brief depiction of these contrasting gestalts. Taken in this "looser" way, modernity refers to the configuration of assumptions and sensibilities closely associated with what has been called the Enlightenment project. The controlling preoccupation of this project has been epistemological. It has generated indefatigable efforts, in both rationalist and empiricist guises, to secure knowledge against the onslaught of particularity. Taking early modern science as a model, reason came to be construed as both ahistorical and universal. Endowed with this capacity, humans were thought capable of the disinterested, objective apprehension of the truth.

As the primary embodiment of this form of rationality, science assumed the culturally dominant role of gatekeeper for the truth. To the extent that other ways of knowing failed to approximate the purported objectivity and disinterested character of scientific rationality, they were discredited and relegated to the private realm of subjectivity and mere opinion. The elevation of science to cultural preeminence had ramifications beyond Western culture: it contributed to the refinement of a colonialist mentality, which regarded non-Western cultures as inferior, mired in superstition, magic, and other "primitive" modes of operation. The "other" was not a voice of reason but the embodiment of irrationality. Thus just as other spheres of inquiry were subjugated to science and its purportedly objective, disinterested approach, so too other cultures were subjugated to Western culture for its self-proclaimed superior grasp of the truth.

Although exiled from the public sphere associated with objectivity, knowledge, and science, religion and theology proved remarkably adaptable to the modernist landscape. Following Schleiermacher's lead, theologians increasingly came to associate religion with an autonomous, self-validating experience of the divine. In this framework religious experience is regarded as primary and controlling and the symbols, beliefs, and doctrines are taken as secondary expressions.[2] The Enlightenment stamp is unmistakable. It is not simply that religion is relegated to the experiential, affective domain but also that the common element in the religious moment is highlighted; the particularities of symbol and belief, attributable to variations in time and place, are decentered. Although a shrewd strategy for preserving the integrity of religion within a modernist framework, its costs and incoherencies have become increasingly visible as this framework wanes in power and influence.

Although the Enlightenment project continues to recruit some participants, there is little doubt that it has been increasingly discredited in recent years. Especially significant have been the many efforts to show that the Enlightenment model of rationality even fails at illuminating scientific inquiry, its supposed anchor. Scientific discoveries in the twentieth century have contributed to the erosion of sharp distinctions between the knower and the known, the subject and

2. The two most sustained analyses and critiques of this modern, liberal trajectory are those by George Lindbeck, *The Nature of Doctrine: Religion and Theology in a Postliberal Age* (Philadelphia: Westminster Press, 1984); and Wayne Proudfoot, *Religious Experience* (Berkeley: University of California Press, 1985). Lindbeck restricts himself, for the most part, to describing this tradition of modernist theology, which he labels "experiential-expressive," and to comparing it to a postliberal or postmodern form, which he calls "cultural-linguistic." This descriptive restraint arises from his sense that arguments inevitably appeal to criteria that are internal to a specific paradigm and hence are ineffective in disproving an alternate paradigm. Proudfoot, in contrast, is more explicitly committed to arguing against the cogency of the liberal, modernist theological tradition. This difference may reflect Lindbeck's explicit postmodern loyalties, which do not surface in Proudfoot's work.

the objective world, and historians and philosophers of science have exposed the historical influences that have shaped scientific debate and progress. The ahistorical, interest-free portrait of reason that has governed the modern epoch has increasingly given way to a contextual, historicist interpretation of rationality. The Enlightenment effort to escape from the particularities of time and place has been widely rejected as an impossible quest, whose intellectual and moral fallout must now be redressed.

The movement of postmodernism clearly involves the abandonment of the Enlightenment project and its animating vision of reason as an ahistorical, disinterested capacity to apprehend objective reality. Far from transcending the particularity of its location, rationality is understood to be fundamentally shaped by its historical context. We think in and through traditions of interpretation, whose symols, biases, and interests inevitably shape the reasoning process. To the extent that modernity is equated with the early modern Enlightenment project, this historicist turn is a move toward a postmodern orientation.

Nevertheless, it does not yet bear the characteristic marks of postmodernism. It is at this point especially that the categories prove limiting. The oppositional contrast between modernism and postmodernism allows no space for the transition between these alternative orientations. Historical precision is thereby sacrificed for typological and rhetorical efficacy. A more careful historical excavation would reveal an extended development within the later modern period in which the turn to the subject generates a deep recognition of the historicity of human life and thought. This emerging historicist perspective calls attention to the intimate, although typically concealed, connections between knowledge and power. The exercise of reason is, from this vantage point, exposed as less pure and less disinterested than the early modernists had thought. Efforts to identify the distinguishing interests of the subject, interests rooted in differences of race, gender, and class, become standard practice.

Postmodernism is clearly an offshoot of the historicist turn. What distinguishes this movement, I would suggest, is largely a matter of emphasis, although an emphasis with significant ramifications. The historicist insight into the multiplicity of perspectives reflecting differences in time, space, and power becomes transmuted into an emphasis upon the multiple worlds produced through human creativity. The accent shifts from perspectives on the world to the multiplicity of worlds within which humans dwell. This metaphorical expression captures the postmodern accent on the multiplicity, autonomy, and legitimacy of the various "worlds" rather than the unending, piecemeal, and provisional efforts to negotiate between their respective "truths."[3]

With this shift science is displaced, no longer regarded as a privileged lens for knowing reality. Its status is relativized along with any other heretofore privileged languages or texts. Not science, with its univocal access to reality, but literature, with its creation and exploration of multiple worlds, emerges as the paradigmatic postmodern genre. With interest transposed to the texts that in effect create their worlds, the particular historical and cultural location of the author fades in importance. The orientation spawned in and through the historicist turn within the modern epoch takes on a decidedly ahistorical cast.

CONFESSIONALISM IS CONFESSIONALISM IS . . . POSTMODERNISM?

It is understandable that theologians would be attracted to movements that seek to undermine the fundamental tenets of modernity. Even though religious thinkers developed successful strategies to accommodate and legitimate religion within the framework of modernity, it was not the whole of religious belief and practice but a truncated form that was validated. The preservation of an underlying religious moment or experience, assimilated to the affective sphere, did not confer independent cognitive significance on the specific beliefs, symbols, and concepts through which this experience was communicated. As faithful expressions of this underlying moment they were accorded

---

3. In his clever lexicon at the end of *Ethics after Babel* (Boston: Beacon Press, 1988), Jeffrey Stout suggests that postmodernism is a form of "ironic eclecticism" or *bricolage*, which he defines as the "selective retrieval and eclectic reconfiguration of traditional linguistic elements in hope of solving problems at hand" (see 293–94). This definition collapses a pragmatic historicist orientation into postmodernism, stretching the latter category to include almost anything that rejects modernism. In Stout's sense Kaufman would be a postmodernist. By limiting its reference to the more exaggerated exaltations of multiple vocabularies that float free from their authorial bases, I am better able to consider the peculiar attractions of this trajectory for some contemporary theological agendas.

some legitimacy, but it was derivative and largely inapplicable to all but the most central symbols and beliefs. Thus although religious thinkers carved out a haven for religion within the modernist paradigm, its size, location, and structure were determined in reaction to the modernist trajectory.

It has also become apparent that the challenges to modernity from a variety of disciplinary perspectives threaten this haven. Its stability is a function of the stability of the fundamental paradigm within which it was forged. Hence the growing challenges to the modernist epoch necessarily impel religious thinkers to rethink the character and support for religious belief and practice.

Postmodernism offers theologians a way not only to contribute to the dismantling of modernity but also to secure for religion a space that is not determined, overshadowed, and marginalized by science. In and through this movement theologians correctly perceive that the incipient signs of a new epoch portend a better future. My fear, however, is that the shifts associated with postmodernism lend themselves all too easily to forms of theology impotent to combat the growing marginalization of theological reflection. Especially disturbing is the way in which elements of postmodernism are appropriated for confessional theologies, theologies that are particularly beguiling because of their avant-garde, academic veneer.

Consider, for instance, how a contextual, historicist interpretation of reason can breathe new life into traditional forms of theological reflection. The recognition that humans reason in and through particular historical patterns provides a crucial legitimation for theology's engagement with a particular religious tradition. Gone is the contrast generated by modernity's framework between parochial (tradition-bound) theological reflection and public (universal and ahistorical) scientific inquiry. Instead, the similarity between theology and science is highlighted insofar as each form of reflection is located within particular traditions of interpretation, which in turn are located within particular historical communities. When this insight is combined with the tendency to affirm the legitimacy and autonomy of the diverse vocabularies—a sort of separate but equal policy—it is a sheer boon for theologians. Even without saying anything more in support of substantive specificities, theologians can enjoy the borrowed status that comes from rubbing methodological shoulders with science. As one theologian has put it, "In a postmodern world Christianity is intellectually relevant."[4] This strikes me as a bit too convenient. A blanket endorsement of intellectual relevance too easily allows a general reprieve for nonscientific inquiry to substitute for piecemeal defenses, a point that postmodernism tends to overlook in its celebration of alternate vocabularies.

Equally problematic is the way in which a contextualist interpretation of reason is appropriated to legitimate a narrow identification with a particular community of faith. George Lindbeck's *The Nature of Doctrine* is a good example of this kind of move. After offering an extremely illuminating analysis of the difference between a modern, liberal theory of religion and a postmodern cultural-linguistic interpretation, Lindbeck uses the latter to defend his own brand of confessional theology. He argues for an intratextual theology, tantamount in his words to "absorbing the universe into the biblical world."[5]

Lindbeck's confessional move has some serious flaws. It turns interpretive traditions into insulated entities, falsely imputing a kind of constancy to them. His recurring analogy between a religion and a grammar is instructive but fails to establish the permanency that he seeks. The issue, however, goes beyond the empirical point that religions, like grammars, evolve, albeit slowly and with a continuity that especially in hindsight is quite visible. The issue is inescapably a normative one, involving questions about the most adequate formulation or reformulation of a tradition. No matter how persuasive the case for constants within a tradition, it does not follow that these are binding on the theologian.

The intratextual theology that Lindbeck advocates is also problematic because it suggests that individuals in the contemporary world should strive to inhabit single communities of interpretation. Lindbeck is well aware that one of the hallmarks of our time is the cacophony of traditions that vie for our allegiance. Most of us are, quite fundamentally, multilingual. We speak in and through multiple vocabularies that reflect different assumptions, attitudes, and values. Although recognizing this situation, Lindbeck regrets it, critical of the eclecticism toward religious belief and practice that it spawns. His intratextual, biblicist orientation is intended to counteract this cacophony, creating a grammatical coherence in its stead. Without some

4. Diogenes Allen, "Christian Values in a Post-Christian Context," in *Postmodern Theology: Christian Faith in a Pluralist World*, ed. Frederic B. Burnham (San Francisco: Harper & Row, 1989), 25.
5. Lindbeck, *The Nature of Doctrine*, 135.

implicit assumption about the adequacy of the biblical worldview, however, it is difficult to see why this tradition of interpretation should be singled out from all the other operative traditions and used as the lens through which to interpret reality. Lindbeck carefully avoids the modernist assumption that one can adopt a neutral standpoint from which to assess the strengths and weaknesses of alternate traditions, but there is little explanation of the rationale that might motivate an individual to undergo the requisite conversion needed to resurrect a biblical worldview.

Here Lindbeck's constructive position reveals little affinity with the animating impulse of postmodernism. The dizzying acknowledgment of the multiple worlds produced through linguistic expression is a far cry from the fideistic appropriation of one of those worlds. Although Lindbeck attempts to ward off the charge of fideism, largely through appeal to the incommensurability of alternate paradigms, which renders apologetics questionable, his position strikes me as a quintessentially confessional one, cloaked in fashionable academic garb. Moreover, it is precisely that veneer that makes it all the more seductive, because despite providing little rationale for appropriating the biblical grammar, it gains credence in and through the borrowed authority that comes from his acute and persuasive identification of the cultural-linguistic framework.

For Lindbeck one of the advantages of his cultural-linguistic approach to religion is the ability to build bridges with scholars in other disciplines who increasingly operate out of the same perspective. There is much truth in this observation; but in the context of Lindbeck's constructive work it obscures an important difference between his brand of theology and academic inquiry in other fields. His appropriation of a cultural-linguistic model for the defense of a biblicist worldview would be not only foreign but academically suspect to the same scholars with whom he seeks connections. Lindbeck appropriates a postmodern framework to serve his primary role as a caretaker of Christianity, not to serve as a device to interpret and critique this tradition.[6]

6. Burton Mack developed the categories of the caretaker and critic of religion in a paper entitled "Caretakers and Critics: On the Social Role of Scholars Who Study Religion," which he delivered at Arizona State University in November 1989. He made a persuasive case, arguing that most scholars of religion continue to operate as caretakers of their tradition, a role that he contended must be left behind if the study of religion is to achieve its academic potential.

A POSTMODERN RELIGIOSITY

Another visible expression of a postmodern theology is that of the deconstructionists, which I will briefly consider in the representative writings of Mark C. Taylor. Although it has received much attention in recent years, deconstructive theology has generated few advocates. Its relatively small following, when compared to the growing influence of Lindbeck's postmodern-confessional alternative, makes it an unlikely prototype for the future direction of academic theology. Although Taylor's version of postmodern theology avoids the narrowly confessional character of Lindbeck's constructive proposal, it appears just as incapable of revitalizing theology within an academic context; but this is so for quite different reasons.

Taylor's postmodern commitments are visible in his continual rejection of any privileged text and of any real beginning or ending. In line with the trajectory extending from G.W.F. Hegel through Martin Heidegger to Jacques Derrida, Taylor critiques the assumptions about representation, presence, and reason that have structured the Western philosophical/theological tradition.[7] To escape the hold of this dominant perspective, he seeks not only to deconstruct its traces but also to think that which has been left unthought in and through this tradition. The specific task of the postmodern religious thinker, then, is to "think what religion within the limits of reason alone leaves unthought."[8] For Taylor this means that "the creative religious thinker must be relentlessly critical of *every* structure of thought and action."[9]

Taylor's version of postmodernism clearly precludes the endorsement of a single text or tradition through which to view the world, which constituted Lindbeck's resolution to the prevailing cacophony. Indeed, the relentless and thoroughgoing criticism that Taylor advocates reflects a sustained antiauthoritarian invective, which runs through his writings.[10] In this he appears faithful to postmodern sensi-

---

7. For his most explicit exploration of this complex of assumptions, see Mark C. Taylor, *Erring* (Chicago: University of Chicago Press, 1984).

8. Mark C. Taylor, "The Cutting Edge of Reason," *Soundings* 61, no. 2–3 (1988): 324.

9. Ibid.

10. It is interesting, however, that his antiauthoritarian strain is combined with the sacralization of texts themselves. Thus even though no single text can be privileged, texts themselves, in and through which the divine presence is manifest, are reverenced. I take this to be the faded, transmuted sacrality of the word of God, transposed to the infinite series of texts. He takes the textual genre of theology as far as it can go in an antiauthoritarian direction. His work is especially interesting and impor-

bilities. It is difficult to avoid the impression, however, that his deconstructive a/theology borders on a form of intellectual play that would be of little interest or relevance beyond the academy. Whereas Lindbeck's decision to inhabit a particular world appears arbitrary and confining, Taylor's perennial deconstructive strategy bears the mark of a Humean skepticism that cannot be sustained beyond one's personal study. His refusal to situate himself renders his theological reflection largely irrelevant to the particular religious beliefs and practices that others hold.

The creative religious thinker in Taylor's postmodern scenario is engaged in a rather esoteric, isolated task. As he expresses it: "To think what reasonable religion leaves unthought is to undertake the impossible and thus endless task of thinking the limen of neither/nor itself. This neither/nor is almost nothing—the almost nothing that is the edge, margin, limen, with which we began and from which we have never really departed."[11] The abstractness and cultivated aura of mystery and paradox that characterize this highly evocative language suggest that Taylor's writings themselves function as vehicles for a form of postmodern religiosity. This would be fully consistent with his understanding of postmodernism, because he insists that "despite its overt atheism, postmodernism remains profoundly religious."[12] This interpretation of his writings is further supported by his explicit criticisms of the shape of religious studies within the modern university. "The price of admission to the sacred precincts of the university," Taylor contends, "has been high. One consequence of the changes that have taken place in the last several decades has been the virtual paralysis of the creative religious imagination."[13] Rather than conform to the university's dulling, truncated version of reason, Taylor advocates that postmodern religious thinkers dare to express the religious within their own scholarly reflections.

Taking Taylor's writings in this way, some of the limitations of this revisioning of the theologian's task become evident. The form of postmodern religiosity that Taylor evidences would appear to be rarified,

---

tant because it reveals the limitations of the textual genre even after the deconstructive purge of privileging any particular text.

11. Taylor, "The Cutting Edge," 326.

12. Mark C. Taylor, *De-constructing Theology* (Chico, Calif.: Scholars Press; and New York: Crossroads, 1982), xx.

13. Taylor, "The Cutting Edge," 317.

attractive to a small coterie of intellectuals who had traversed a similar path. It is so disengaged from the actual religious beliefs and practices of the culture that it would have little effect in their critique or transformation. In other words, it is a religious vision for fellow intellectuals with postmodern affinities, and certainly not a strategy for evoking transformation within embodied religious belief and practice. Moreover, despite a heavy accent on critique it inhabits such an abstract plane that it offers little overt leverage for moral and political transformation.

The writings of thinkers such as Taylor and Lindbeck are critical in helping to expose and undermine the problematic assumptions of the modernist epoch. Their constructive proposals for the future of theology, however, hold far less promise. Despite sharing many of the same criticisms of modernism, in his recent work Kaufman proposes a rather different model for the future of theology. In my judgment, this model provides some important clues for the transformation of theology, which may help it secure greater impact and legitimacy beyond its own professional borders.

THEOLOGY AND CONTEXTUALIZATION:
TOWARD A NEW THEOLOGICAL PARADIGM

The vision of theology that Kaufman has developed in the last fifteen years suggests a way to move beyond modernism without resorting to the postmodern strategies and alternatives identified thus far. Operating from a pragmatic, historicist orientation, Kaufman attempts to reconstitute theology as a form of cultural critique that abandons authoritarian modes of argumentation as well as confessional agendas. For Kaufman, theology is a public enterprise which gains its substance and relevance through the operative religious symbols and beliefs of the culture at large. The task of the theologian includes the interpretation, evaluation, and reconstruction of such symbols and beliefs. Moving toward this vision of theology means abandoning the systematic, ahistorical, textually driven mode of theology for one that is far more contextual in its attention to embodied religion. This trajectory is already visible in Kaufman's own corpus of writings, evident in a comparison of his early *Systematic Theology: An Historicist Approach* and *Theology for a Nuclear Age*, which was written about two decades later. Fully extended, this trajectory leads toward even more funda-mental changes in the genre of theology.

We can begin to get a clearer picture of Kaufman's vision of theol-ogy by considering briefly the theological strategies that he rejects. His most extended criticisms are directed to theologies that continue to evoke the traditional authorities of the Bible, tradition, or ecclesiastical pronouncements for support. Although such warrants were eminently reasonable in light of traditional assumptions about divine revelation, they now appear both circular and problematic. "Many of the most important theological questions with which we must concern our-selves today," Kaufman contends, "are begged by the authoritarian approach."[14] Rather than regard religious symbols, myths, and rituals under a "sacred canopy," Kaufman roots them within the creative reli-gious human imagination. Therefore, he writes that "all Christian God-talk, and everything associated with it (prayer, worship, medita-tion, repentance, obedience), belongs to a specific world-view, a specific interpretation of human existence, created by the imagination in one particular historical stream of human culture to provide orien-tation in life for those living in that culture."[15] Not only does this his-torical perspective proscribe the appeal to traditional theological authorities; it also legitimates a far more extensive revisioning of the operative symbols, myths, and rituals.

Kaufman is equally critical of the line of modern theology stem-ming from Schleiermacher, which has sought to root theology within some prelinguistic religious experience. This focus upon experience fails to recognize the extent to which it is informed, shaped, and perhaps elicited by the language that we speak.[16] Therefore, like Proudfoot and Lindbeck, Kaufman rejects the turn to religious experi-ence and emphasizes a "cultural-linguistic" approach to religion and theology. Unlike Lindbeck, however, Kaufman does not primarily seek to sustain the coherence or continuity of a biblical grammar. Hence he does not advocate a biblical intratextual theology but insists upon the need to engage the culturally prevailing religious symbols and beliefs. He writes:

14. Gordon D. Kaufman, *Theology for a Nuclear Age* (Philadelphia: Westminster Press, 1985), 18.
15. Ibid., 23–24.
16. See Gordon D. Kaufman, *An Essay on Theological Method* (Missoula, Mont.: Scholars Press, 1975), 4–8.

If my understanding of theology, as ultimately rooted in the common language and in general human experience, is correct, it has a general cultural significance, and there is no reason for it to be restricted to the parochial confines of the church or to be regarded as an esoteric or subrational discipline. Whether the church as an institution lives or dies, theology has an important cultural role to play—so long as people continue to use and understand the word "God."[17]

The connection between theology and the interpretation of the symbol "God" is a historically contingent one, as Kaufman acknowledges. The important point is that theology engages the primary religious beliefs and practices of a culture and, in this engagement, contributes to their interpretation, evaluation, and reconstruction. To the extent that theology does engage the religious life of a culture, it will avoid the tendency to function primarily as a form of personal religiosity that may have little appeal or relevance beyond a small professional circle.

The model of theology that informs Kaufman's recent work has ramifications for the genre that, in my judgment, are not fully realized in his writings. They begin to emerge most clearly in his last book, *Theology for a Nuclear Age*. Unlike his earlier emphasis upon the peculiar logical features of the concept of God, in this work he considers several operative Christian interpretations of eschatology and divine providence that affect attitudes and responses to the possibility of a nuclear holocaust. The move from conceptual clarification to cultural analysis is telling. It reflects a refocusing, away from symbols, concepts, and texts taken in isolation to their instantiation in local contexts.

The reasons for moving in this direction are several. Perhaps the most compelling, and certainly one that is instrumental in shaping Kaufman's theological method, is the desacralization of the Bible and its dethronement as arbiter of divine truth. For over a millennium Christian theology was, for the most part, biblical commentary. The Bible was not simply the authoritative text that adjudicated between various theological alternatives; it was the central source or wellspring that nourished, structured, and controlled theological reflection. Underlying this mode of theology was the assumption that the Bible was sufficient for the articulation of faith. The paradigm of theology as biblical commentary was transformed during the twelfth and thir-

17. Ibid., 16.

teenth centuries with the rise of the medieval universities and the influence of the liberal arts on theological reflection. Commentary on Scripture was supplemented by dialectics, a form of reasoning that helped to turn theology into a systematic, speculative enterprise, more at home in the university than the monastery. Although the influence of dialectics in theology placed a premium on deductive logic, coherence, and systematization, scriptural touchstones continued to ensure its truthfulness. The rationale and legitimacy underlying theology lay in the sacrality of the text from which it proceeded and to which it eventually returned. The deconstruction of biblical authority eliminates the anchor for this textual genre, making room for its transmutation.[18]

Recent work on the multivalent meaning and function of religious myths and symbols provides additional impetus for moving beyond the textual bias in theological reflection. If religious myths, symbols, and rituals, rather than possessing a univocal meaning, assume their meaning and function in particular contexts, then their interpretation and critique demand careful attention to their embodiment within a particular time and place. This point has emerged from many quarters, although in theology it has been most powerfully and effectively made in theologies of liberation. The meaning and effect that a symbol or narrative has are not discernible apart from the context within which it is uttered or enacted. Thus what might appear in the abstract to be a noble idea or vision can assume, depending upon the speaker, context, and audience, a very different meaning and function.

The debate between some feminist and womanist theologians illustrates a variation on this point. The classic feminist analysis of the meaning and patriarchal effects of the symbol of God, which is found, for instance, in Mary Daly's *Beyond God the Father*, has been challenged by womanist theologians from the perspective of the black cultural experience. The sweeping feminist critique of the inherent patriarchal effect of traditional God-talk continues in the line of classical textual theology, albeit from a different angle. Its limitations become visible when inhabitants of different contexts identify quite different meanings and functions for the same symbols and narratives. The implica-

---

18. Friedrich Schleiermacher's recasting of theology as the analysis of the contents of the Christian consciousness is an important historical ancestor for this transmutation in the genre. Indeed, it can be interpreted as the liberation of the Schleiermachian model for theology from its modernist moorings.

tions of this sort of debate are far-reaching, going beyond the mandate to include more voices within the theological arena. At a more fundamental level, such arguments point to the need to move beyond the focus upon texts or symbols in isolation. Because the meaning and effect of texts and symbols are inextricably embedded in contexts, their interpretation and critique should also be locally rooted.

If theology were to develop along this trajectory, then the nature of theological expertise would be substantially reconfigured. Greater attention to the local embodiment of religious myths, symbols, and practices calls for historical and cultural expertise, which has not often been emphasized in theological scholarship. All too often theologians have pursued an ahistorical engagement with the great theologians of the past, regarding their positions as perennial Christian options rather than as strategies peculiar to a specific place and time. In the contextualization of theology the premium placed on philosophical and exegetical skills would be muted as theologians became more attentive to the interplay between text and context.[19]

Interpretation and critique of religious perspectives and behaviors call for competence in behavioral-explanatory approaches to religion. This line of development would locate theology more deeply and thoroughly in the domain of religious studies and reduce the gap that currently isolates the history of religions from theology. Such repositioning would not eliminate the normative and constructive aims of theology by making the history of religions paradigmatic for theological reflection, but it would connect these aims more closely to the enactment of religion in concrete contexts, thereby curbing the tendency to traffic in ahistorical verities isolated from instantiation in a particular time and place. This repositioning can also be described as moving from an essentialist orientation to one that is more empirically grounded. Critique and construction are not eliminated so much as they are transformed and harnessed self-consciously to cultural conversations. Recasting theology in this fashion would also have an impact on traditional theological sensibilities. The disdain for popular or folk religion, for instance, would be tempered as such religion

19. Lindbeck proposes a similar contextualization of theology, although locating it within carefully circumscribed intratextual (i.e., biblical) parameters. Paraphrasing Clifford Geertz's defense of "thick description" within cultural anthropology, Lindbeck also suggests that the theologian needs to become more like an ethnographer to avoid treating religion as an isolated symbol system that is divorced from real life. See Lindbeck, *The Nature of Doctrine*, 115.

became a central focus of attention. Moreover, the antipathy to religious syncretism, an aversion akin to a sense of pollution, would similarly be muted as theologians moved beyond the unifying parameters of a sacred text and immersed themselves in the far messier morass of lived religion.

The waning of the modern epoch has generated a variety of proposals for extending the genre of theology while theologians seek a paradigm that is compatible with the emerging intellectual and social landscape. Kaufman's recent work charts a direction for theology that moves it beyond modernism without succumbing to the textual or confessional bias so prevalent in forms of postmodern theology. His is a contextual revisioning of theology, which follows largely from the displacement of the Bible as the authority and anchor for theological reflection. This trajectory calls for some significant changes in the expertise, sensibilities, and primary conversation partners of the theologian. It will be no small task to incorporate such changes without eliminating the critical and constructive concerns that animate the enterprise of theology. Nevertheless, commitment to this task, in my view, offers us the best means for securing a role for theology that is not only academically sound but culturally relevant.

5

Regulae fidei and Regulative Idea: Two Contemporary Theological Strategies

WAYNE PROUDFOOT

The prospects for theology are not easy to gauge. Perhaps the best way to address the topic is to examine some present proposals in the light of the recent past and to highlight common themes. George Lindbeck and Gordon Kaufman have recently published programmatic statements about the nature of theology and theological method.[1] Although these statements are very different, in form as well as content, I will use them to articulate and to comment on some problems that confront the contemporary theologian.

From a distance Lindbeck and Kaufman might appear quite similar. They could both be described as liberal theologians, despite Lindbeck's rejection of that term and his proposal of new concepts of religion, doctrine, and theology for a postliberal age. Each has noted affinities of his method with pragmatism, at least in the current broad sense of that term. Both received their doctorates from Yale, and Lindbeck has been a member of the Yale faculty through most of his professional career. Nevertheless, the work of each differs significantly from the other's. Lindbeck has been active in ecumenical discussions, particularly those between Roman Catholics and Lutherans. These discussions about the possibility of reconciling communal norms of belief

---

1. George Lindbeck, *The Nature of Doctrine: Religion and Theology in a Postliberal Age* (Philadelphia: Westminster Press, 1984); and Gordon Kaufman, *An Essay on Theological Method*, rev. ed. (Missoula, Mont.: Scholars Press, 1979).

and action that initially appear to oppose each other have strongly influenced his views on religion, doctrine, and theology. Kaufman belongs to the Mennonite tradition, a religious community in which comparatively little emphasis is placed on explicitly articulated doctrine. Lindbeck and some of his colleagues at Yale see themselves as building on the work of Karl Barth, whereas Kaufman is less enthusiastic about that work.

These details are not isolated facts or preferences; they are shorthand ways to place two prominent figures within contemporary American Protestant theology. Despite their differences, their proposals for understanding religion and theology are both centrally addressed to the same topic: the logical status of religious and theological language. This topic has been addressed in different ways, but for similar ends, by the major Protestant thinkers since Friedrich Schleiermacher. Despite some ingenious and even brilliant contributions that have been offered along the way, the topic is not able to bear the burden that has been placed on it: to ensure that religious language, especially language about God, is construed in such a way that it is radically independent of, and therefore cannot conflict with, the languages of science or of any domain of inquiry outside the religious. Schleiermacher developed an elaborate typology of religious and theological language to support his claim for the radical autonomy of theology.

> Our dogmatic theology will not, however, stand on its proper ground and soil with the same assurance with which philosophy has so long stood on its own, until the separation of the two types of proposition is so complete that, e.g., so extraordinary a question as whether the same proposition can be true in philosophy and false in Christian theology, and *vice versa*, will no longer be asked, for the simple reason that a proposition cannot appear in one context precisely as it appears in the other: however similar it sounds, a difference can always be assumed.[2]

The theological statement "God created the world" differs in logical status from, and therefore cannot support or conflict with, the same sentence occurring in a treatise on physics or metaphysics. Conflict between theology and any other domain of inquiry is precluded.

Lindbeck sets out what he calls a cultural-linguistic theory of religion and doctrine as a contribution to a postliberal theology. Doctrines

---

2. Friedrich Schleiermacher, *The Christian Faith*, 2d ed., trans. H. R. Mackintosh and J. S. Stewart (Edinburgh: T. & T. Clark, 1928), Proposition 16, postscript.

are grammatical rules that provide identifying criteria for the proper use of language in a religious community. These rules have a fundamentally different status from propositions or assertions about the world. Kaufman views theology as imaginative construction, along with other domains of intellectual activity; but he regards religious language, especially talk about God, as having a distinctive status. The concept of God is not subject to rules that are internal to a community and its doctrine. It is a public concept. It has, however, a peculiar logical status as the most comprehensive or fundamental concept by which people understand themselves. The task of theology is to take responsibility for this concept and to shape it to serve human ends, one of which may be to criticize those ends.

Although they differ greatly in their conceptions of the character of theology, both Lindbeck and Kaufman begin by identifying the logical status of doctrine or of the concept of God in such a way as to establish autonomy for doctrinal statements or uses of that concept and to preclude conflict with nonreligious statements. They thus continue a form of prolegomena to theology that can be traced back at least to Schleiermacher.[3] This task is finally impossible to carry out. One cannot identify the logical status of religious doctrine or of the word "God" in such a way that it remains invulnerable to our changing beliefs and desires. If that could be achieved, then the doctrine or word would be isolated from the ongoing inquiries by which we become aware of and transform those beliefs and desires. In this essay I consider briefly the similarities and differences in these projects and use them to point to some problems for contemporary theology.

REGULAE FIDEI

Lindbeck distinguishes at the outset between propositions and rules. Propositions are used to make truth claims, whereas rules are second-order statements that identify and govern the proper use of concepts and sentences in a particular domain. A rule such as "Drive on the right side of the road" or "A preposition must agree in number with its antecedent" might conflict with another rule but cannot conflict with a statement about the world. With this distinction and the claim that religious doctrines are rules rather than propositions, Lindbeck has

---

3. See Schleiermacher's discussion of religious language in *The Christian Faith*, propositions 16–17.

achieved the desired result: religious doctrines can never conflict with the results of science or with any other beliefs about the world.

> It seems odd to suggest that the Nicaenum in its role as a communal doctrine does not make first-order truth claims, and yet this is what I shall contend. Doctrines regulate truth claims by excluding some and permitting others, but the logic of their communally authoritative use hinders or prevents them from specifying positively what is to be affirmed.[4]

Nothing in the Nicene creed, qua doctrine of a religious community, can conflict with any first-order claim. "I believe in God the Father, Maker of Heaven and Earth," whatever it might mean, cannot conflict with theories of cosmology. "It is simply that the logic of rules and propositions is different."[5] This is precisely what Schleiermacher achieved by redescribing religious doctrines as expressions of communal modifications of the feeling of absolute dependence, and by claiming that a sentence in theology differs in meaning from the same sentence as it is used in philosophy or physics.[6]

Religions, according to Lindbeck, are cultural systems governed by grammatical rules, and therefore are analogous to languages.

> In the account that I shall give, religions are seen as comprehensive interpretive schemes, usually embodied in myths or narratives and heavily ritualized, which structure human experience and understanding of self and world. . . . Stated more technically, a religion can be viewed as a kind of cultural and/or linguistic framework or medium that shapes the entirety of life and thought.[7]

A religion is an interpretive scheme that is used to identify and describe "the maximally important."[8] Stress is placed on the code rather than on what is encoded.

Religions are interpretive schemes with their own criteria for intelligibility and appropriateness. Lindbeck cites Clifford Geertz and Peter Winch in support of his cultural-linguistic theory of religion.[9] Like Geertz, he holds that proper understanding comes from "thick description," the elucidation of a text or action in terms of the grammatical rules that govern the proper use of concepts or practices in a

---

4. Lindbeck, *The Nature of Doctrine*, 19.
5. Ibid., 103.
6. See n. 2.
7. Lindbeck, *The Nature of Doctrine*, 32–33.
8. Ibid., 33.
9. Ibid., 20.

particular culture. Like Winch, he holds that a religion has its own rules for judging intelligibility and appropriateness and cannot legitimately be justified or criticized by appeal to criteria imported from some other interpretive scheme, such as science or philosophy.

This redescription of religion and doctrine enables Lindbeck to argue, with Barth and against Schleiermacher, that religious narrative and doctrine inform the religious life and shape, but are not shaped by, experience. "A scriptural world is thus able to absorb the universe. It supplies the interpretive framework within which believers seek to live their lives and understand reality."[10] Religion is neither subject to nor dependent upon some extrareligious interpretive scheme.

Faithfulness to a scriptural tradition is construed as intratextuality, correspondence to the semiotic universe encoded in holy writ.[11] Criteria for intelligibility and rhetorical appropriateness are internal to the system. Doctrines are second-order propositions making only intrasystematic truth claims. The logic of religious discourse is radically independent of external norms.

Theology is properly descriptive, according to Lindbeck, and thus intratextual. "The task of descriptive (dogmatic or systematic) theology is to give a normative explication of the meaning a religion has for its adherents."[12] Some allowance is made for ad hoc apologetics, rhetoric directed to particular persons or issues, but not for attempts to justify religious belief or doctrine by appeal to extrasystematic evidence or arguments.

In fact, Lindbeck's book is a clear instance of apologetics. His redescription has rendered a religion as a cultural-linguistic system radically independent of concepts and beliefs that are not governed by its internal rules. In this regard his project is similar to that of Schleiermacher.[13]

Like his nineteenth-century predecessors, Lindbeck wants to allow for Christian claims of superiority and exclusiveness. Adherents often claim that their religions are better than others. He also wants to argue that religions as interpretive schemes capture something real that is not exhausted by the systems of conventions themselves. This poses a

10. Ibid., 117.
11. Ibid., 116.
12. Ibid., 113.
13. For an analysis and critique of Schleiermacher's project, see Wayne Proudfoot, *Religious Experience* (Berkeley and Los Angeles: University of California Press, 1985), chap. 1.

problem. Judgments of correctness or superiority and distinctions between appearance and reality, he has said, are internal to interpretive schemes. How, then, can he speak intelligibly of the relation of these schemes to reality?

Lindbeck says that a religion as a comprehensive interpretive scheme can be said to correspond to reality and, therefore, to be ontologically true. To invoke the idea of correspondence but still shield religious doctrines from extrasystematic criteria, he proposes that the entire scheme be viewed as one statement.

> As actually lived, a religion may be pictured as a single gigantic proposition. It is a true proposition to the extent that its objectivities are interiorized and exercised by groups and individuals in such a way as to conform them in some measure in the various dimensions of their existence to the ultimate reality and goodness that lies at the heart of things. It is a false proposition to the extent that this does not happen.[14]

This image of a gigantic proposition corresponding to some (what?) ultimate reality and goodness does not fit easily with the rest of the argument, despite Lindbeck's excursus on the issue of religion and truth. It is, however, an acknowledgment that extrasystematic claims are intrinsic to religious belief and life, even though the burden of his redescription has been to ensure that religious doctrine and practice are autonomous and subject only to intrasystematic appraisal.

The result is a theory of religion and doctrine that insulates both from conflict with any external beliefs or practice. Religious tradition and doctrine are redescribed so that they are compatible with the results of science and with any other extrareligious beliefs. This is an apologetic strategy and is quite similar to Schleiermacher's program, with which Lindbeck contrasts his own.

Attention to the distinctive character of narrative has also been employed to identify a logical status for religious language that would preclude any conflict between religious claims and those of science, broadly considered. Lindbeck describes faithfulness as intratextuality and commends recent work on narrative in theology, especially Hans Frei's discussion of realistic narrative.[15] Study of the way in which biblical narrative forms personal and communal identity is important for theology. Problems arise, however, with arguments for the auton-

---

14. Lindbeck, *The Nature of Doctrine*, 51.
15. Ibid., 120. See Hans Frei, *The Eclipse of Biblical Narrative* (New Haven: Yale University Press, 1974).

omy of narrative that portray it as sharply distinct from and thus incapable of conflicting with ordinary beliefs and explanations. Recent theological interest in story and narrative is rooted in Barth's identification of saga as neither history nor myth and in H. Richard Niebuhr's concept of internal history as opposed to external history.[16] Each of these was in part an attempt to fix a status for the word of God, as revealed and preached, that would differentiate it from and establish it as autonomous with respect to mundane beliefs and explanations. Although this is usually done in the name of confessional theology and associated with a rejection of apologetics, it is itself an apologetic ploy. It is an attempt to preclude conflict between religious and theological statements on the one hand, and nonreligious beliefs, intentions, and desires on the other hand. Such attempts are, finally, futile.

REGULATIVE IDEAS

Lindbeck writes that religion viewed as a cultural-linguistic framework "functions somewhat as a Kantian *a priori.*"[17] Like Lindbeck, Kaufman argues for the peculiar logical status of distinctively religious language. His argument focuses not on doctrinal norms but on the concept of God, with brief reference to analogous concepts in other traditions. Unlike Lindbeck, Kaufman does not hold that criteria for the proper use of religious language are tradition-specific; nor does he stress the internal and traditional context of religious norms. On the contrary, he calls for a public theology and rejects parochial appeals to authority.[18]

Although agreeing with Lindbeck that religious beliefs and practices are linguistic and cultural systems, Kaufman argues that they can and should be criticized and reformed in the light of public, openly debated criteria of intelligibility and appropriateness. In a review of *The Nature of Doctrine*, he writes:

A clear exposition of the theological significance of the cultural-linguistic conception of religion has been needed for some time, and

---

16. See Karl Barth, *Church Dogmatics*, vol. 3, part 1, trans. G. W. Bromiley and T. F. Torrance (Edinburgh: T. & T. Clark, 1958), 81–94; and H. Richard Niebuhr, *The Meaning of Revelation* (New York: Macmillan, 1941), chap. 2.

17. Lindbeck, *The Nature of Doctrine*, 33.

18. See Kaufman, *An Essay on Theological Method*, 8.

Lindbeck's achievement in this regard assures the lasting significance of his book. One might wish, however, that he had not been so intent to put his important insight exclusively into the service of the theologically conservative enterprise of ecumenical debate, with its diverse parties all wishing to keep their theological cake even at the very moment they are consuming them [*sic*].[19]

Like Lindbeck, and like Schleiermacher and many in his wake, Kaufman focuses on the proper construal of religious language. He faults traditional theology for its "failure to recognize certain peculiarities of the logical status and function of the concept of God."[20] Following Immanuel Kant, he holds that "God," like "world," is a concept of a different order from the concepts and categories that structure judgments about objects of experience.

"God" and "world" stand at the limits of experience. They do not enter into particular judgments but are presupposed by those judgments. They are regulative ideas and represent the comprehensive unity that is assumed in the act of distinguishing between particulars. When I identify a particular object in space and time or predicate properties of the object, I make this identification or predication against the background of an ideal of the world as a unified whole of all that exists. This ideal can never be an object of my experience and, therefore, cannot be an object of knowledge, but it is a limiting idea that must be assumed to give a proper account of my experience and my knowledge. For Kant the idea of God is an even more comprehesive unity, embracing all that is possible as well as all that is actual.

Kaufman writes that "the peculiar logical status of the central concepts with which theology deals demands radical reconception of both the task of theology and the way in which that task is carried out."[21] Once it is recognized that the word "God" does not refer to an object, cannot function in an explanation, and is not a matter of how things are but is indispensable and presupposed by all experience, certain naive conceptions of the theological task can be discarded. The theologian becomes more self-conscious and self-confident about her role in shaping this limiting concept to contribute to human life. "God" need not be conceived as male rather than female, as lord rather than servant, or even in personal rather than impersonal terms, although rea-

19. Gordon Kaufman, "Review of George Lindbeck, *The Nature of Doctrine: Religion and Theology in a Postliberal Age,* " *Theology Today* 42 (1985–86):241.
20. Kaufman, *An Essay on Theological Method*, 24.
21. Ibid., 28.

sons can be given for constructing the concept one way rather than another and Kaufman has often argued for the superiority of personal over impersonal language for this purpose.[22]

Like Lindbeck, Kaufman wants to distance theology from first-order claims about the world. First-order theology, he argues, is executed when theologians claim to explain God and the world as they really are. Second-order theology emerges when the theologian realizes that her concepts are constructs of the imagination. Third-order theology, the task to which Kaufman is committed and calls his colleagues, comes into being when the theologian actively takes control of these concepts and images of God and the world, deliberately shapes them to humane ends, and seeks to interpret experience in the light of them.[23]

In *An Essay on Theological Method* Kaufman acknowledges his debt to Kant but not to the details of Kant's argument.[24] He endorses the Kantian claim that the concept of God is universal and, therefore, indispensable.

> I would like to suggest that with the word "God" we are attempting to indicate the last or ultimate point of reference to which all action, consciousness and reflection can lead. . . . This idea of an ultimate reference point (whether conceived as "God" or in some other way) is no optional or dispensable one.[25]

More recently, in *The Theological Imagination*, he places less emphasis on the Kantian framework and on the universality of such an ultimate reference point and more on the development of the idea of God in Western culture.[26] The Kantian background persists, however, and shows itself in an ambiguity that informs the understanding of theology as construction.

Throughout *The Theological Imagination* the reader is told that the concept of God and all of the concepts with which the theologian works are products of human construction. They are not given but constructed by the human imagination. There seem to be two possible

22. See Gordon Kaufman, *God the Problem* (Cambridge: Harvard University Press, 1972), chap. 4.
23. See Kaufman, *An Essay on Theological Method*, 37–38.
24. Ibid., 24–25.
25. Ibid., 11–12.
26. The shift is indicated in the preface, where Kaufman says he no longer views "God" as an idea or concept but sometimes refers to it as symbol or image and realizes that conceptual analysis of the term is insufficient. Gordon Kaufman, *The Theological Imagination: Constructing the Concept of God* (Philadelphia: Westminster Press, 1981), 14.

interpretations of this claim, both of which derive from Kant and neither of which leads to the conclusion that theology is constructive in
the manner that Kaufman suggests.

The first interpretation is that all of our concepts are the products of
the human mind and its history. We have no access to innate ideas or
immediate impressions as a foundation for knowledge. Even perception is constituted by judgment and by the constructive activity of the
mind. This Kantian point is not widely disputed; but that all of our
concepts are human constructions does not imply that they are subject
to self-conscious choice and alteration in the way that Kaufman suggests. This interpretation does not differentiate theology from any
other human endeavor. The concepts of physics, of ethics, of the arts,
and of every other discipline and pursuit are products of human construction, but the constraints on construction are quite different in
each of these areas. The physicist constructs models and hypotheses
and reconstructs theories and concepts, but she does so in order to
solve problems, to provide a better explanation of the data, and to
advance inquiry. One need not deny that observation is theory-laden
and that there are no uninterpreted data to recognize that the physicist
operates under certain constraints. Although one could describe the
constraints on the construction of theories in physics as pragmatic,
they are not the same as those that Kaufman proposes for theology. On
this first interpretation, to say that theological concepts and doctrines
are the product of human construction does not differentiate them
from anything else.

A second interpretation is possible as well for at other points Kaufman describes the imaginative and constructive activity behind the
use of the word "God" and other theological concepts in such a way as
to distinguish it not only from physics but from ordinary inquiry.

> God is not a reality immediately available in our experience for observa-
> tion, inspection, and description, and speech about or to God is there-
> fore never directly referential. Thus, we are unable to check our
> concepts and images of God for accuracy and adequacy through direct
> confrontation with the reality *God*, as we can with most ordinary objects
> of perception and experience.[27]

This could be read as a restatement of the earlier point, because nothing is immediately available for observation, inspection, and descrip-

27. Ibid., 21.

tion. But the contrast with "ordinary objects of perception and experience" shows that something else is meant. The constructive character of theological and metaphysical concepts is being contrasted with those employed in ordinary judgments.

This contrast derives from a different Kantian claim. Particular metaphysical concepts such as the self, the world, and God differ from the concepts that inform ordinary experience. Ordinary concepts are constructions of the human mind but our judgments within experience are governed by categories of understanding, and we have procedures for revising and checking those judgments. By contrast, the concepts of self, world, and God have no place at all in experience. They are regulative ideas that stand at the limits of experience and serve to orient us in our thinking. Kant argues that these ideas can never be employed in judgments that yield knowledge, but neither can they be dispensed with; they are required for orientation and presupposed by ordinary judgments. That Kaufman has this Kantian background in mind is shown by his description of the concept of God as a limiting idea, his emphasis on the role of theological and metaphysical concepts in orienting thought and action, and his claim that the principal terms of the Christian metaphysical scheme are God, humanity, and world.[28]

In later work Kaufman does not claim that the concept of "God" or its analogue is universal or indispensable. One can then ask, as he does:

> Why might one be inclined to move toward construction of such an ulti-
> mate relativizing principle? Why not be satisfied with a concept of
> nature or the world as the ultimate context within which human
> existence falls? Only if one is aware of certain important values which
> "God-talk" can provide and certain serious dangers against which it can
> help protect, will one feel impelled to move beyond anthropology and
> cosmology to theology.[29]

The portrayal of theological construction as subject to choice in this way is unconvincing. If the concept of "God" is universal and indispensable, then the question makes no sense. If it is not, then it is difficult to see how an individual or community could choose "to move beyond anthropology and cosmology to theology" in such a

28. Ibid., 238–62, esp. 250.
29. Ibid., 50.

way that the theological concepts are vested with sufficient authority to provide orientation and to protect against idolatry.

The recognition that cultures characterized by monotheistic beliefs and practices benefit from a system of symbols that includes an ultimate point of reference, which can be employed to relativize parochial values and claims, does not show that such benefits can be produced by self-consciously adopting a monotheistic symbol system to bring them about. Religious beliefs are authoritative because those who hold them take them to be descriptive or revelatory of how things actually are, not because they produce certain benefits. One might well decide, from psychological and sociological considerations, that basic confidence or some kind of trusting orientation toward the cosmos is a desideratum. Kaufman says that the symbol of God as creator, sustainer, and perfecter of our humanity through love and forgiveness provides a powerful and significant object of devotion. One cannot, however, choose to adopt a certain set of symbols and concepts as a basis of trust or as an object of devotion. Trust depends upon one's conception of the world and of one's place in it. It rests upon certain tacit explanations and cannot be secured by choice. One cannot decide to adopt a certain concept or categorial scheme because it will provide a trusting orientation for life.

Metaphysical and theological claims are to be assessed, for Kaufman, according to the degree to which they raise consciousness about the human situation and further liberation.[30] But liberation, as Marx and Freud saw, requires the identification of false consciousness and the awareness of ideological constraints by arriving, through inquiry, at a more accurate understanding of one's actual situation, social and personal. The raising of consciousness and the furthering of human liberation are brought about by the search for a more adequate explanation of the forces that act upon oneself and one's world. The resulting knowledge must be appropriated in such a way as to inform practice and transform perception; but pragmatic criteria and liberation cannot be separated from intellectual inquiry.

Kaufman recognizes that a set of symbols that is to supply a framework for orientation and foci for devotion and loyalty must have some connection with "the real world," that is, the actual situations in which people find themselves.

30. Ibid., 257.

To see these possibilities as ultimately normative for human existence is to hold them to be grounded in and expressive of "reality" in a way not true of significantly different modes of life. Speech about the Christian God as "real" or "existent" expresses symbolically this conviction that free and loving persons-in-community have a substantial metaphysical foundation, that there are cosmic forces working toward this sort of humanization.[31]

Like Lindbeck, who states that a religion is true to the extent that it enables individuals to conform themselves to "the ultimate reality and goodness that lies at the heart of things," Kaufman here acknowledges the truth claims that are implicit in religious belief and practice. Those claims provide the authority and force by which religious concepts and beliefs are able to provide a framework for orientation, critical leverage, and foci for devotion.

Kaufman's project seems to have begun with the idea that the concept of "God" or of some ultimate point of reference is universal and indispensable but that different cultures have shaped and developed that idea in different ways. Now that we have become self-conscious about that process, we can actively engage in the criticism and transformation of that idea as it has come down to us and can shape it to humane ends. Having moved from tacit reliance on Kant's transcendental claim that the concept of God is universal, Kaufman portrays the theological option as one that a culture might or might not adopt. Constructive theology is no longer a matter of shaping a concept that is indispensable, but rather one of constructing a concept and associated language and investing with them sufficient authority to fulfill certain functions: to provide an object of trust and loyalty and a criterion for criticizing parochial beliefs and loyalties. That is a large order for constructive theologians to fill.

CONCLUSION

Both Lindbeck and Kaufman identify what they take to be the peculiar logical status of distinctively religious language. Lindbeck focuses on doctrine as normative for a religious community, Kaufman on the concept of God. That peculiar logical status is explicated in such a way as to insulate those doctrines or that concept from conflict with nonreligious beliefs. Both adopt protective strategies that ensure that tra-

31. Ibid., 49.

ditional religious beliefs and practices can be reconstrued or reshaped for contemporary application.

Both strategies can be criticized. In contrast to Schleiermacher, Lindbeck proposes a redescription of religious doctrine that does not depend upon a dubious anthropology and a romantic theory of linguistic expression; it does, however, require him to draw a sharp distinction between what he calls first- and second-order propositions, that is, between statements about the world and regulative statements that function like syntactic rules. Religious doctrines are such regulative statements and religions are interpretive schemes that function like the Kantian a priori; hence both are of a different order from scientific statements. Willard Quine, one of the most distinguished recent pragmatists, has shown that such a distinction is only relative, even in the linguistic case.[32] One cannot identify certain statements as grammatical or logical rules and shield them from the kind of reassessment to which ordinary beliefs are subjected. At any particular moment some rules may be taken as given and some beliefs as not subject to scrutiny, but all are corrigible, including those we think of as grammatical rules or logical relations. There is, finally, no difference in status or in relation to experience between statements of rules and statements of belief. To describe religious doctrine as rule and religion as interpretive framework does not preclude the possibility that both might conflict with ordinary and scientific beliefs. In the course of inquiry one infers to the most coherent explanatory account, revising rules, beliefs, and practices until a reflective equilibrium is reached. Ironically, the dichotomy between second-order rules and first-order propositions that is central to Lindbeck's program derives not from Wittgenstein's later work but from logical positivism.

Even if such a dichotomy were possible, it would surely be anachronistic to view the Nicene and Chalcedonian symbols and other formulations of religious doctrine as rules only, where "rule" is described in such a way as to render it innocent of first-order statements. These doctrines developed out of inquiry elicited by particular problems: what is the relation of Jesus to God, of Christians to Jews, of the kingdom of God to the message of the prophets, and of the authority of the Bible to Greek philosophy? Doctrinal formulations were

32. See Willard van Orman Quine, "Two Dogmas of Empiricism," in idem, *From a Logical Point of View*, 2d ed. (Cambridge: Harvard University Press, 1961), chap. 2.

often constructed so as to rule out unacceptable answers to these questions; they would allow room for further inquiry but acknowledge the limitations of human insight into divine mysteries. These formulations were not, however, constructed to be radically independent of all first-order claims about the world.

Recognition that the concept of God is a human construct allows one to take an active role in formulating a conception of the world, an idea of God in relation to that world, and a reconception of the world as experienced in the light of that idea of God. Kaufman describes this three-step process as the "order of theological construction."[33] He has written convincingly on how such contemporary issues as the emergence of feminist consciousness and the threat of nuclear war should affect the images by which God is conceived. Given a conception of God that we have inherited, awareness of such issues can provide criteria for shaping that inheritance in specific directions. When a question is raised about the authority or dispensability of the idea of God or of an ultimate point of reference, however, functional criteria alone will not serve to establish it in such a way as to enable it to fulfill those functions and to provide an object of loyalty and a critical perspective.

Theology must somehow reconstitute itself as genuine inquiry. The most common protective strategy in Protestant thought since Schleiermacher has been to stress the autonomy of religious and theological language, to decouple it from nonreligious beliefs and practices, and to leave inquiry about the world to the sciences, broadly considered. That decoupling has permitted scientific inquiry to flourish without ecclesiastical interference and has served apologetic purposes in the short run. The cost, however, has been to remove theological reflection from the actual inquiries in which we continually engage, and to court the risk of irrelevance.

---

33. Kaufman, *The Theological Imagination*, 46.

PART III

THEOLOGY, HISTORICITY, AND SOLIDARITY

6

The Crisis of Hermeneutics and Christian Theology

FRANCIS SCHÜSSLER FIORENZA

Among contemporary theologians, few have contributed to the understanding of modern theology as much as Gordon Kaufman. He has consistently profiled the sharp contrasts between traditional and modern theology. Against an uncritical theology based on authority he has proposed a theology ordered toward modernity. Against ahistorical views of the world he has consistently elaborated the theological implications of a historical and evolutionary worldview. Against a view of theology as a retrieval of past traditions he has sought to elaborate a constructive modern theology. These essays in honor of Kaufman, therefore, appropriately deal with modernity and the crisis of modernity, as modernity itself is challenged and our modern culture is considered by many as postmodern.[1]

This essay addresses one aspect of the crisis of modernity: the crisis of modern theology as a crisis of interpretation or, more specifically, as a crisis of the conception of theology as hermeneutical. A crisis of hermeneutics signifies that many controversies and disagreements exist, not only because individuals and groups have different beliefs and share different values but also because individuals and groups have

1. See Jean-François Lyotard, *The Postmodern Condition: A Report on Knowledge* (Minneapolis: University of Minnesota Press, 1984); Jean-François Lyotard and Jean-Loup Thébaud, *Just Gaming* (Minneapolis: University of Minnesota Press, 1985); and Steven Connor, *Postmodernist Culture* (New York: Blackwell, 1989).

basically different interpretive approaches to their beliefs, values, and practices. These interpretive approaches deeply affect how persons understand and come to their beliefs and practices and constitute the very rationality with which people approach, articulate, and explain their identity in relation to their particular cultural and political situations.

For modern theology the crisis of hermeneutics is not simply about how one interprets the Christian tradition. The issue is much more fundamental because it deals with questions of how one even begins to undertake such a task of interpretation and whether theology is primarily hermeneutical or not. Because interpretation has been central to both traditional and modern theology, however, such a crisis of hermeneutics is at the same time a crisis of both traditional and modern theology. It is a crisis affecting the conception of the theological task and the very nature of theology.

THEOLOGY AS HERMENEUTICAL

A historical sketch of the shift from traditional theology to modern theology and from modern theology to the crisis of modernity will show the contours of this crisis of hermeneutics. Whereas traditional theology understood the theological task as a hermeneutics of authority, modern theology understood the theological task as a hermeneutics of religious subjectivity. When one becomes acutely aware of the historicity of both modern religious subjectivity and traditional theological authorities, an interpretive crisis emerges. The awareness of this double historicity characterizes the contemporary hermeneutical task within theology.

The crisis of hermeneutics, then, entails not only that traditional approaches to the question of the meaning of religious or Christian identity are no longer adequate but also that modern responses are inadequate and invalid because the interpretation of identity has become a complex interpretive endeavor. This complexity and radicality of hermeneutics challenge theology to move beyond traditional and modern conceptions of its hermeneutical task.

Traditional Theology:
A Hermeneutics of Authority

The hermeneutical problem revolved around the meaning of revelation given in the Scriptures and its authoritative interpretation. For

Augustine the major hermeneutical issue in interpreting the Scriptures was whether the words of the Scriptures were seen only as material signs or were understood in their spiritual meaning as referring to the transcendent God and to the spiritual realities of the Christian faith.[2] One failed to interpret the Scriptures if one failed to grasp the spiritual meaning of the words.

The basic hermeneutical problem for Augustine arose from assumptions influenced by Neoplatonic background theories. These assumptions led to a hermeneutical theory quite distinct from contemporary theories of whatever type.[3] Augustine argued that to interpret properly the literal meaning of the Scriptures, one had to understand the transcendent spiritual realities to which they referred. This interpretive problem required personal self-transcendence as the preparation for grasping the spiritual meaning of the Scriptures. Through spiritual purification, converting one's energies from the visible material goods of life to invisible spiritual goods, one prepared oneself to interpret correctly the Scriptures and their Christian identity.[4] In cases of doubt as to correct interpretation, Augustine offers two rules: opt for that which serves the love of God and love of neighbor, and follow that which has been traditionally taught in those episcopal sees that trace their origin to the apostles.[5] Theologians, scholastic as well as modern, have often neglected the first rule to focus on the second. The decisive criteria of correct interpretation have been the authorities of tradition.[6]

2. See esp. Augustine, *On Christian Doctrine*, bk. 1, (Indianapolis: Bobbs-Merrill, 1958); and *Spirit and Letter*, Vol. VIII in *Augustine: Later Works*, trans. John Burnaby (Philadelphia: Westminster Press, 1955).

3. One should not simply identify traditional theories or movements, such as fundamentalism, with Augustine's interpretive approach toward the Scriptures; see Francis Schüssler Fiorenza, "The Challenge of Fundamentalism to Roman Catholic Theology," in *The Struggle over the Past: Fundamentalism in the Modern World*, ed. William Shea (Washington, D.C.: University Press of America, 1991). For an analysis of the Neoplatonic background, see Cornelius Mayer, *Die Zeichen in der geistigen Entwicklung und in der Theologie des jungen Augustins*, 2 vols. (Würzburg: Augustinus Verlag, 1974).

4. Augustine develops six steps of purgation in *On Christian Doctrine*, bk. 2, vii, 9–11.

5. Augustine, *On Christian Doctrine*, bk. 1, xxxvi.40–xl.44. "The rule of faith should be consulted as it is found in the more open places of Scripture and in the authority of the church" (bk. 2, ii.2). One should accept those Scriptures according to the "authority of the greater number of catholic churches, among which are those which have deserved to have apostolic seats and to receive epistles" (bk. 2, viii, 12 [p. 41]).

6. Whereas the historical-critical method of modern scientific exegesis excludes in principle the type of spiritual purgation recommended by Augustine, the contrasting contemporary existential hermeneutical theory underscores the correlation between

The appeal to authoritative traditions, however, became a much more complex interpretive endeavor in medieval times. Peter Abelard's influential *Sic et Non* (Yes and No) demonstrated that the authorities of tradition often conflicted with one another.[7] Abelard's rules, borrowed from the canonical tradition, sought to resolve the conflicts among authorities (attending, for example, to linguistic ambiguities, shifts in circumstances, specific intention, and so forth) but failed to do so; then Abelard urged reliance upon that authority which had the most weight, that is, the most authority. Abelard's procedure of displaying the conflicts of authorities and attempting to resolve them had the logical consequence of implying a critique of authorities while acknowledging authority.[8]

Thomas Aquinas explained the resolution of theological arguments as a task of weighing authorities.[9] One argued from the authority of Scripture properly and with certainty, from the doctors of the church properly but only with probability, and from philosophy only extrinsically and only with probability. Aquinas presupposed, however, a harmony between the truth in the Scriptures, the proper authority of theology, and the truth of philosophy, an extrinsic authority for theology. The proper role of philosophy within the theological task was primarily instrumental or propaedeutic.[10]

The centuries after Thomas Aquinas led to a significant change in the relation of theology to tradition and authorities. The number of authorities that theologians appealed to increased. The influential sixteenth-century Spanish theologian Melchior Cano listed ten sources of theological authority that came to be decisive for theological argumentation.[11] The first two, Scripture and unwritten oral tradition, constituted the indispensable authorities of revelation. The next five constituted the interpretation of revelation: the universal church, the

---

the life-relation of pre-understanding and understanding. Various liberation thinkers emphasize the same point in their critique of scientific objectivity, in addition to justice and an option for the poor.

7. See Peter Abelard, *Sic et Non*, ed. Blanche Boyer and Richard McKeon (Chicago: University of Chicago Press, 1976–77).

8. Andrea Nye, "An Arsenal of Reasons: Abelard's Dialectic," in idem, *Words of Power* (New York: Routledge & Chapman, 1990), 85–102.

9. See Thomas Aquinas, *Summa Theologiae* I, q.1., a.8, "Whether sacred doctrine is argumentative." For a commentary on Thomas Aquinas's use of authority in theological arguments, see Edward Schillebeeckx, "Scholasticism and Theology," in idem, *Revelation and Theology*, vol. 1 (New York: Sheed & Ward, 1967), 223–58.

10. See *Summa Theologiae*, I.q.1, a.5 to q.2; and q.1, a.8 to q.2.

11. See Melchior Cano, *De locis theologicis* (1524).

general councils of the church, the Pope, the church fathers, and the scholastic theologians. The last three were not properly sources of theological authority: human reason, philosophy, and human history. These ten sources constituted sources of authority that provide the bases for theological argument about Christian identity.[12]

Modern Theology:
A Hermeneutics of Experience

In the modern period a shift took place that led to a reversal of what counted as authority. What was previously probable became knowledge; what was knowledge became only probable. This shift led to a new paradigm of interpretation within theology. Opinions are no longer probable merely by virtue of the external authorities that support them. Instead, intrinsic evidence or personal experience determines the probability of our opinions concerning which authorities should be followed.[13] In other words the hermeneutical problem has shifted. Authority no longer resolves issues of identity; instead, subjective experience determines what counts as an authority.[14] As Jürgen Habermas has noted, in modernity "religious life, state, and society, as well as science, morality, and art are transformed into just so many embodiments of the principle of subjectivity."[15]

The causes of this shift were varied and many: the rise of nominalism with its critique of classical metaphysics, the theological debates of the late scholasticism regarding theological errors, Martin Luther's appeal to Scripture to criticize medieval ecclesiastical practice and doctrines, and the Renaissance's contribution to the development of historical consciousness. The conflict of authorities could no longer be readily resolved. Philosophers René Descartes and Immanuel Kant and theologian Friedrich Schleiermacher became the paradigmatic figures of modernity. They attempted to relate philosophy and theology to its grounding in human subjectivity.

12. See Eugene Marcotte, *La nature de la théologie d'après M. Cano* (Ottawa: University of Ottawa, 1949); Elmar Klinger, *Ekklesiologie der Neuzeit* (Freiburg: Verlag Herder, 1978); and Albert Lang, *Die theologische Prinzipienlehre der mittelalterlichen Scholastik* (Freiburg: Verlag Herder, 1964).

13. See Ian Hacking, *The Emergence of Probability* (Cambridge: Cambridge University Press, 1975), esp. chaps. 3 and 5.

14. See Jeffrey Stout, *The Flight from Authority: Religion, Morality, and the Quest for Autonomy* (Notre Dame, Ind.: University of Notre Dame Press, 1981); and idem, *Ethics after Babel* (Boston: Beacon Press, 1988).

15. Jürgen Habermas, *The Philosophical Discourse of Modernity* (Cambridge: MIT Press, 1987), 18. Habermas follows Hegel's interpretation of modernity.

In theology the interpretive question shifted from weighing author-ity to interpreting the religious dimension of experience.[16] Modern theology, from Schleiermacher to Roman Catholic modernism, sought to explicate religious beliefs as interpretations of religious experience and to ground religious beliefs and traditions in that experience. Instead of considering the doctrinal formulation as primary, modern theology appealed to the primacy of religious experience. Despite these important shifts, however, the theological task remained basically a hermeneutical task.

THE CRISIS OF MODERN THEOLOGY

The shift from external authority to personal experience that charac-terizes modern, liberal theology is now increasingly questioned. It is becoming more and more evident that human subjectivity does not provide a foundational certainty. Consequently, the turn toward the subjective and the foundational reliance on experience are being challenged, just as the reliance of traditional theology on external au-thorities was challenged. As this crisis becomes widespread, the con-temporary situation is increasingly labeled as "postmodernist."[17]

Two particular developments present the crisis of modern theology as a crisis of theology's interpretive task. On the one hand, there is the universality of interpretation, through which all aspects of human his-tory, knowledge, and experience become subject matters in need of interpretation. This development results in part from the continuing theological task of interpretation itself. On the other hand, there is the limitation of interpretation that results from the insight into the limita-tions of human subjectivity. These two tendencies constitute the crisis of modernity and especially of theology's interpretive task.

Universality of Interpretation

The term "universality of interpretation" refers to the inescapable linguisticality and historicity of the subject matter of theology. Both

---

16. Schleiermacher's defense of his own project links the appeal to experience with the demands of modernity. See his *Two Letters: On the Glaubenslehre*, trans. James Duke and Francis Fiorenza (Chico, Calif.: Scholars Press, 1981).

17. For a survey of the meanings of "postmodern," see the special issue *Modernity and Postmodernity* of *New German Critique* 33 (Fall 1984).

traditional theology and modern theology were based on a hermeneutical approach to authoritative texts. They sought to decipher texts so as to uncover their foundational truth. Traditional theology deciphered the text as a sign and as foundational authority pointing to transcendence. Modern hermeneutics deciphers the religious text as an expression of the authority of the religious dimension of human experience. Awareness of the universality of hermeneutics brings to the fore the historicity of both the traditional and modern sources of authority.[18]

Before the awareness of the universality of interpretation, theologians often sought to isolate spheres or areas that were foundational because they were independent of human interpretation. Theologians often distinguished between principles of faith, that is, between the revelation in Scripture and Scripture's later theological interpretation in early Christian doctrines. In neo-Scholastic Roman Catholic theology they sharply differentiated dogma from doctrine. In liberal Protestantism they distinguished between a "basal religious experience" and the subsequent reflective doctrinal formulation. Each of these distinctions inadequately acknowledges the universality of interpretation and that there are no principles of faith, no dogmas of theology, and no human experiences free from historically conditioned human interpretation.

This awareness of the universal interpretive nature of theology's subject matter has been most sharply articulated within liberal Protestantism by Ernst Troeltsch.[19] Although the neo-orthodox critique of nineteenth-century liberalism tended to push the issue of historicity into the background, it still dealt with it. Karl Barth retrieved God's Word as the foundation of theology, yet he still distinguished between primary objectivity (God's eternal Word) and secondary objectivity (the Scriptures). Such a distinction acknowledged the historicity of the written Scriptures insofar as it prevented a literal objectification of God's Word.[20] H. Richard Niebuhr drew out the implications of

18. See Jürgen Habermas, "On Hermeneutics Claim to Universality" in *The Hermeneutics Reader*, ed. Kurt Mueller-Vollmer (New York: Crossroad, 1985), 293–319.

19. See Ernst Troeltsch, *Der Historismus und seine Probleme* (Tübingen: J.C.B. Mohr, 1922; Aalen: Scientia, 1961). See also Sarah Coakley, *Christ without Absolutes* (Oxford: Clarendon, 1988).

20. See Karl Barth, *Church Dogmatics*, 2 vols. (Edinburgh: T. & T. Clark, 1956), 1:1–44, 2:457–537.

finitude in the face of radical monotheism for our understanding of not only the human world but also the Scriptures, Christ, and the Christian community. He underscored the limited and interpretive nature of the appearance of faith in history.[21]

The awareness of the interpretive and historical character of all appeals to "objective" as well as "subjective" foundations of faith has become especially acute within contemporary theology and religious studies.[22] Historical criticism increasingly includes analyses of the social world of early Christianity as well as of later periods of Christianity. These analyses have enlarged our knowledge of the relation between social world and religious and moral ideas.[23] They have constructed the social location of the Jesus movement at the origins of Christianity.[24] Such social analyses also have uncovered the shifting and conflicting interpretive self-definitions at the very origin of Christianity and have shown the degree to which these self-definitions are intertwined with particular life practices and social worlds. Thus Christians are challenged to examine religious beliefs and moral ideas in relation to the sociopolitical context and practice of these beliefs and ideals.

The historical-critical method with its historical and social analyses has uncovered the entanglement of traditional theological authorities within conceptual, social, and political frameworks. Current philosophical and social analyses have exposed this same entanglement for human experience. They have demonstrated that the Cartesian ego, the Kantian a priori forms of understanding, and the Schleiermachian basal religious experience represent not what is prior to interpretation but what is concrete and particular, historically and socially conditioned. The human subject is not an "unencumbered self" but a self embedded in social, cultural, and political contexts.[25] The universal

21. See H. Richard Niebuhr, *Radical Monotheism and Western Culture* (New York: Harper, 1943), 38–63.

22. The use of historicity has been at the center of much of Gordon Kaufman's work; see his *Relativism, Knowledge, and Faith* (Chicago: University of Chicago Press, 1960).

23. See Wayne A. Meeks, *The Moral World of the First Christians* (Philadelphia: Westminster Press, 1986); and Elisabeth Schüssler Fiorenza, *In Memory of Her* (New York: Crossroad, 1983).

24. See Gerd Theissen, *Sociology of Early Palestinian Christianity* (Philadelphia: Fortress Press, 1978).

25. The criticism that contemporary liberal and Kantian ethical theories presuppose an abstract conception of the human self has been argued by Michael J. Sandel, *Liberalism and the Limits of Justice* (Cambridge: Harvard University Press, 1982).

ego and the transcendental subject are particulars as well as culturally determined subjects.[26]

This point has been elaborated especially by feminist philosophers and theologians, as well as by neopragmatic philosophers and deconstructive literary critics. Judith Plaskow's analysis of the doctrine of sin in the theologies of Reinhold Niebuhr and Paul Tillich provides a paradigmatic critique of a "substitutional universalism," whereby a particular (male) experience is passed off as a universal human experience. Plaskow has demonstrated that the two theologians' interpretations of human experience reflect not a universal self but concrete particularities of male experience. Her reflection on Doris Lessing's descriptions of women's experience leads to a considerably different theological interpretation of sin.[27]

The example of Plaskow's feminist criticism shows that just as one can no longer appeal to classical authorities without at the same time asking the interpretive question, so too one cannot simply appeal to personal experience to confirm interpretation. Personal experiences are themselves interpretive and have themselves influenced the interpretation. The experiences themselves need to be subjected to criticism. A person's experiences may more closely represent a person's individual bourgeois existence than interpretation of religious experience or the Gospels. The interdependence between interpretation and experience affects the transcendental appeal to human subjectivity.

The Limits of Interpretation

The contingency or context dependency of language brings us to the limits of hermeneutics because it pushes us to the insight that language mediates not only meaning and freedom but also oppressive power. Not only is reality experienced as interpreted (the universality of hermeneutics), but what is experienced is not just meaning, truth, and freedom, but also the lack of meaning, the absence of truth, and the force of domination (the limits of hermeneutics). In short, the limits of interpretation represent the other side of the universality of hermeneutics.

Hermeneutical reflection is incomplete unless it reflects on these limits. It is on the issue of the limits of hermeneutics that modern and

26. See Manfred Frank, *What Is Neostructuralism?* (Minneapolis: University of Minnesota Press, 1989).

27. See Judith Plaskow, *Sex, Sin, and Grace: Women's Experience and the Theologies of Reinhold Niebuhr and Paul Tillich* (Washington, D.C.: University Press of America, 1980).

postmodern thought divide. For Habermas recognition of the distortion and domination within cultural language and within the values of the tradition is a reflective step on the way to the emancipation of the subject.[28] The point of completing hermeneutical reflection through insight into the limits of hermeneutics is to overcome these limits. Critical reflection on distortions of communication leads to emancipation, just as a critical reflectivity of psychoanalytic insight liberates by uncovering the hidden distortions of consciousness so that where id once was, now ego should be.[29] Critical theory points to the inadequacy of a hermeneutical approach alone insofar as cultural traditions are permeated not only with meaning and truth, which have a claim upon us, but also with oppressive power, from which we must be liberated. Nevertheless, critical theory, as represented by Habermas, criticizes hermeneutics but still seeks to complete the project of the Enlightenment and modernity.[30] It criticizes distorted communication and tradition for the sake of the self-reflective liberation of the human self.

The critique of hermeneutics in contemporary French poststructuralist thought undermines even this appeal to subjectivity and thus goes beyond modern hermeneutics in a radical fashion.[31] Linguistic phenomena cannot simply be explained with reference to the human subject. Human subjectivity has to pass through a forest of signifiers with a resulting indeterminacy of signification.[32] The consequence of such indeterminacy, as expressed by Michel Foucault, is: "There is nothing absolutely first to interpret, because at bottom, everything is already interpretation, every sign is itself not the thing which is offered to interpretation, but an interpretation of other signs."[33] This critical analysis argues that the meaning of signs relates neither to an uninterpreted objective reality nor to an uninterpreted human subject. Consequently, human subjectivity is not transparent to itself and cannot be an absolute starting point of philosophical or theological

28. See Jürgen Habermas, *Kultur und Kritik* (Frankfurt: Suhrkamp Verlag, 1973).
29. See Jürgen Habermas, *Knowledge and Interest* (Boston: Beacon Press, 1971).
30. See Habermas, *The Philosophical Discourse of Modernity.*
31. See Diane P. Michelfelder and Richard E. Palmer, *Dialogue and Deconstruction* (Albany, N.Y.: SUNY Press, 1989).
32. See Jacques Derrida, *Writing and Difference* (Chicago: University of Chicago Press, 1978), 278–93.
33. Michel Foucault, "Nietzsche, Freud, Marx," in idem, *Nietzsche* (Paris: Cahiers de Royaumont, 1967), 189. Translated text quoted by Peter Drews, *Logics of Disintegration* (London: Verso, 1987), 206.

reflection, as in modern Romantic hermeneutics or transcendental phenomenology.

Eschewing Cartesian Anxiety

The increased awareness of both the universality and limits of hermeneutics leads to the recognition that knowledge and meaning lack firm foundations. This absence of certain foundations produces a "Cartesian anxiety" for those who identify truth and knowledge with Cartesian certitude in "clear and distinct ideas."[34] Others who equate objective natural standards with truth and values view this indeterminacy of meaning as "Nietzschean" relativization of all values—a nihilism. This lack of certitude points to the breakdown of modern theology with its emphasis upon the human subject's religious experience and its view of the theological task as the explication and thematization of religious experience. Modern theology cannot give religious language and theological reflection an immediacy and certain grounding by appealing directly to human subjectivity.

The equation of truth and knowledge with certitude, immediate experience, or clear and distinct ideas represents a distinct interpretive attitude that has not only permeated a whole philosophical era but also deeply influenced the theological understanding of Christian faith and truth. Absolute certitude, secure foundations, and conceptual exactitude came to characterize the proper interpretive attitude of faith. In contemporary philosophy the collapse of this Cartesian search for foundations resulted from the awareness that observational experience, cognitional structures, and the formation of concepts and hypotheses were thoroughly interpretive. In theology this collapse results from the awareness that the historical and experiential bases of faith and theology are themselves interpretive endeavors.

Awareness of the effects of universality and the limits of hermeneutics upon the objective and subjective foundations of faith has had several consequences for understanding the theological task. First, insofar as contemporary theology has become aware of the interpretive nature of the foundations of faith it has increasingly eschewed the Cartesian search for certitude in its formulations of Christian identity. Contemporary theology has increasingly become aware of its own

---

34. Richard J. Bernstein, *Beyond Objectivism and Relativism: Science, Hermeneutics, and Praxis* (Philadelphia: University of Pennsylvania Press, 1983).

fragility and that of faith, not as fault but as a part of the interpretive nature of the human world. Second, the inadequacy of experiential approaches has led to the expansion of the hermeneutical circle and to a "revisionistic" conception of a method of correlation as the most adequate theological method.[35] Such a method claims to be a "self-critical" interpretive attitude insofar as it seeks to take into account that personal experience is caught within the web of contextual interpretation. We must ask if such a method deals adequately with ideologically distorted theological interpretations of faith and critically acknowledges the limits of hermeneutics for appeals not only to traditional objective foundations but also to transcendental subjectivity.

BEYOND A HERMENEUTICAL THEOLOGY OF CORRELATION

The absence of a secure foundation undergirding faith and theology means that faith seeking understanding is a complex interpretive endeavor, entailing diverse elements.[36] This lack of secure foundations within either tradition or personal experience has led to a broadening of the hermeneutical circle and to a method of correlation. The question is whether the complexity of the interpretive endeavor and the dilemma of classical and modern hermeneutics require going beyond the "hermeneutical circle" and the method of correlation. In my opinion, the crisis of hermeneutics and modern theology does require passage beyond that circle, not to a hermeneutical triangle, as some maintain, but to a process that includes a multiplicity of diverse elements.

Beyond the "Hermeneutical Circle"

The "hermeneutical circle" serves to describe a certain classic process of interpretation: one moves from the whole to the part and back again to the whole. To understand a verse one has to understand the whole text; to understand the whole text one has to understand individual

---

35. See the three chaps. by David Tracy in Robert M. Grant with David Tracy, *A Short History of the Interpretation of the Bible* (Philadelphia: Fortress Press, 1984, 2d rev. ed.). See also Tracy, *Plurality and Ambiguity* (New York: Harper & Row, 1987).

36. See Francis Schüssler Fiorenza, *Foundational Theology* (New York: Crossroad, 1984), 285–323; and idem, "Systematic Theology: Task and Methods," in *Systematic Theology: Roman Catholic Perspectives*, ed. John Galvin and Francis Schüssler Fiorenza (Minneapolis: Fortress Press, 1991), 1–87.

verses. Within this circular movement, one continually corrects and modifies one's understanding of the text, be it the whole or the part. The emergence of the historical-critical method has broadened the circle in that such a method views the text against its total cultural context. Interpretation thus moves back and forth between the text and a particular historical-cultural context or expands the scope and views a text or an epoch against a much broader, even universal, historical context.

The emergence of modern hermeneutics in the nineteenth century brought human subjectivity fully into the hermeneutical circle. Interpretation moved from the text and its style to the subjective experience of the author and back to the text. In the early twentieth century, interpretation sought to overcome the focus on the subjectivity of the author. A critique of the dependence of the hermeneutical circle on the author was elaborated by Martin Heidegger in his exposition on interpretation in *Being and Time*.[37] His notion of pre-understanding shifts the direction of the circle. Interpretations move from the pre-understanding and questions of the reader to the text and back. The questions that the reader brings to the text are corrected by the reading of the text. The reader's pre-understanding of a text is corrected by an understanding of the text, which leads to a new understanding and in turn becomes pre-understanding, and so forth. This emphasis on pre-understanding and projected meaning sought to overcome the subject-centeredness of a nineteenth-century hermeneutic that focused on auctorial intention. Nevertheless, even this hermeneutic remained caught within subjectivity.

The subject-centeredness of the modern hermeneutical circle emerged and became dominant within modern theology, especially in the method of correlation.[38] This method sought to mediate the subjectivity of religious experience with the objectivity of religious tradition.[39] Tillich correlated questions of ultimate concern with the biblical

37. His awareness of this subject-centeredness led Heidegger to move away from his conception of the hermeneutical circle in *Being and Time* (New York: Harper, 1962) to look for a more primordial relation between language and being as a means of going beyond the circle. Cf. Martin Heidegger, *On the Way to Language* (New York: Harper, 1971). See John D. Caputo, *Radical Hermeneutics* (Bloomington and Indianapolis: University of Indiana Press, 1987).

38. Hans Küng has recently argued that the method of correlation is the new paradigm for modern theology. See his *Theology for the Third Millenium* (New York: Doubleday, 1988).

39. See Ragnar Holte, *Vermittlungstheologie*, Acta Universitatis Upsaliensis, vol. 3 (Uppsala: University of Uppsala, 1965).

symbols.[40] Karl Rahner correlated the human quest for self-transcendence with the central dogmas of the Christian faith. The theological task consisted in the hermeneutical explication of a basic correspondence between the human search for meaning and the explicit religious symbols of Christian faith.[41] This method amounted to a transfer of the hermeneutical circle to theology. It sought to overcome the subjectivity of modern theology by correlating subjectivity and objectivity. Nevertheless, it understood theology primarily as a hermeneutical task.[42]

The formulation of the theological method as a method of correlation turned the hermeneutical circle into a "theological circle." In Tillich's understanding of theological method the theological circle is much tighter than that of a philosopher of religion. Tillich claims that, although cultural traditions partly determine the experiential basis of every philosophy of religion, the philosopher attempts to elaborate more universal concepts. The theologian, however, not only stands within a cultural tradition but also "enters the theological circle with a concrete commitment" that underpins the theological task.[43] A revisionist conception of the method of correlation seeks to broaden correlation through the language of analogy in order to avoid the collapse of correlation into identity.[44] Nevertheless, its underlying conception of theology remains hermeneutical.

Beyond Correlation

The hermeneutical circle and the theological method of correlation remain transcendental and subject-centered, despite attempts to overcome this aspect.[45] In a quite different philosophical context, analytical philosophers sought to grasp the complexities of the interpretive pro-

---

40. Tillich's de facto use of the method of correlation does not always coincide with his definition. In addition, the notion of correlation in terms of question and answer differs from the correlation between form and content. For diverse assessments of Tillich's use of correlation, see John Clayton, *The Concept of Correlation* (Berlin: de Gruyter, 1980); and Langdon Gilkey, *Gilkey on Tillich* (New York: Crossroad, 1990).

41. See Karl Rahner, *Foundations of Christian Faith* (New York: Crossroad, 1978).

42. See David Tracy, *The Analogical Imagination* (New York: Crossroad, 1986).

43. See Paul Tillich, *Systematic Theology*, vol. 1 (Chicago: University of Chicago Press, 1951), 9–11.

44. See David Tracy, "The Uneasy Alliance Reconceived: Catholic Theological Method, Modernity and Postmodernity," *Theological Studies* 50, no. 1 (March 1989): 548–70.

45. See the critical observations by Hans W. Frei, "The 'Literal Reading' of Biblical Narrative in the Christian Tradition: Does It Stretch or Will It Break?" in *The Bible and the Narrative Tradition*, ed. Frank McConnell (New York: Oxford University Press, 1986), 36–77.

cess and to shift the focus from human subjectivity by broadening the hermeneutical circle to a triangle.[46] The triangle brings in a third element, namely, background theories.[47] As well as the life-relation of persons, which constitutes their pre-understanding and influences their interpretations, these implicit theoretical assumptions equally impact upon understanding and interpretation. The term "triangle" refers to this interconnection between life-relation, background theories, and understanding. The background assumptions, life-relation, and concrete interpretations point to the relativity of our self-definitions and the need critically to challenge and revise them.

The introduction of background theories and assumptions seeks to break out of both the classic and the modern hermeneutic circles. As noted above, background theories modify the circle by introducing a third element;[48] but even though they cut through the hermeneutic circle, they are still basically hermeneutical and subject to change. Theories about the external, physical world as well as about the social world are subject to change, revision, and interpretation. There is also a subjective element to such theories. Nevertheless, as constituting the social and external world in which we live they limit and check the authority of the tradition as well as the expressiveness of the self.[49] The advantage of background theories is that they provide limits to the indeterminacy of meaning and place boundaries on the hermeneutical retrieval of a tradition.

Consideration of background theories places constraints on the understanding of theological method as hermeneutical. The systematic interpretation of the claims of a tradition's religious classics has to deal with multiple and changing background theories. The three-storied world cosmology of biblical times no longer exists. A

46. W. H. Newton-Smith uses "triangle" in belief, meaning, and action; see his "Relativism and the Possibility of Interpretation," in *Rationality and Relativism*, ed. Martin Hollis and Steven Lukes (Cambridge: MIT Press, 1982), 114. See also Newton-Smith, *The Rationality of Science* (Boston: Routledge & Kegan Paul, 1981).

47. Jeffrey Stout takes over the phrase "hermeneutical triangle," borrowed from W. H. Newton-Smith, and uses it primarily to include background theories; see Stout, "The Relativity of Interpretation," *The Monist* 69 (1986): 103–18.

48. A similar function to the introduction of background theories is served in Paul Ricoeur's hermeneutical theory by the introduction of the complementarity of methods of explanation and methods of understanding; see Ricoeur, *Hermeneutics and the Human Sciences*, ed. John B. Thompson (New York: Cambridge University Press, 1981), 131–64.

49. A further question, whether one should differentiate between background theories about nature and those about society, cannot be discussed here. Against a too facile understanding of this distinction, see Hilary Putnam, *Realism with a Human Face* (Cambridge: Harvard University Press, 1990), 135–78.

Ptolemaic astronomy has been superseded by a Copernican astronomy. Monarchical societies and their assumptions have in many cases been replaced by democratic societies. The Neoplatonic theory of signs has been displaced by contemporary semiotics. An analysis of background assumptions places restraints on the retrieval of the tradition by demonstrating that the tradition has been formed in part by assumptions about the natural world and conventions of the social world. When these assumptions are no longer valid, the theological task can be neither simply a hermeneutics of the tradition's classics nor simply a task of retrieval or correlation. Instead, it must be constructive and reconstructive.[50]

The Christian belief in creation illustrates how background theories push theology beyond correlation to reconstruction. Within the last century several developments have taken place: modern science has increasingly produced evidence and new theories about the origin of the universe and human life; biblical studies have become aware of the significance of literary forms of understanding the Bible; and historical studies of early Christian writers such as Origen and Augustine have shown their interpretations of Genesis were neither literalist nor fundamentalist. At the same time, the growth of modern democracies has led to changes in the structural organization of society. The changes in diverse background theories—from natural science, literary criticism, and the social world—have together led to a new interpretation. The result is that the meaning of the biblical doctrine of creation has come to be seen neither in specific details nor in a specific social order, but rather in the theological affirmation of covenantal relation between God and humans.

The shift in the perception of creation from a belief in a divine providence ordering all life and society into distinct hierarchies to a belief in the God-given rights and equality of all involves a significant transformation.[51] This transformation results from a new equilibrium among diverse elements: our reading of Scripture, our scientific background theories, and our social human experience. The shift from an understanding of creation as "all are created different or unequal" to

---

50. The elaboration of the constructive task of theology has been consistently argued by Gordon Kaufman, *An Essay on Theological Method*, 2d ed. (Missoula, Mont.: Scholars Press, 1979).

51. See Jacob Viner, *The Role of Providence in the Social Order* (Princeton: Princeton University Press, 1972).

"all are created equal" and the shift from a vision of human creation excluding evolution to one including evolution show the degree to which Christian belief in creation does not refer to a pre-given reality or entail an interpretive discovery of an essence or an underlying identity. Instead, the very meaning of creation is constructive, forged in a hermeneutical reconstruction of past traditions, new background theories, and new experiences. The theological task concerning the Christian tradition is more than hermeneutical, because it involves not only interpretation or correlation but also creative reconstruction.

The Interpretive Dilemma
for Theology

The transformation from belief in divine creation and providence as the foundations for social and political inequality to belief in social and political equality shows how background assumptions affect the understanding of traditional Christian doctrines. Background theories are constraints upon interpretation and experience, but they are also determined by experience. Because background assumptions are subject to change and depend on diverse factors, the hermeneutical dilemma becomes even more complex. Background theories are themselves caught up in the universality and limits of hermeneutics.

Warrants from contemporary experience and practice, as articulated in diverse communities of discourse, are significant and often determinative for the understanding and appropriation of background assumptions. Consequently, although changes in background theories challenge an understanding of theology as hermeneutical, the introduction of these theories does not break the hermeneutical circle. The hermeneutical dilemma remains: If there are no uninterpreted standpoints and no uninterpreted background theories, then how does a theologian articulate the meaning of Christian faith and identity?

INTERPRETATION AND IDENTITY

An interpretive decision has to be made as to what is decisive and essential to Christian faith and what is not, what is paradigmatic and what is not, what is primary and what is not. A decision as to what constitutes the identity of a faith involves much more than the interpretation of a tradition. It is not simply an act of uncovering an identity already present; rather, it is a decision based on considered judgments about what constitute priorities and paradigms in the face of conflicts and changes in the facticity of the tradition. Such decisions involve judgments about overarching beliefs, values, and practices of the tradition; about whether beliefs and values fruitfully relate to contemporary practice; and about possible background theories. But how does one make such decisions? How does one set priorities when he or she acknowledges the universality of interpretation and recognizes the interpretive nature of all foundations, or when one recognizes the contingency of language and tradition as both constituted by power and constituting power? Is one so caught up in the infinite play of meaning that it is meaningless to talk about Christian identity? How does a theologian deal with the indeterminateness of meaning, the conflict of interpretations, shifts in background theories, and disagreements about fundamental priorities?

Solidarity with Suffering

Rather than resign before these questions by equating Christian theology with a "gamely play" of an elite bourgeoisie or with a continued search for uninterpreted foundations, we should bring the interplay of diverse factors to bear on the hermeneutical dilemma. Three of these factors are solidarity with suffering, communities of discourse, and integrity as reconstructive. Each must be conceived in a way that avoids traditional as well as modern foundationalism.

The commitment to a transformative praxis in relation to suffering takes seriously the experience and pervasiveness of suffering. We encounter suffering. This suffering is diverse. There is, for example, the loss of loved ones, the pain of illness, and the agony of emotional isolation. There is also economic, social, and political suffering. Much suffering is inescapable, but much is not. Indeed, much suffering results from political oppression, social discrimination, ethnic hatred, and economic greed. Images of such suffering fill our lives. Television bombards us with images of jet fighters attacking food convoys in starving nations. The faces of starving children glare out in critique of our comfortable existence. Our tabloids display the pictures of bloodied dead bodies of groups at war with one another. The images of the bodies of Jesuit educators in a country already known for its death squads become ineradicably imprinted on our imaginations. Our hospitals and shelters are deluged with cases of battered wives and abused children—the most visible manifestations of patriarchy and sexism.

Suffering brings us to the bedrock of human existence and cuts through the hermeneutical circle. It is a source of "local knowledge" that points out the inadequacies of ideological, social, and economic systems. As such, suffering provides a source for the "insurrection of subjugated knowledges" against dominant ideologies.[52] Suffering is a source of critique of modernity, as various contemporary liberation theologies have shown. The suffering today of the poor and of poor nations exhibits the illusory nature of modernity's belief in scientific method and technological advances as infallible means for the advancement of the human race.[53]

Suffering is, so to speak, at the seam between interpretation and reality. Although it is not without interpretation and one's horizon deeply affects one's suffering, our bodily existence is affected in a way that gives suffering a "mediated immediacy."[54] Language about the "hermeneutical privilege of the oppressed" is justified to the extent that it points to this immediacy. Such a "privilege," however, should not be interpreted in a foundationalist sense that excludes the significance of background theories, the conditioned nature of all knowledge, and the possibility of self-criticism.

Indeed, my emphasis that suffering takes place at the intersection of reality and interpretation should not be taken to exclude the role of interpretation in relation to suffering.[55] Protest movements arise more from relative than from absolutely deprived groups. Often the lessening of deprivation allows for an increased ability to mobilize the interpretive resources for critique. Nevertheless, suffering challenges metanarrative claims of progress and protests against ideological justification.

Suffering is a "retroductive" warrant, not because it justifies the

52. See Michel Foucault, *Power/Knowledge*, ed. Colin Gordon (New York: Pantheon, 1980), 80–82. I borrow Foucault's notion of "local knowledge," which expresses not an indeterminate signification of an eclectic knowledge but one that is rooted in the "bedrock of existence" and which rises up to challenge established patterns.

53. A perceptive analysis of suffering and liberation theologies is provided by Rebecca Chopp, *The Praxis of Suffering* (Maryknoll, N.Y.: Orbis Books, 1986).

54. The phrase "mediated immediacy" is borrowed from Karl Rahner but given a different application here.

55. The interpretive nature of solidarity is an important point underscored by Richard Rorty, *Contingency, Irony, and Solidarity* (New York: Cambridge University Press, 1989), 141–98.

status quo but because it challenges such justifications.[56] It is retroductive rather than deductive in that it moves backwards from experience, not from ideas and principles. It moves from a negative experience, a contrast experience, to a more universal challenge. Suffering often produces a claim with a negative universality, which positive social or political programs do not have. The presence of suffering challenges structures and programs so that often, although there is disagreement over how to ameliorate suffering, agreement exists about the evil of suffering.

Communities of Discourse

The idea of a community of discourse relates to the hermeneutical crisis in connection with the importance of solidarity with suffering. "Community of discourse" is a notion that has been introduced to avoid conceptions of rationality as abstract and universal. What is to be interpreted as well as who does the interpreting exists not in abstract but concrete communities.[57] Current discussions about hermeneutics and rationality revolve around the significance of communities of discourse.[58] The nature of rationality and interpretation is not a problem primarily between an individual subjectivity and an objective reality but a problem of the interrelations between discourse and power, between dominative discourses and excluded discourses, and between those who are included in the community discourse and those who are oppressed and excluded from that discourse.

Just as society has its victims, so discourse has those who are excluded from discourse. The "other" is not simply the other of signification but also represents those whose voices are not present within the tradition, are not present within the discourse interpreting the tradition, and have no voice in interpreting their identity and self-determination.[59] In the absence of secure objective or experiential foundations, the community of discourse plays a pivotal role. It

56. See Johann Baptist Metz, *The Emergent Church: The Future of Christianity in a Postbourgeois World* (New York: Crossroad, 1986).

57. See David Rasmussen, ed., *Universalism vs. Communitarianism: Contemporary Debates in Ethics* (Cambridge: MIT Press, 1990).

58. See the debate between Bernstein and MacIntyre in Richard J. Bernstein, "Nietzsche or Aristotle? Reflections on Alasdair MacIntyre's *After Virtues*," in idem, *Philosophical Profiles* (Philadelphia: University of Pennsylvania Press, 1986), 115–40; and Alasdair MacIntyre, *Practical Rationality: Whose Justice? Whose Rationality?* (Notre Dame, Ind.: University of Notre Dame Press, 1988).

59. See Francis Schüssler Fiorenza, "Politische Theologie und liberale Gerechtigkeits-Konzeptionen," in *Mystik und Politik*, ed. Edmund Arens (Düsseldorf: Patmos Verlag, 1989), 105–17.

becomes imperative that those voices excluded from dominant discourse become introduced to the discourse. If a society based on a principle of justice seeks to develop a different principle in relation to the disadvantaged, then similar principles need to be incorporated in the practice of discourse. To the extent that the certainty of both the objective and the personal have been superseded by a multiplicity of interpretations, experiences, and theoretical assumptions, it becomes necessary to make the community of discourse as inclusive as possible. One cannot simply appeal to experiential evidence as the warrant for truth; one has to bring the interpretation of conflicting paradigms and traditions into dialogue and conversation with the neglected and often repressed voices of the other. Solidarity with victims needs to become also a solidarity that seeks to give voice to the voiceless, so that they can enter into conversation about the interpretation of their identity as well as Christian identity.

The interpretation of religious identity for two basic reasons requires a conversation and dialogue in openness to the voices of victims. First, because understanding and interpretation take place only in relation to pre-understandings that are rooted in different life experiences and practices, it becomes necessary to incorporate into the community of discourse previously silenced or repressed voices. Second, because only concrete historical communities exist, when the pre-understandings, experiences, and life practices of repressed and silent voices are kept from public discourse, limited and distorted interpretations are allowed to continue without restraint. The voices of feminist theologians pointing to sexism, of African-American theologians pointing to racism, and of the poor and oppressed pointing to exploitation amply illustrate how radically different voices change the construction of the identity of the tradition.[60]

Integrity as a Reconstructive Principle

Integrity is an elusive concept. Its root suggests the notion of wholeness and its common usage refers to honesty and an absence of deceit. As an interpretive concept integrity has a specific force, because it signals a standard or principle of interpretation that enables interpretation to convey truth and moral authority. In legal philosophy a

60. For a feminist analysis, see Elisabeth Schüssler Fiorenza, "The Politics of Otherness: Biblical Interpretation as a Critical Praxis for Liberation," in *The Future of Liberation Theology*, ed. Marc H. Ellis and Otto Maduro (Maryknoll, N.Y.: Orbis Books, 1989), 311–25.

conception of law centered in integrity differs from one centered in convention.[61] Conventionalism, as used in legal philosophy, refers to law as the result of conventions and consensus. A conception centered in integrity suggests that integrity should ground consensus, that the ideas, standards, or principles of law should in fact be critical of de facto conventions and consensus. A conception based on integrity rather than convention presupposes a difference can exist between principles and conventions or between ideals and concrete practice.

Integrity is narrower and stricter than coherence or consistency. It concerns priorities, principles, and paradigms, whereas consistency refers to uniformity and coherence to harmony. To ask for the integrity of a belief, law, or practice is to explore its ideals, standards, and principles. Quite often tensions and conflicts emerge among beliefs, laws, and practices. There is not only the conflict between ideals and practices but also between diverse ideals. To inquire about the integrity of a belief, tradition, or practice is to ask not how these cohere or correlate with one another but what critique, change, or expansion is required in the face of inconsistencies and conflicts.

Integrity requires that one set priorities when there are conflicts and inconsistencies within the tradition, face squarely all the challenges to the tradition, include neglected and excluded voices, and take honestly and seriously changes in background assumptions. It requires an ethics of accountability, not only in the interpretation of belief and traditions but also in the face of suffering and of communities that challenge those beliefs and traditions. Integrity, therefore, is not so much insight into a pre-given essence as reconstructive interpretation resulting from an ethics of accountability.

Integrity requires, for example, that, when confronted with the experience of the Holocaust, Christians face squarely how Christian identity for two millennia involved a self-identity at the expense and disparagement of the Jewish faith. Such an experience requires a retroductive reformulation of Christian identity. If one accepts a post-Darwinist evolutionary biology that challenges traditional Aristotelian conceptions of human nature as teleological, then integrity requires that one not make Aristotelian conceptions of human nature or gender the basis of understanding natural law and human gender.[62] Integrity

61. See Ronald Dworkin, *Law's Empire* (Cambridge: Harvard University Press, 1986), 175–275.
62. For the relation between Aristotelian conceptions of human nature and political theory, see Amos Funkenstein, *Theology and the Scientific Imagination* (Princeton: Prince-

requires, as Kaufman has reminded us, that in the face of a nuclear age one reconstruct one's theological traditions in relation to human responsibility.[63]

One approaches Christian tradition with some pre-understanding or initial understanding of Christian identity. Initially, one has at least an awareness of the difference between the facticity of the tradition and the ideals of the tradition. What the tradition considers to be paradigmatic often stands in stark contrast to the factual events within the tradition. One can argue that the plundering of the crusaders or the torture of the Inquisition does not represent what is Christian identity but rather a betrayal of what the Christian tradition claims to be its paradigmatic identity. The crucial dilemma, however, occurs when historical-critical and social analyses show the inconsistencies and conflicts in the understanding of what is ideal and paradigmatic for identity. Inconsistencies and conflicts require a reflective theological decision as to what constitutes Christian identity with regard to the integrity of the tradition; the social, political, and practical consequences of beliefs; and related theoretical assumptions. These decisions about priorities lead to a postinterpretive, reconstructive or reforming stage beyond initial understanding. In this stage the considered judgment of what is essential to the tradition is brought to reform or to critique elements at variance with the ideal and paradigmatic. Such reconstructions and reforms are made on the basis of considerations of what constitutes the tradition's identity and integrity, taking into account the experience of suffering and of those excluded from the community of discourse in light of relevant background theories and retroductive warrants.

CONCLUSION

The interpretative dilemma for theology is that religious beliefs and practices do not exist as bare facts but have value, purpose, and interpreted meaning. The value, purpose, and meaning need to be taken into account when discussing religious beliefs and practice. Such beliefs and practices are themselves sensitive to their very purpose

---

ton University Press, 1986), 342–63. The term "post-Darwinian" was chosen deliberately in view of the political and racial challenges to Darwin's own assumptions.

63. See Gordon Kaufman, *Theology for a Nuclear Age* (Philadelphia: Westminster Press, 1985).

and values and must be interpreted in relation to them. Such interpretation should explain not only the actuality of existing religious beliefs and practices but also their integrity.

This integrity, however, is not a pre-given fact, principle, or essence. It emerges as a result of a reconstructive interpretation that has to deal with conflicts of interpretation and divergent priorities concerning the meaning of Christian identity. This interpretation must attend to background theories and retroductive warrants within a community of discourse that takes into account excluded and oppressed voices.

In our modern society the Christian communities are communities of discourse. They are held together by their symbols, beliefs, and practices, which serve as a source of unity and identity, not as external possessions but as shared meanings and interpreted practices.[64] Conversation and dialogue about the interpretation of central beliefs and practices enable communities to articulate communal meaning and identity. It is not the foundational or authoritative insistence upon these beliefs and practices but the conversation about their meaning that enables the churches as communities of discourse to articulate their identity.[65] Attention to the diverse elements of this interpretive process helps make possible this dialogue on the interpretation of identity. In bringing the values and beliefs of their traditions into discourse, the churches as communities of discourse also have a role to play in modern and postmodern society.[66] As parts of the larger community of discourse in which religious and ethical values are at the center, particular Christian communities can, precisely as communities of discourse, contribute to and "thicken" the ethical and moral level of discourse in the public life of society. Such public conversation should encourage society's discourse to be self-critical and critical of the pretension of modernity.

---

64. See Anthony P. Cohen, *The Symbolic Construction of Community* (New York: Ellis Horword & Tavistock, 1985).

65. See Francis Schüssler Fiorenza, "Presidential Address: Foundations of Theology: A Community's Tradition of Discourse and Practice," *Proceedings of the CTSA* 41 (1986):107–34; and idem, "Theory and Practice: Theological Education as a Reconstructive, Hermeneutical, and Practical Task," *Theological Education* 23 (1987):113–41.

66. See Francis Schüssler Fiorenza, "Die Kirche als Interpretationsgemeinschaft. Politische Theologie zwischen Diskurethik und hermeneutischer Rekonstruktion," in *Habermas und die Theologie*, ed. Edmund Arens (Düsseldorf: Patmos Verlag, 1989), 115–44.

7

Black Theology and the Quest for a God of Liberation

SIMON S. MAIMELA

Black theology, as part of the worldwide theological movement known as liberation theology, is directed against major social evils of our time and claims to offer a new way of doing theology that contributes to the overcoming of human oppression. It differs from other theologies by its conscious decision to take a stand for black humanity over against white domination and oppression. This consciously accepted partisanship means that black theology attempts in particular to be a critical reflection on the historical praxis in which powerful white Christians dominate and oppress powerless black Christians. Black theology further represents an articulated form of black resistance to white power structures in general. It hopes thereby to inspire and arm oppressed blacks in their struggle for the liberating transformation of unjust racist social structures in which they live.

Beginning with their concrete experiences of oppression and suffering in white-dominated societies, where Christian faith has been and continues to be used as an instrument of legitimizing white people's political and economic domination of people of color, black Christians have become increasingly aware that there is something wrong in their so-called Christian countries. They have become suspicious not only about the situation of injustice and oppression under which they have suffered, often at the hands of white Christians, but also about white theologies that unashamedly have given tacit support to the privileged status of white people in relation to people of color.

THE CLAIMS OF
HISTORICAL CONSCIOUSNESS

The rise of black theology, as that of all other contemporary theologies of liberation, is without doubt related to the emergence of the national and political movements of the twentieth century, in which peoples of color began to revolt against colonial and racial domination. I believe, however, that for us to have a correct perspective on this theology it is also important to place it within the broad background of modern historical consciousness, namely, the new human awareness of the relativity and the questionable nature of all human convictions, including religious beliefs and theological claims. Put somewhat differently, by "modern historical consciousness" we refer to the modern awareness of the historical and relative character of all human claims to know or possess the truth. As a result of this awareness there has emerged an increased recognition that individuals, communities, and human institutions, as well as their religious beliefs and concepts, are products of a long history. All individuals and their modes of thought are constituted, conditioned, and influenced by their place in history and society. Historical consciousness also involves the recognition that human beings are products not only of history but also of social structures, that is, of a network of interrelationships that we deliberately shape and by which we are, in turn, created and shaped.

This new historical consciousness has produced the modern belief that truly free human beings are those who have the right to take power into their own hands in order to create the world and future they want, in fulfillment of the fundamental human aspirations for freedom and justice. If, in the face of injustice and sociopolitical and economic oppression, it were to be agreed that human beings, not the gods, are the creators of exploitative social structures, it then would be just a matter of time before modern historical consciousness would reach the momentous conclusion that some people are oppressed and suffer because they have been denied by the ruling elite the right to become architects of their own destinies. What is new in this situation is the awareness by oppressed groups and individuals that they are poor not by accident or because of laziness on their part but because they are made poor and dependent by human oppressors who deny their voices in the shaping of human society and history.[1]

It is important to note how modern historical consciousness conditions the way in which contemporary women and men understand and relate to the causes of human suffering in the world, particularly needless suffering that is caused by unjust social structures designed to benefit the dominant few at the expense of the oppressed majority. In the past, beginning with the Constantinian era, the church allowed itself to be hijacked and taken over by the ruling classes. In consequence, traditional theology was adapted to serve the interests of the powerful and dominant segments of society by trying to persuade the poor and the oppressed majority to accept suffering and poverty as part of the divine design. Indeed, traditional theology has taught and continues to teach that God can and often does inflict or tolerate pain and suffering for some inscrutable divine purpose and that, therefore, the poor and oppressed would do best to accommodate themselves to their earthly suffering.

Modern historical consciousness has challenged the traditional way people understand and relate to human suffering. Aware that human beings create all social structures and institutions in order to realize human aspirations and self-fulfillment, modern historical consciousness no longer accepts the inequitable social arrangements between the rich and poor on the basis of the church's teaching that such an unjust order derives directly from the hand of the God the Creator. The secularization process, which began in the sixteenth century and was given impetus by the antidogmatic and critical outlook of the Enlightenment in the seventeenth and eighteenth centuries and by the liberalism of the nineteenth century, effected a separation between faith and social life, between private religion and public activity. Building on insights derived from that process, modern historical consciousness has produced a slow but definite transformation of human self-understanding. One important outcome has been a shift of focus from understanding reality exclusively in terms of the gods as

1. See Simon S. Maimela, *Proclaim Freedom to My People* (Johannesburg: Skotaville, 1987), 9–10. See also Karl Hertz, "The Two Kingdoms Debate—A Look at the American Situation," in *Lutheran Churches—Salt or Mirror of Society?* ed. Ulrich Duchrow (Geneva: Lutheran World Federation, 1977), 245–47.

the primary agents in human history to perceiving humans as creative subjects and agents, who must take responsibility for shaping social structures in the production of human history and destiny.[2]

This perception was given a fundamental grounding by G.W.F. Hegel, who argued that in the dialectical process of history, in which humans through labor transform their environment, humans create themselves, attain an awareness of their true being, and gradually become creators of their own destiny and their historical freedom. Karl Marx developed this line of thought much further when, through critical analysis of the capitalist society and the role of labor in the transformation of the world, he created categories of historical science that not only enabled modern men and women to reflect on the meaning of human action in the transformation of this world but also made social criticism more effective. These insights have enabled modern men and women to have a greater understanding and control of what historical initiatives must be taken if the present oppressive social structures are to be transformed and reoriented toward a society in which every person can live freely and more humanely.

A central outcome of modern historical consciousness is the increasing appreciation that just as all social structures are human creations, theology also is and has always been human work, which is grounded in and reflects human history and the experiences of particular people. As human speech about God, theology is always related to particular historical situations that color, condition, and limit theological assertions precisely because they are influenced and shaped by the sociocultural conditions of their age and time. Put differently, historical consciousness has enabled modern women and men to accept the fact that no theology is a universal language. Rather, because what people think and say about God cannot be divorced from their locus in society and history, theologies are particular and culturally conditioned modes of speaking about God. James Cone has articulated this relationship between theological reflection and social situation.

> What people think about God cannot be divorced from their place and time in a definite history and culture. While God may exist in some heavenly city beyond time and space, human beings cannot transcend history. They are limited to the specificity of their finite nature. And even when theologians claim to point beyond history because of the

2. See Simon S. Maimela, *Modern Trends in Theology* (Johannesburg: Skotaville, 1990), 74–78, 172–77.

possibility given by the Creator of history, the divine image disclosed in their language is shaped in time. Theology is a subjective speech about God, a speech that tells us far more about the hope and dreams of certain God-talkers than about the Maker of heaven and earth.[3]

The assertion that all theology is necessarily perspectival and not universal, because every theology is colored by the concerns and hopes of particular women and men who engage in specific causes and struggles to make life fulfilling for themselves, flies in the face of much of traditional Western theology. That theology often claimed it was possible to speak of "God-in-himself" or, at least, of God revealed to us. As it has been realized that every theology is closely intertwined with the sociopolitical conditions that give rise to it, contemporary theology has increasingly rejected the claims that truth is the correspondence of thought to reality and that theology is the description, exposition, or interpretation of God's revelation to humanity. Instead, we have become aware that all theologies are reflections of socially and historically conditioned human perspectives on the significance and meaning of human life. As human perspectives on life, all theologies serve certain human needs by promoting specific human activities, at the same time suppressing others that are regarded as unsupportive of our fuller humanization.

To summarize, the basic claim of modern historical consciousness is that people, both as individuals and communities, and their institutions, ideas, symbols, and myths are all influenced and conditioned by their loci in history and all reflect particular social experiences. Because of the relativity of all human perspectives, there is no such thing as an objective, universally valid human experience or knowledge. This holds true also for theology as a human product, because theologies represent human perspectives on life, each embodying and serving the interests of particular groups of people in society.

THE CONCEPT OF GOD IN
BLACK THEOLOGY

Black theologians have worked out the insights of historical consciousness in the development of a black hermeneutic, which has made possible both the rereading of the Bible from a black perspective and the construction of black theology. In what follows I will outline the

3. James H. Cone, *God of the Oppressed* (New York: Seabury Press, 1975), 41.

positive role that the Bible plays in black theology and, at the same time, show the disadvantages of tying black theology too closely to the Bible.

Accepting the claims of modern historical consciousness that human beings, their knowledge, and their thought patterns are irrevocably historical and therefore conditioned by history and culture, black theologians such as Cone have alleged that white theology, which often neglects the political and economic interests of oppressed persons of color, is by definition a theology of oppression, serving the interests of white oppressors. It does so by constructing an authoritarian concept of God and by teaching oppressed persons that this God, as the Supreme Being in the universe, establishes different social classes in every society. Thus the God of white theology has often insisted that there will always be rich and poor in every society and has implied that inequitable power and privilege are the result of God's will. To ensure that the unequal distribution of material resources and power remains unchallenged by the poor and the underdogs, white traditional theology has often taught that God establishes law and order in every society and demands obedience to the authority of both the church and state.[4] Napoleon Bonaparte, an astute politician, understood long before Marx published his Communist Manifesto (1848) that religion has sociopolitical and economic functions that prevent the poor from rising to challenge unjust social conditions. Concerning the theology of his age, he states:

> As far as I am concerned, I do not see in religion the mystery of the incarnation but the mystery of social order: it links the idea of inequality to heaven which prevents the rich person from being murdered by the poor. . . . How can there be order in the state without religion? Society cannot exist without inequality of fortunes and the inequality of fortunes could not subsist without religion. Whenever a half-starved person is near another who is glutted, it is impossible to reconcile the difference if there is not an authority to say to him: "God wills it so, it is necessary that there be rich and poor in the world, but afterwards in eternity there will be a different distribution."[5]

Agreeing with Napoleon's observation and suspecting that traditional theology has been coopted by the ruling classes, who use it to

4. See Victorio Araya, God of the Poor (Maryknoll, N.Y.: Orbis Books, 1987), 27–28. See also Jack Nelson-Pallmeyer, The Politics of Compassion (Maryknoll, N.Y.: Orbis Books, 1986), 19.
5. Quoted by Carter Lindberg, "Through a Glass Darkly: A History of the Church's Vision of the Poor and Poverty," Ecumenical Review 33 (1981):37.

give religious sanction to the sociopolitical and economic bondage to which people of color are subjected, Cone notes:

> White theology has not been involved in the struggle for black libera-
> tion. It has been basically a theology of the white oppressors, giving reli-
> gious sanction to the genocide of Indians and the enslavement of black
> people. From the very beginning to the present day, American white
> theological thought has been "patriotic," either by defining the theologi-
> cal task independently of black suffering (the liberal northern approach)
> or by defining Christianity as compatible with white racism (the conser-
> vative southern approach). In both cases theology becomes the servant
> of the state, and that can only mean death to black people.[6]

This hermeneutics of suspicion, which assumes that in all human societies "anything and everything involving ideas, including theology, is intimately bound up with the existing social situation in at least an unconscious way,"[7] has helped black theologians to begin unmasking the reality of oppression and the ideological mechanisms that underpin and morally justify the social forces that foster and perpetuate domination of people of color. According to Juan Luis Segundo, one of those mechanisms is the ideology that claims to be color-blind and allows white Christians to construct the entire social edifice in which the cause of the oppressed people's suffering is not even mentioned or discussed.[8]

For black Christians, insights into these mechanisms of oppression began as they related their own experiences of dehumanization to the biblical message of the God of love, as proclaimed in the Scriptures, and started asking questions: Why did God create me black? Why does God allow white Christians to oppress black people, whom God also loves, simply because of their color? What does God say and what is God willing to do about this situation of oppression? By asking such questions, it began to dawn on believing blacks that the reality of the politics of white domination differed from what they found in the Bible. In the Bible, God is not revealed as a category to be manipulated for the maintenance of the privileged status quo of white domination; rather, for many blacks God is portrayed as the liberator God, who battles injustice and human misery to establish justice and freedom for

6. James H. Cone, *A Black Theology of Liberation*, 2d ed. (Maryknoll, N.Y.: Orbis Books, 1986), 22. See also Allan A. Boesak, *Farewell to Innocence* (Maryknoll, N.Y.: Orbis Books, 1976), 30–36, 107–16.

7. Juan Luis Segundo, *The Liberation of Theology* (Maryknoll, N.Y.: Orbis Books, 1976), 8.

8. Ibid., 28.

the oppressed.[9] Black theologians, therefore, found it significant that the God of the exodus is portrayed as the God of mercy who condescended from his or her throne of justice, not to just any human situation but to the deep dungeon of slavery in which the oppressed were suffering, to bring them out and create a new people.[10] The same God, it was said, continued to express divine concern for the underdogs by calling and sending the Hebrew prophets to denounce the injustice and exploitation that were perpetrated by the powerful against powerless widows and orphans. God's advocacy for the powerless and oppressed was, according to black theologians, taken to new heights by the coming of Jesus, in and through whom God chose to be born by poor parents and to live as a poor and oppressed human being, who suffered and was crucified as a rejected outcast in order to give the oppressed poor and the downtrodden new life and hope. Therefore, for black theologians the incarnation is the event that clearly demonstrates that God takes the side of the oppressed, the defenseless, the outcasts, the excluded, and the despised. Desmond Tutu puts it eloquently:

> In the process of saving the world, of establishing His Kingdom, God, our God demonstrated that He was no neutral God, but a thoroughly biased God who was for ever taking the side of the oppressed, of the weak, of the exploited, of the hungry and homeless, of the refugees, of the scum of society. . . . So my dear friends we celebrate, worship and adore God, the biased God, He who is not neutral, the God who always takes sides.[11]

Agreeing with Tutu, other black theologians have called upon every theologian to become candid and to declare on which side of the liberation struggle he or she stands, thereby declaring whose interests his or her theology serves. They challenge the church to take a preferential option for the poor, who struggle for liberation. In support of their challenge, they point out that this divine preferential option for the poor and the oppressed is central to the biblical mes-

---

9. See Cone, *God of the Oppressed*, 4–5, 8–11, 122–24. See also Boesak, *Farewell to Innocence*, 16–25; and Takatso A. Mofokeng, *The Crucified among the Crossbearers* (Kampen: J. H. Kok, 1983), 24–108, 160–85, 238–63.

10. Cf. Exod. 3:7.

11. Quoted by Simon S. Maimela, "Archbishop Desmond Tutu: A Revolutionary Political Priest or Man of Peace?" in *Hammering Swords into Ploughshares*, ed. Buti Tlhagale and Itumeleng Mosala (Grand Rapids: Wm. B. Eerdmans, 1986), 16.

sage, running through the pages of both the Hebrew Scriptures and the New Testament.[12]

As might be expected, the assertion that the church should take a preferential option for the poor and be the advocate and defender of the oppressed has invoked great hostility from both conservative and liberal theologians, who interpret it to mean that God is now portrayed as being against the rich and against white Christians. Bound by the ideology of justification by faith through grace alone, many white theologians resist any meaningful discussion of God in relation to the problems of racial oppression and suffering. In their view such a discussion would necessarily lead to the problem of work righteousness, namely, that poverty would be sacralized and portrayed as a virtue by which the poor can demand special favors from God. Alternatively, it is argued that the poor would be portrayed as sinless people who merit God's favors. Against this view white theologians are quick to add that all people, be they white or black, are saved by God's grace and not by good works and that therefore questions of wealth and poverty and of oppressor and oppressed are of little importance to theological discourse.

What is often missed by critics of liberation theology is that what is at stake is not whether the poor are sinners or should be favored by God. Rather, liberation theology has asserted that its talk about God's preferential option for the poor witnesses to the transcendental and universal love of God, the love that unconditionally accepts the unacceptable, the rejected, and the worthless.[13] This divine love demonstrates its historical efficacy by seeking the little and marginalized ones of this world simply because they are poor and defenseless before the cruel reality of historical structures of injustice, which threaten to destroy the lives of millions of poor people.

In order to overcome this threat, liberation theology asserts God assumes the role of advocate for the cause of poor persons, regardless of their moral and personal dispositions. God chooses to be their advocate simply because they need God's defense. Therefore, what is at stake is not their merit, virtue, or worthiness, on account of which the poor could solicit God's acceptance. The justice of God's kingdom demands that the poor must have life in all its fullness. For that to hap-

12. Cf. Pss. 107:4–6; 113:7; 118:7; 140:12; Isa. 25:4; Prov. 14:31; 22:23; Matt. 5:3ff.; Luke 1:53; 4:18–19; 6:17, 20–23.
13. Cf. Rom. 5:6–8.

pen, God assumes the role of advocate out of mercy and love, by making the cause of the defenseless and poor God's own cause. Karl Barth, one of the foremost theologians of the twentieth century, who cannot be accused of one-sided partisanship for the poor, says concerning God's preferential option for the poor and the underdogs:

> God always takes His stand unconditionally and passionately on this side and on this side alone: against the lofty and on behalf of the lowly; against those who already enjoy right and privilege and on behalf of those who are denied it and deprived of it.[14]

To appreciate the significance of what is being suggested here, it is important to note that in the black theological perspective, wealth and poverty are consequences of the fundamental sin of a breach of fellowship between God and humans.[15] The Book of Genesis tells us how, after this tragic rupture, the consequences of sin were incarnated between human beings and manifested in destructive social relationships.[16] God steps in to correct the malady of social sins as it is manifested in the human domination and oppression of fellow beings. Therefore, God's advocacy of the poor and oppressed should be understood as a precondition for the liberation of both the rich and the poor, the oppressor and the oppressed. God assumes the role of advocate for the poor in order to become the advocate for the rich and powerful who must be liberated from the bondage of their wealth, power, and oppressive tendencies, which prevent them from becoming partners with the poor and oppressed in their struggle against the social consequences of sin and from building up the values of the kingdom of God together and alongside God.

In taking up the cause of the oppressed, God declared that the divine self is not prepared to put up with the social situations in which the poor and the powerless are oppressed and humiliated.[17] Consequently, black theologians argue that just as God liberated Israel not only from spiritual sin and guilt but also from sociopolitical oppression and economic deprivation, God will liberate oppressed black people from their personal sins, their guilt, and the historical structures of evil, exploitation, and oppression.

14. Quoted by Araya, *God of the Poor*, 44.
15. Cf. Genesis 3.
16. Cf. Genesis 4.
17. See Maimela, "Desmond Tutu," 44–50. Cf. idem, *Proclaim Freedom*, 96–97, 106–8, 115–20.

Challenging those who doubt that God continues, in acts of divine grace, to condescend and impinge on the lives and situation of the underdogs in order to transform those lives, Cone rhetorically asks:

> Without the certainty that Christ is with us as the historical Jesus was present with the humiliated and weak in Palestine, how can black people account for the power and courage to struggle against slave masters and overseers in the nineteenth century and the Ku Klux Klan and policemen in the twentieth? What is it that keeps the community together when there are many scares and hurts? What is it that gives them the will and the courage to struggle in hope when so much in their environment says fighting is a waste of time? I think that the only "reasonable" and "objective" explanation is to say that the people are right when they proclaim the presence of the divine power, wholly different from themselves.[18]

Drawing their inspiration from a theological vision in which God is portrayed as the liberator of slaves from the Egyptian captivity, black theologians began to reject the dominant white expressions of Christianity and to develop a black theology of liberation, one of whose tasks is confronting, questioning, and rejecting any vision of a "god" who fails to hear the cry of the poor and oppressed. Inspired by the vision of God the liberator attested to in the Scriptures, black theology of liberation has attempted to provide the struggling black masses with alternative biblical and theological models (visions), with which to resist the extreme demands of white racial oppression and to work for the liberation of all God's people. It is hoped that as the black masses are encouraged and empowered to become subjects of their own history and destiny, they will assume the role of agents of their own liberation and become creators of just and humane social structures. Thus freedom, justice, and human rights may become the common property of the majority of the human family.

BLACK THEOLOGY, THE BIBLE AND BLACK EXPERIENCE

It should be clear that the emergence of black theology, which is directed against the major social evils of our time, has resulted in a major qualitative paradigm shift in theological discourse, a real departure from the Constantinian model in which the church and its theolo-

18. Cone, *God of the Oppressed*, 122.

gians were alienated from the poor and the oppressed. Because of this paradigm shift, black theologians have been able to construct a concept of God that is different from that of the white theologies they criticize. The God of black theology is a God who cares for dominated and oppressed black people; who not only listens to the cries of the powerless, the suffering, and the downtrodden but also is willing to do something about human suffering; and who seeks the lost, binds the brokenhearted, rescues the afflicted, and is the comforter of the weak. Because of the love, concern, and care that this God shows to those who call on him or her, the God portrayed by black theology is able to elicit human responses of faith and trust. This portrait of God, developed within black theology, is impressive enough to move, inspire, and involve those who have encountered God's love in acts of love and liberation toward their human fellows. This is the God about whom Tutu could testify:

> We worship an extraordinary God who says that in order for your worship of me to be authentic, in order for your love of me to be true, I cannot allow you to remain in your spiritual ghetto. Your love for me, your worship of me, are authenticated and expressed by your love and your service of your fellows.[19]

However, despite the paradigm shift in theological discourse that I have noted, black theology in my view suffers from serious contradictions, which must be faced and overcome if this theology is to be taken seriously. For instance, although wanting to enjoy the benefits of modern historical consciousness—on the basis of which they are enabled effectively to confront and expose the complicity of white theology in the legitimation of white socioeconomic interests—black theologians appear unwilling to accept the full consequences of modern historical consciousness for black theology. They claim for black theology a privileged position on the grounds that the black theological rereading of the Bible is the only correct one. Hence black theology's concept of God is assumed to be free from ideological distortion and therefore more faithful to the biblical portrayal of God as liberator.[20] Not surprisingly, black theologians are anxiously trying to convince their readers that their construction of a liberative God is based on the Christian revelation as enshrined in both Hebrew and

19. Quoted by Maimela, "Desmond Tutu," 49.
20. See Boesak, Farewell to Innocence, 97–122; and Cone, God of the Oppressed, 84–107.

Christian Scriptures. Because black theologians such as Cone are still very traditional in their use of Scriptures, Segundo has commended black theology for being one of the serious theologies that have completed the so-called hermeneutic circle.[21]

Most black theologians share with Segundo two serious misconceptions. The first misconception is the almost naive—if not unsophisticated—belief that the Bible is normative for Christian theology and can therefore be used as a direct source of theology. In consequence, in the dispute between white and black theologians regarding the use or misuse of the Christian faith in the furtherance of sectarian socioeconomic and political interests, theologians assume that it is appropriate to appeal to biblical texts to authorize their proposals, hoping thereby to convince their opponents about the "biblicalness" and hence the legitimacy of their theological claims. The futility of trying to prove that one's theology has the Bible as its direct source is beautifully illustrated by Cone's dismal failure to explain convincingly to black humanist William Jones where in the Bible it is mentioned that God the liberator, whom black theologians have constructed, will in fact liberate the oppressed black people. Jones's basic argument is that up to now there is no historical evidence to prove that the liberative God of Exodus, who became incarnate in the person of Jesus Christ, is actually carrying out the project of liberating black people from white oppression.[22] Even when Cone grudgingly admits the validity of Jones's argument, he does not persist in trying to prove that there is a straight line between the Bible and his theological construction. Instead, he abruptly shifts the argument from an attempt to prove that the concept of God in black theology is biblically grounded to a personal confession, when he states in a dogmatic fashion his belief that his theology has the Bible as its source, especially the biblical account of Jesus' cross and resurrection.[23] Because personal confession is not amenable to rational discussion, the discussion between Jones and Cone became unfruitful and ended in a deadlock.

I believe Cone should have been more candid from the outset, admitting that the concept of a liberative God in black theology is not necessarily derived from the Bible. Instead, it is the imaginative con-

---

21. See Segundo, *The Liberation of Theology*, 25, 31–34.
22. See William Jones, *Is God a White Racist?* (Garden City, N.Y.: Doubleday, 1973).
23. See Cone, *God of the Oppressed*, 187–92, 267–68.

struct of black theologians, who find the construals of God's presence in the traditional theology unacceptable because there God is portrayed as not hearing the cries of suffering people and therefore is incapable of inspiring and mobilizing oppressed blacks in the struggle for their historical liberation.

In addition to Cone's feeble and unpersuasive response to Jones's critique, amounting to "the Bible tells me so," I find it amazing that even those black theologians who use the materialist interpretation of the Bible continue to cling to the view that the Bible could function as a direct source of black theology.[24] By materialist interpretation is meant the recent attempts by biblical scholars to read the Bible in light of the concrete sociopolitical and economic conditions prevailing when it was written. The assumption here is that behind biblical stories, both individual and communal, stand concrete sociopolitical and economic conditions embodying and serving the particular interests of the writers. These conditions must be brought into mutual dialogue with the sociopolitical and economic conditions of interpreters if biblical stories are to shed light on our contemporary problems. In other words, a materialist reading of the Bible makes it clear that what constitutes the biblical canon resulted from long ideological struggles between the dominant and dominated groups and cultures among Israelite people. In consequence, the Bible contains not neutral and objective records of actual events but the partisan perspectives of dominant groups that won this ideological struggle.

If all theologies are socially conditioned modes of human speech about God that tell us "far more about the hopes and dreams of certain God-talkers,"[25] then it is surely naive for black theologians to continue to believe that the Bible can be used as the final court of appeal, as if theological claims expressed there had a status different from all others. Ideas and claims to truth both in the Bible and in black theology are human constructions without ontological privilege or certainty, held by human beings to serve human needs. For black theologians to be consistent in their appropriation and use of the

---

24. See Takatso A. Mofokeng, "A Black Christology: A New Beginning," *Journal of Black Theology in South Africa* 1 (May 1987); idem, "Black Christians, the Bible and Liberation," *Journal of Black Theology in South Africa* 2 (May 1988); Itumeleng Mosala, "The Implications of the Text of Esther for African Women's Struggles for Liberation," *Journal of Black Theology in South Africa* 2 (November 1988); and idem, *Biblical Hermeneutics and Black Theology in South Africa* (Grand Rapids: Wm. B. Eerdmans, 1988).

25. Cone, *God of the Oppressed*, 41.

insights of modern historical consciousness and to outgrow their naivete, they would be well advised to read David Kelsey's very perceptive analysis of the uses of Scripture in theology. Kelsey demonstrates that the Bible has never provided and could never serve as the direct source of theological proposals, because theological positions are a result of irreducible and radically different imaginative construals of the mode of God's presence in the world and are influenced and conditioned by the time and place in which they were written.[26] Therefore, because all theologies are imaginative human constructs, to continue to view different theologies as having the Bible as their direct source betrays a lack of theological sophistication.

The second misconception is rooted in the naive understanding of the uses of Scripture in theology, which seems to indicate that, in direct contradiction to the paradigm shift that has occurred in black theological discourse, black theologians continue to work with the traditional understanding of the duty of theologians—interpreting or mediating the word of God to humanity as that word is found "revealed" in the Bible. When theology is thus understood as a translation or an exposition of the biblical message to a particular community, the duty of theology is seen as peeling off the cultural wrappings in which the "revealed truth" is enshrined. After "discovering" this truth, theologians try to apply it to Christian social practice. José Míguez Bonino has eloquently expressed this traditional understanding of the relationship of the Bible to theology:

> Truth belongs, for this view, to a world of truth, a universe complete in itself, which is copied or reproduced in "correct" propositions, in a theory which corresponds to this truth. Then in a second moment, as a later step, comes the application in a particular historical situation.[27]

Agreeing with Míguez Bonino's characterization of traditional theology, Hugo Assmann notes:

> The basic structures of traditional theological language . . . aim at establishing an absolute truth without any intrinsic connection with practice, which is seen as something that comes later, as a consequent application of the "truth." "Truth" understood in this way possessed a world of its own, a world of thought reality, not reality that exists. . . . Truth existed "of itself" in a sort of Kingdom of its own, and any account taken of its

26. See David H. Kelsey, *The Uses of Scripture in Recent Theology* (Philadelphia: Fortress Press, 1975), 97–216.

27. José Míguez Bonino, *Doing Theology in a Revolutionary Situation* (Philadelphia: Fortress Press, 1975), 88.

historical dimension was something subsequent to, and pretty well independent of, the establishment of the truth.[28]

Whether they are aware of it or not, black theologians continue to assume that biblical truths are relatively fixed and stable, readily ascertainable to those freed from the ideological captivity under which white theologians suffer, and, above all, not themselves to be subjected to critical appraisal and reconstruction by the present generation of theologians but simply to be accepted as the bases of theological interpretation. Attempts by black theologians to give the so-called biblical truths privileged status, as if such truths were not themselves socially conditioned human constructs created to serve human needs, are a repudiation of the very historical consciousness that grounded many of the insights of black theology. Black theologians must not only become subjects of their liberation but also take full responsibility for the kind of theology they have opted to construct, without craving for some "sure" biblical foundation with which to authorize their proposals. As feminist theologian Sharon Welch correctly points out, to continue using "Scripture and the person and work of Jesus as criteria for faith and theological reflection . . . is still to avoid the costs and risk of history."[29] She further notes that to try to ground liberation theology in either the Bible or the person and work of Jesus is to "abdicate liberation theology's uniqueness: its reconceptualization of theology in the light of a particular experience of the relation between theory and practice."[30] Refusing to abdicate her responsibility as a theologian of liberation, Welch correctly opts to ground feminist theology "in the experience of sisterhood, in the process of liberation from sexism" in the same way that "Latin American theologies of liberation are grounded in the resistance and solidarity within base Christian communities."[31] This grounding of theology in the experience of liberation is similar to what Míguez Bonino refers to as the "Copernican" hermeneutics, from whose perspective:

> Theology . . . is not an effort to give a correct understanding of God's attributes or actions but an effort to articulate the action of faith, the

---

28. Hugo Assmann, *A Theology for a Nomad Church* (Maryknoll, N.Y.: Orbis Books, 1975), 74, 76.
29. Sharon D. Welch, *Communities of Resistance and Solidarity: A Feminist Theology of Liberation* (Maryknoll, N.Y.: Orbis Books, 1985), 25.
30. Ibid.
31. Ibid.

shape of praxis conceived and realized in obedience. As philosophy in Marx's famous dictum, theology has to stop explaining the world and start transforming it.[32]

This is not meant to suggest that black theologians should ignore the Bible in their theological reflection. Indeed, they have to use it because they are a part of the Christian community for whom the Bible occupies an important place and whose religious vocabulary and grammar of faith it has decisively shaped. The continuing appeal to Scripture by black theologians answers questions about the "Christianness" of their theological reflection.[33] It must be borne in mind, however, that although reference to the Bible identifies our historical Christian identity, it does not establish the "truth" of our theological claims. It is high time that black theologians accept the full consequences of modern historical consciousness, which has made it clear that divine absolute or revealed truth is not directly accessible to historical beings even as they appeal to Scripture to help authorize their theological proposals. There is no neutral, uninvolved, or pure divine truth-in-itself on which black theologians could lay their hands in the Bible or anywhere else in order to directly prove their case. We have many sociological Bibles, not "the Bible" to which we all could appeal to adjudicate disputes among Christians.[34] Put somewhat differently, we have as many Bibles as we have churches and Christian groups, which are themselves historical embodiments of the Christian faith; and some of them are deformed, others reformed, and still others revolutionary.

Therefore, instead of wasting their energies in search of the biblical norm with which to ascertain the "biblicalness" of their theological truth-claims, black theologians must underpin their theological quest for a liberating God with pragmatic or moral arguments. They must simply tell foes and admirers alike that the oppressed black community needs an alternative theology that can be employed as an instrument in the struggle for their historical liberation and survival. An alternative theology is needed because, as Gordon Kaufman correctly points out, traditional theology has proposed different sorts of gods in the past, many of which have not been conducive to the further

---

32. Míguez Bonino, *Doing Theology in a Revolutionary Situation*, 81.
33. Cf. Kelsey, *The Uses of Scripture*, 153; and Segundo, *The Liberation of Theology*, 31, 37–38.
34. See Kelsey, *Uses of Scripture*, 102–8.

humanization of the human species.[35] Black people know this all too well. Therefore, black theologians must candidly admit that they have found it morally necessary to take upon themselves the responsibility of searching for new ways of talking about God's presence in the world, hoping to construct a theology that will lead to black liberation, self-realization, and fuller humanization.

Black theologians should follow the example that Welch has set and should ground black theology in the process of liberating oppressed blacks from white domination, rather than trying to ground black theology in some "revealed" truth supposedly deposited in the pages of the Bible.[36] Grounding black theology in the black experience of being freed from white racialism, in my view, follows logically from the fact that black theologians have opted to do theology from the perspective of oppressed black people. What I suggest here is not a novel idea; the young and angry Cone came close to this conclusion when he wrote that the sole reason for the existence of black theology was

> to put into ordered speech the meaning of God's activity in the world, so that the community of the oppressed will recognize their inner thrust for liberation is not only consistent with the gospel but is the gospel of Jesus Christ. . . . Black theology will not spend much time trying to answer critics because it is accountable only to the black community. . . . There is only one principle which guides the thinking and action of black theology: an unqualified commitment to the black community as that community seeks to define its existence in light of God's liberating work in the world.[37]

The preferential option for oppressed blacks was chosen not because it is prescribed for or imposed upon black theologians by the Bible but on moral grounds, when black theologians decided to confront and reject the dominant white expressions of Christianity in which God is portrayed as a God who does not hear the cries of the poor and oppressed black people. By opting to develop an alternative vision of a God who battles against the social injustices under which black people suffer, black theologians, consciously or unconsciously, declared that they were no longer prepared to leave the ideological terrain of religion and biblical interpretation to white theologians who

35. See Gordon D. Kaufman, *The Theological Imagination: Constructing the Concept of God* (Philadelphia: Westminster Press, 1981), 187.
36. See Welch, *Communities of Resistance and Solidarity*, 26.
37. Cone, *A Black Theology of Liberation*, 10.

misused the Christian faith to justify morally the sociopolitical and economic interests of white people and the white domination of people of color. Instead, by choosing to contest the white monopoly over theological discourse, black theologians have effectively opted to enter "the battle for truth" on the side of the oppressed black community. Therefore, in the struggle for liberation, the one and only truth that matters will be the one that proves itself effective: liberating the black people from oppression and thus leading them to realize their fuller humanity, regardless of whether that truth is allegedly also found "revealed" in the Bible. By insisting that the divine truth consists in nothing other than an effective action that transforms our unjust world and untruthful human relationships (sin in the traditional language), black theology will consciously opt for pragmatic or moral criteria for evaluating truth-claims of all theologies, thus making it clear that the only God they are prepared to and can afford to worship is the God who will truly further black liberation and the creation of a just and more humane world.[38]

---

38. For a perceptive discussion of the sort of moral criteria that are called for here, see Gordon D. Kaufman, *An Essay on Theological Method*, rev. ed. (Missoula, Mont.: Scholars Press, 1979), 75–76; and idem, *The Theological Imagination*, 182–84, 190–206.

8

Toward a Dialogical Theology of Mission

M. THOMAS THANGARAJ

In this essay I attempt to work toward a theology of mission, taking into account some of the issues that Gordon Kaufman has raised with regard to theological method. That is, I will propose a theology of mission and utilize Kaufman's methodology as the framework for theological inquiry.

As I read Kaufman, two major concerns stand out in his methodology. The first is the discovery of a context for theological discussion that is wider than a purely ecclesial context. The second is a forthright recognition that it is human beings who engage in theological thinking, using their imaginative and constructive capabilities. The first concern is closely related to our growing awareness of the historically diverse character of human life. Kaufman writes:

> We live now in a single interconnected and interdependent world, whether we like it or not, and it is no longer possible either to ignore the other ways of being human or to move toward eliminating them. We must learn instead to encounter these others on equal terms, seeking, as sympathetically as we can, to understand and appreciate both their insights into the human condition and the forms of belief and practice they recommend and inculcate.[1]

---

1. Gordon D. Kaufman, "Religious Diversity, Historical Consciousness, and Christian Theology," in *The Myth of Christian Uniqueness*, ed. John Hick and Paul F. Knitter (Maryknoll, N.Y.: Orbis Books, 1987), 4.

He refers to this wider context as "the open market place of human experience and ideas."[2] The discovery of such a wider context for theology can be of use to Christian theologizing only when we accept the importance of dialogue and conversation between various theological and religious points of view. Kaufman has ably argued that interreligious dialogue has become crucial in today's theological agenda, because the problems that we face at the end of modernity demand a pooling of our spiritual and intellectual resources for their solution.[3]

The second concern Kaufman's methodology raises relates to the human character of the theological enterprise. He sees recognition of this as vital because of the way in which it can free theologians from an enslaving authoritarianism and for a much more imaginative and creative reconstruction of theology in a setting of dialogue and interchange.

> To acknowledge forthrightly and regularly that our theological statements and claims are simply *ours*—that they are product of our own human powers imaginatively to envision a world and our human place within that world—is to set us free from these all too easy but false moves toward authoritarianism, ... [and provide us] with a powerful incentive to engage in dialogue and other interchange—on equal terms—with representatives of other religious and secular points of view.[4]

I now turn to how we may construct a theology of mission that gives serious attention to these two major concerns of Kaufman's work.

THE STARTING POINT

What is the starting point for such a reconstruction of a theology of mission? Traditionally, a theology of mission has taken a so-called biblical view of mission as its starting point, because it has been widely assumed that the Bible is the primary and perhaps the only source book for every Christian theological statement or claim. For some theologians a vision of the church has functioned as the starting point for developing a theology of mission. I, however, begin my reconstruction differently.

2. Ibid., 13.
3. Ibid.
4. Ibid.

My own experiences with interreligious dialogue confirm the possibility of using such conversations as a framework for a theology of mission. I have been a regular member for several years of two dialogue groups, which meet periodically at Madurai in South India for dialogue, prayer, and discussion. One is the Saivite–Christian Dialogue Group and consists of Hindus who belong to the Tamil Saivite tradition within Hinduism and of Christian theologians. The second is a larger group of Christians, Hindus, and Muslims: the Religious Friends Circle. In participating in these dialogue meetings, it has become clear to me that one cannot possibly enter serious and constructive dialogue with a fixed idea of what the theology of mission is about. An appropriate theology, adequate to our present context, instead must emerge within the process of dialogue itself. That this is capable of happening—that it has happened in the dialogue groups in which I have participated—means that the starting point for theological reflection can be conceived in new, larger, and more productive ways. There are times, and this seems to be one, when our citizenship on the planet Earth becomes the starting point for theological reflection; at other times, the sharing of a common concern over a particular issue or event may trigger the theological exploration.

If we want to engage in such a discussion in the wider context of theology, then we simply cannot begin with the mission of the church as such. The very employment of the word "church" leaves a large majority of humans outside the circle of discussion, because church is not the most inclusive category as far as humanity is concerned. Coming from a multicultural situation, in which the reality of the church has been that of a tiny minority within India's large Hindu and Muslim population, I am aware of the divisive character of the word "church." Therefore, one has to look for an alternative starting point.

One may suggest that we begin with *missio Dei*—the mission of God—because "God" is the most inclusive word in the English language. One can twist Anselm's words and say that God is "that than which nothing more inclusive can be conceived." Although it is quite possible to conceive of God as the most inclusive category, historically it has not functioned that way. From the known beginnings of human history, a sizable part of humanity has understood and lived out its existence without any reference to this word. The employment of the word "God" does exclude many groups of humans, whether they call themselves atheists, humanists, or Buddhists. Therefore, if we want to begin our reconstruction at a point where it is possible dialogically to engage the whole of humanity, *missio Dei* cannot be the starting point.

MISSIO HUMANITATIS

Another possibility is to begin with the idea of the mission of humanity. The word "humanity" does include all human beings, irrespective of either their faith in God or their membership in any religious community. Here again we are faced with a difficulty. Although all humans can be dialogically engaged in the discussion of the mission of humanity, our understanding of what it means to be human is varied and sometimes contradictory. How can we proceed with a discussion of the mission of humanity when we do not agree on a common view of the human? Kaufman also is aware of this particular difficulty.

> Some suggest we should attempt to overcome our traditional parochialism by moving to what they claim is a "universally human" position, one that penetrates beneath all the "accidental" and "historical" differences among humans and their religions to some supposed "essential oneness" we all share. . . . But there really is no such universally human position available to us; every religious (or secular) understanding and way of life we might uncover is a *particular* one.[5]

Although the meaning of "the mission of humanity" cannot be fixed by an essentialist definition of the human, there do, however, seem to be resources that can help us to understand and develop an appropriate meaning for this term, one larger than the meanings held by the church in the past.

First, the word "mission" is not the private property of Christian discourse. It is a word in the English language and thus part of normal human discourse. Mission is a public word. For example, the Georgia Department of Human Resources has drawn guidelines for its work which it has titled *DHR Directions: Mission, Philosophy, Goals and Strategies, and Values of the Georgia Department of Human Resources.*[6] The document opens by saying, "The mission of the Department of Human Resources is to assist Georgians," and refers to itself as "the mission statement." In earlier times, especially in India, the word "mission" was closely and often solely related to the work of the

5. Ibid., 5.
6. Georgia Department of Human Resources, Atlanta, 1989.

Christian churches in India; but today in the city of Madurai, for example, one comes across Meenakshi Mission Hospital and Hindu Mission Hospital.[7] Moreover, the word "mission" is not a peculiarly religious word; national governments talk about their political missions, and even James Bond (007) refers to his activity as a mission to be accomplished! The public character of the word "mission" makes it possible for us to engage in a discussion about the idea of *missio humanitatis* in a larger human context.

Second, if one seriously takes into account the emerging historical consciousness, which is affecting almost all human groups and nations in every part of the world,[8] then one can venture a few basic affirmations about the nature of the human from a historicist perspective, which can account for the diversity of interpretations of the human in history. These are not fully developed theological or religious affirmations in themselves; rather, they are meant to provide a basic framework within which the multiplicity of theological, religious, and secular understandings of the human can be recognized, located, and explicated. The value of these affirmations is that they offer us "ways of relativizing and opening up our basic symbol system," so that we can move to speak of a *missio humanitatis*.

I will mention here three such affirmations.[9] First, humans are self-conscious beings. This simply means that there is an internal relation in every human being, wherein the self is able to relate to its own self. This internal relation can also be called reflexive consciousness. Such a

---

7. Meenakshi is the name of the presiding goddess in the largest Hindu temple in Madurai, and the Hindu Mission hospital is, in a sense, the Hindu counterpart of the Christian Mission Hospital that was started by Christian missionaries several decades ago.

8. By "historical consciousness" I mean an intense awareness that human beings are fundamentally historical creatures who, although they create their own historical traditions and cultural expressions, are significantly shaped and oriented by the same history and culture. It also includes a recognition that humans create these traditions in diverse and different ways. Although it is more accurate to say that the kind of historical consciousness we refer to grew out of the Western theological, philosophical, and scientific traditions, we live in a period of human history in which such consciousness has come to pervade larger and larger portions of humanity. E.g., the sociopolitical life of India, both during the independence struggle and after independence in 1947, bears ample witness to this emerging historical consciousness. The democratization in Eastern Europe during the last several months, the struggle of the Tamils in Sri Lanka to establish a nation of their own, and other such recent events testify to the emergence of a historical consciousness on a global level.

9. In dealing with these three affirmations I am heavily dependent on Kaufman's lectures delivered at the Institute for Teachers of Systematic Theology, organized by the Board of Theological Education of the Senate of Serampore College at Bangalore, India, in June 1988. As far as I know, these lectures have not appeared in print.

reflexive consciousness is not merely something that humans possess; it is constitutive of what it means to be human. Our being human is constituted by the understanding of human that we hold. Different religious and theological traditions may name this consciousness differently: for example, soul, mind, *atman*, or *jiva*. In each case, however, humans hold these ideas about themselves and these ideas shape the way they think and live in the world.

Second, humans are historical beings. By historicity we mean that creativity by which humans transcend the limitations of time and space in order to create history and, in turn, to be shaped and constituted by history; that is, historicity is creativity in human relations and in relation to the world and a recognition that one is shaped by the traditions within which one is situated. Even when a religious tradition envisions history as an illusion, that vision is itself an expression of the historical creativity of the human and shapes and influences the way in which the people of that particular religious tradition live in the world. Although located in the natural and material world, humans can create artificial worlds of their own, such as those of religion, art, music, and culture, and can in turn be influenced by them.

Third, humans are ecological beings. They are a part of the network of ecological interdependence. Humans are not disembodied historical spirits; they are "the dust of the earth." Kaufman uses the phrase "bio-historical beings" in referring to this aspect of the human. Here again, one can see that humans shape and are shaped by the natural world around them. We live at a time when we are beginning to recognize the demonic consequences of an undue emphasis on the history-making character of the human, consequences of ecological imbalance in the world of nature. Therefore, there is an increasing desire on the part of all religions and secular traditions to reiterate the ecological nature of the human.

The three affirmations I have made show that while there is, in fact, a multiplicity of understandings of the human, we can recognize the interconnectedness of these differing views at the levels of self-consciousness, historicity, and ecological interdependence. Such recognition makes it possible for humans to engage in discussion toward developing a common understanding of the mission of humanity.

My claim so far is that although our understandings of what it means to be human are multiple and varied, it is possible to engage in an open dialogue about the mission of humanity on the basis of the public character of the word "mission" and the self-conscious, historical, and ecological character of the human. Now the question is, What is *missio humanitatis*?

To answer this question, I will return to the word "mission." This word, in its Latin root, means "being sent." It is also, at least in the biblical tradition, linked to the Greek word "apostello," which means "I send." Thus mission means "being-sent-ness." If humans are self-conscious, historical, and ecological beings, then what is the being-sent-ness of the human? I will organize my explication around three words: "responsibility," "solidarity," and "mutuality." These words in no way exhaust the meaning and understanding of mission, either Christian or otherwise, but they do point to some of the major elements in a contemporary idea of mission as far as *missio humanitatis* is concerned.[10]

Responsibility

One of the ways in which we can describe the nature of the being-sent-ness of the human, that is, the *missio humanitatis*, is to explicate it as an act of responsibility. H. Richard Niebuhr, in his book titled *The Responsible Self*, has ably outlined the history, meaning, and characteristics of this word.[11] He discovers four elements in responsibility: response, interpretation, accountability, and social solidarity. He maintains that an act is responsible when one acts in response to action upon oneself with an interpretation of the larger context in which that interaction takes place and with a sense of accountability to oneself that enables a continuing community of social actors.[12]

Although I am unable here to go into the details of Niebuhr's explication of this concept, I do want to show the relevance and usefulness of his interpretation of this concept for an elaboration of the idea of *missio humanitatis*. The being-sent-ness of the human can be seen as the response of the human to all that is going on around us. We do

10. One may ask whether responsibility, solidarity, and mutuality are already informed by a Christian bias in the understanding of *missio humanitatis*. While it is true that a Christian theologian cannot at any given moment suspend all Christian perspectives and look at a theological issue in a vacuum, it is possible, in a dialogue setting, to relativize one's particular standpoint for a time and work toward a more inclusive understanding of the issue at hand.

11. See H. Richard Niebuhr, *The Responsible Self* (New York: Harper & Row, 1963), 47–68.

12. Ibid., 65.

respond to persons, things, events, natural phenomena, and so forth as they impinge on us. There is a "going-forth-ness" involved in our "missionary" mode of existence that can be seen as our response to everything around us. This going-forth-ness also involves a returning-back-to-ourselves in the form of interpretation of events and persons. The response and interpretation, in turn, evolve into a sense of accountability. In responding to and interpreting all that goes on around us, we do see ourselves as accountable to ourselves, others, and the wider context of human existence. Thus the mission of humanity is simply the act of taking responsibility.

Our picture of the human as a self-conscious, historical, and ecological being can be filled out, to some extent, by this concept of responsibility. The very element of self-consciousness is a missionary mode of being human. Self-consciousness is an interpretation of oneself that guides one's responses to events and things and for which one is accountable. In this sense self-consciousness is one's mission to oneself—a mission expressed in the relation of the self to its own self. By contrast, the historical and ecological dimensions of human existence portray our connectedness to history, culture, and the material world in which we live and to which we respond. To the extent that our responses are also shaped by our ideas of this world, we become accountable not simply for our ideas and responses but also to and for that to which we are connected as historical and ecological beings. In this sense our connectedness with the historical and ecological world in which we live constitutes our mission of responsibility to and for that world.

Thus the mission of humanity is to take responsibility for ourselves, others, and the world. This is possible and desirable because we are all bound to each other in history and in ecology, living in an interconnected and interdependent world. Am I my brother's or sister's keeper? Yes, and that is what *missio humanitatis* means.

Solidarity

I have not dwelt here on the fourth element in the idea of responsibility suggested by Niebuhr, namely, the concept of social solidarity, but it plays a significant role in our understanding of the mission of humanity. Niebuhr himself deals with social solidarity in a separate chapter, following the discussion of the meaning of responsibility.[13]

13. Ibid., 69–89.

For Niebuhr the idea of solidarity is linked to the need for a "continuing discourse or interaction among beings forming a continuing society."[14] Although this is true and valid, our perception of solidarity is developed from a different angle.

The word "responsibility" has the danger of implying that it is something we do for others: *we* take responsibility *for* others. In human history through the ages we have seen individuals, groups, and nations arrogating for themselves responsibility for the destiny of others. Such an assumption of the *missio humanitatis* has often resulted in disastrous and oppressive consequences, as the two world wars bear witness. Moreover, the present ecological crisis is a supreme example of a kind of *missio humanitatis* that has led humans to take oppressive responsibility over nature and, by so doing, to reach the brink of destroying the very sustaining context of human and other life.

Therefore, if the mission of humanity is an act of responsibility, it is to be done in a mode of solidarity. Response and responsibility do not always mean an "over-against-ness"; rather, they involve much more a "being-with-ness." Our act of being responsible to and for all that is around us has to be coupled with a mode of being in solidarity. Without a sense of social solidarity, with both other humans and nature, there is no creative responsibility, individual or social.

Here again, we may recall the character of the human as self-conscious, historical, and ecological and see the relevance of the idea of solidarity to such a view of the human. The interconnectedness of the historical and ecological characters of the human places human beings in a situation of solidarity. The missionary character of the human does involve an expression of solidarity. Thus the mission of humanity is to be in solidarity with others in the acting out of one's responsibility. *Missio humanitatis* is both responsibility and solidarity.

Mutuality

By the very use of the phrase "the mission of humanity" we have, to a large extent, universalized the concept of mission. All humans have a mission to accomplish in terms of responsibility and solidarity. If all humans are self-conscious, historical, ecological beings, then all humans are necessarily "missionary" beings, namely, beings who experience a being-sent-ness or going-forth-ness in their very being human. We need, however, to reiterate and strengthen this aspect of

14. Ibid., 65.

inclusivity and universality by bringing a third element into the idea of *missio humanitatis*: mutuality.

Mutuality means that humans have a mission to one another. Mission is possible only in a spirit of mutuality in the sphere of interhuman relations. There are no longer "missioners" and the "missioned." All are missionaries, in a relationship of mutuality. This is highly significant if we take seriously the multireligious and pluralistic character of the context in which we attempt to explicate the mission of humanity, because only in this way can there be an "open market place of human experience and ideas" in which we can learn from each other.

Often in our history we have seen mission as an I–It relationship rather than an I–Thou relationship. In the modern missionary movement the very employment of the term "mission field" to denote a group of people or nations is symptomatic of the kind of I–It relationship the missionary enterprise has entailed. This particular problem has also been quite apparent in the way humans have exploited nature and natural resources for our own advantage. The world of nature has been quite often seen as an "it" to be subdued and conquered, and we are now beginning to reap the destructive consequences of such an I–It relationship. Therefore, *missio humanitatis*, if it is to be a responsible vision, must include a spirit of mutuality both in our interhuman relations and in our relation to the world of nature.

We began our inquiry into the theology of mission with an affirmation of the importance of open dialogue and interchange. One is further enabled to sustain such a spirit of dialogue in one's theological exploration only by conceiving of mission as an exercise in mutuality. Without mutuality, mission sinks into parallel monologues that never meet.

To sum up our discussion on *missio humanitatis*, we can say that the mission of humanity is an act of taking responsibility, in a mode of solidarity, shot through with a spirit of mutuality.

MISSIO DEI

So far we have given form and content to the concept of the mission of humanity, as seen from a historicist perspective. This has been done without any reference to the central and guiding concept of theology, namely, the concept of God. Hence our exercise has not yet moved to the level of a theological exploration. As any theologian of mission would rightly demand, only when we allow the concept of God to "preside over" our discussion of mission do we begin to move toward a theology of mission. As we step into that dimension of our discussion, we need to recognize what is happening to our circle of dialogue partners.

When we bring the word "God" into a discussion of mission, we are making a point of departure that means that some of our dialogue partners begin to see themselves as being outside the circle of discussants. The nontheists of the world are tempted to say goodbye to us. Even the theists face a difficulty in continuing in the conversation, because none of us speaks of God in a vacuum. Our vision of God is shaped and formed by a particular religious and theological tradition that informs us. In a sense we cannot discuss a theology of mission as such but only a Christian theology of mission. Our *missio Dei* is normatively determined by our understanding of *missio Christi*. Therefore, the theists of religious traditions other than Christianity are in no way in a better position than the nontheists in joining our conversation.

Nevertheless, I believe it is possible to continue the dialogue in the open marketplace of ideas because of the basic framework within which we have understood the mission of humanity. Although the particular explications of responsibility, solidarity, and mutuality may vary according to the religious or secular tradition out of which one undertakes them, it is still possible to sustain the dialogical posture because of the concept of mutuality built into the *missio humanitatis*.[15] I will now investigate how the three basic elements in the mission of humanity acquire a theological dimension as we move toward a Christian theology of mission.

Cruciform Responsibility

When we place the concept of responsibility within the Christian theological context, we need to say that it becomes redefined primarily as response to God and being responsible to God. In the central

15. I had occasion to present these ideas about a possible theology of mission to a group of theological students in India. The students were highly skeptical of sustaining the conversation with the other religious and secular partners once we introduce the idea of God in Christ. Interestingly, however, the Hindu theological professor who was present at the seminar maintained that as long as one operates within the framework of responsibility, solidarity, and mutuality, it would still be possible for a Hindu to continue in the conversation, even though a Hindu may bring his or her own particular understandings with regard to the elaboration of these basic concepts.

affirmation of the Christian faith—namely, that God is the creator of all—God's ultimacy in terms of God's responsibility for creation is made clear. If God is ultimately responsible, then human responsibility can only be exercised in partnership with God. God is primarily in mission and we are only God's co-missioners. This radical and monotheistic affirmation of Christianity acts as the great relativizer of human responsibility. Humans can never claim ultimate responsibility for the earth and those who dwell on it. This protects us from a destructive and idolatrous understanding of human responsibility. Such an affirmation in no way belittles the seriousness with which humans have to exercise their missionary responsibility, because as humans are understood to be created in the "image of God," they are also undertood to share in the divine responsibility for the whole of creation; but they can exercise that responsibility only with a due recognition of their relativity in relation to the ultimacy of such responsibility. Humans can act as responsible beings only in humility and prayer. Prayer becomes both the attitude with which and the mode in which humans act out their missionary responsibility. Karl Barth's claim that Christian theology is an act of prayer also holds good for the Christian's missionary responsibility.[16]

This relativized understanding of human responsibility is highlighted in the vulnerability that is manifested in the central symbol of the Christian faith, the cross. The missionary responsibility, seen in the light of the cross, can only be expressed as vulnerability. Kosuke Koyama, contrasting the crusading and cruciform missionary modes, argues rightly that the cruciform reponsibility is specifically a Christian theological understanding of human responsibility.[17] The Christian missionary activities during the grand era of modern Christian missions often have forgotten this thrust of their faith. Missionary activities in the eighteenth, nineteenth, and twentieth centuries often have been dominated by a conquest mentality that is in complete contrast to the cruciform responsibility that we are explicating here. The cross is the climactic point at which God's missionary vulnerability is revealed. Indian theologians such as Keshub Chandra Sen and Vengal Chakkarai have referred to Jesus' cry on the cross, "My God, my

16. See Karl Barth, *Church Dogmatics*, vol. 1, no. 1 (Edinburgh: T. & T. Clark, 1975), 23.

17. See Kosuke Koyama, *Three Mile an Hour God* (Maryknoll, N.Y.: Orbis Books, 1979), 51–55.

God, why have you forsaken me?" as the supreme manifestation of divinity.[18]

The Christian theological understanding of mission needs to take seriously the vulnerability and openness involved in the exercise of one's missionary reponsibility. The image of God in the human is but the image of the crucified God. This is all the more significant since it is God, and God alone, who is ultimately responsible for the whole of creation and thus relativizes every human responsibility.

Liberative Solidarity

Solidarity, the second element in the *missio humanitatis*, also gains significant direction when placed under the discipline of the Christian theological orientation. Although in our earlier portrayal the concept of solidarity looked absolutely open to all, it gains a slightly narrower definition within the framework of *missio Dei* and *missio Christi*. God has expressed God's solidarity with humanity in creating them in God's own image. In the process of God's own missionary journey through the history of humankind, however, the solidarity of God with the whole of humanity is achieved through God's specific and preferential solidarity with those who are oppressed, poor, and marginalized.

One can interpret the biblical account of the history of Israel, the ministry of Jesus, and the life of the early church as indicative of this particular mode of solidarity that is expressed in God's involvement in the world. This solidarity is not limited to the people of Israel. The prophet Amos asserts, "'Are you not like the Ethiopians to me, O people of Israel?' says the Lord. 'Did I not bring up Israel from the Land of Egypt, and the Philistines from Caphtor and the Syrians from Kir?'"[19] Further, Jesus in speaking to the crowds on the shores of Galilee expressed this solidarity by saying "Blessed are you poor, for yours is the kingdom of God."[20] The point here is that God's ultimate solidarity with the human race is achieved through God's penultimate solidarity with those who are poor, oppressed, and exploited.

Latin American liberation theologians have helped theologians all over the world to rediscover this biblical and theological under-

18. See Robin Boyd, *An Introduction to Indian Christian Theology*, rev. ed. (Madras: Christian Literature Society, 1975), 31, 181–82.
19. Amos 9:7.
20. Luke 6:20.

standing of solidarity. God's preferential solidarity is for the sake of liberation of the poor; thus it is always liberative solidarity. Feminist theologians too have emphasized this understanding of liberative solidarity.[21]

It is interesting to note that in the work of the modern missionary movements (Roman Catholic and Protestant) in India, the oppressed classes among the Indian people were always the first attracted to the gospel of Christ. In my own family's history I can easily see how my ancestors who belonged to the lower castes in the Hindu social hierarchy saw the Christian gospel as a message of liberation and the missionaries as being in liberative solidarity with them. Thus the *missio Dei* for early Indian Christians was a mission of liberative solidarity.

Eschatological Mutuality

The third element in the *missio humanitatis*, mutuality, needs now to be reconstructed in the light of the Christian theological standpoint. An overly Christocentric orientation of Christian theology and a narrowly defined understanding of the finality of Christ have tended to keep the idea of mutuality outside the discussion of mission. Mutuality often has been seen as contradictory to the call of mission itself. This is so, I believe, because of the way in which the idea of the Holy Spirit has been neglected and marginalized in Christian theological thinking.

In one of his farewell addresses recorded in the Fourth Gospel, Jesus tells his disciples, "I have yet many things to say to you, but you cannot bear them now. When the Spirit of truth comes, he will guide you into all the truth . . . and he will declare to you the things that are to come."[22] Here the Spirit signifies both the incompleteness of the present and the fullness of the eschaton. When one recognizes this aspect of Christian talk about the Holy Spirit, one is enabled to be open to mutuality. Because the Spirit is significantly related to the eschatological in the New Testament, it is fair to refer to a Christian understanding of mutuality as eschatological mutuality.

Our missionary responsibility demands eschatological mutuality, "for now we see in a mirror dimly, but then face to face. Now I know in part; then I shall understand fully, even as I have been fully under-

---

21. Cf. Rosemary R. Ruether, *Sexism and God-Talk* (Boston: Beacon Press, 1983), chap. 8; and Lynn Rhodes, *Co-Creating: A Feminist Vision of Ministry* (Philadelphia: Westminster Press, 1987), chap. 4.
22. John 16:12–13.

stood."[23] As John writes in one of his letters, "Beloved, we are God's children now; it does not yet appear what we shall be, but we know that when he appears we shall see him as he is."[24] Therefore, our being-sent-ness involves listening to other religious viewpoints, learning from other religious and secular traditions, and mutually enriching one another toward the eschaton. The kind of eschatological mutuality we are referring to invites us to join the groaning of the whole of creation toward the day of freedom and liberation. As Paul writes, "not only the creation, but we ourselves, who have the first fruits of the Spirit, groan inwardly as we wait for adoption as sons [and daughters], the redemption of our bodies."[25]

MISSIO ECCLESIAE

We are now in a position to say that the mission of the church is the working out of its commitment to cruciform responsibility, liberative solidarity, and eschatological mutuality. One may wonder if, by the route we took in formulating a theology of mission and by the kind of conclusions we have reached with regard to the mission of the church, we have lost sight of some of the traditional yet significantly important issues related to the mission of the church. Evangelism, conversion, church growth, social service, verbal proclamation of the message of salvation in Christ, and so forth have all been lost on the way, one may think.

I would argue, however, that that is not necessarily the case, although certainly each of these terms needs to be redefined within the new perspective that I have been developing. In particular, our understanding of the elements of mission must be shaped by a spirit of dialogue and mutuality. The church will and should continue to bear witness to the love of God expressed in the life, ministry, death, and resurrection of Christ; but it can do so only in a setting of mutual witness, allowing our partners in dialogue to witness to us regarding their experience and vision of the mighty and salvific acts of God. Similarly, conversion will have to be defined as a two-way traffic wherein we are all converted to and by each other, which is different from an understanding of conversion as contributing to church growth. All acts of

23. 1 Cor. 13:12.
24. 1 John 3:2.
25. Rom. 8:23.

service will now be seen in the light of the liberation of peoples and nations from oppression and injustice, rather than in acts of charity which alleviate the suffering of a selected portion of humanity. Moreover, such acts of service will have to be envisioned as acts of cooperation and joint ventures with people of other faiths and ideologies.

In a way our understanding and practice of Christian mission will have to be judged by a new set of principles and norms. It is this kind of adventurous and dialogical theology of mission, I believe, that is required of us at the end of modernity.

PART IV

THEOLOGY AND
CORPORATE/CORPOREAL IDENTITY

9

In Defense of
Realism

JOHN B. COBB, JR.

I

Gordon Kaufman and I share a common project, that of constructive Christian theology. That project has become uncommon in recent years, so this is no minor bond. It differs, on the one side, from any effort to repristinate past thinkers and, on the other side, from the religious studies approach in which Christian faith and Christian theology are treated from the outside. We understand ourselves as Christian thinkers, living at the end of modernity, accepting responsibility to construct a way of thought appropriate for contemporary believers.

We share also many other concerns. We agree that our task cannot be merely intellectual or academic, if that means ignoring the most pressing issues facing humanity. Kaufman undertakes to rethink the faith in light of the nuclear threat. I have responded more extensively to the environmental challenge. But these differences do not separate us. We both know that both issues are important.

In addition, we both draw on common sources. The pragmatic tradition is important to both of us. We are each influenced by liberation and feminist thinkers. We both know that all thinking is profoundly affected by historical and cultural factors and by the social location of the thinker.

Despite all these similarities, one especially important difference does separate us. We differ radically in our evaluation of Immanuel

Kant. For Kaufman, Kant is the great hero of modern philosophy. For me, he is the villain of the piece.

Obviously, I am being overdramatic. I share Kaufman's admiration for Kant's brilliance, originality, and rigor. No thinker has had a more profound or pervasive effect on the development of a civilization, altering the way it understands itself and its own intellectual activities. Furthermore, I agree that there is something profoundly true about the direction of this alteration. The human mind, in very important respects, does create its world. Nevertheless, I believe it has been catastrophic that the emergence of this profound insight was accompanied by neglect and even denial of the equally important truth that the human mind is acted on by the body and through the body by the wider world. Thus the truth of idealism has been grasped as opposing the truth of realism. Whereas the dominant intellectual project inaugurated by the discovery of the truth of idealism should have been to integrate it into a wider, realistic context, it has in fact been to understand the creative activity of mind as if the physical body and the physical world were themselves its creatures.

The terms "idealism" and "realism" are used in many ways. They tend to be used chiefly to label quite specific philosophical positions to which few people adhere today. In this narrower usage Kant was himself not an idealist, because he affirmed that a noumenal reality did exist behind the phenomena. Similarly, those who have taken the linguistic turn distinguish themselves from idealism.

In this essay, by contrast, I am using the terms much more broadly. By "realism" I mean the clear affirmation that a world exists independently of human experience or knowledge. By "idealism" I mean that very widespread tendency in the nineteenth and twentieth centuries so to accent the creative and determinative character of human thinking, imaging, or speaking as to minimize or deny the importance of physical processes, relatively uninfluenced by human mentality, in shaping the world. The tendency is to argue that, or as if, the world has the character it has only because it is structured in that way by human thought or language or imagination. There are important differences among those I call idealists as to whether some of this structuring is universal or whether it is all relative to cultural or even individual activity.

For idealists philosophy is quite separate and distinct from science. Prior to Kant, and for the early Kant as well, philosophy was continuous with science, interacting with it in the process of trying to understand the world. Beginning with Kant's mature work, however, science was assigned by philosophy roles that could no longer impinge upon philosophy. As a result, since Kant philosophy and science have gone their separate and increasingly fragmenting ways. Any attempt to make sense of the world as the sciences show it to be falls outside both the sciences and philosophy.

In my view this is an intellectual and spiritual disaster. People can no longer look either to science or to philosophy to orient them to the world and give guidance for living. One might suppose that this would provide free space for the Christian faith, and, indeed, there have been serious theologians who made such claims. But whereas in intimate interaction with science and philosophy Christian theology could make plausible claims to give guidance to thought and life, in isolation from them it is reduced to arbitrary assertion.

With no responsible guide to life and thought, the field is left open to fundamentalisms, cults, and charismatic leaders of all sorts. Highly trained scientists are as likely to succumb to authoritarianism in the realms of ethics and religion as are persons with little education. Philosophy commits suicide, and theology disappears as a cultural force.

Inattention to what is actually taking place in the physical world has been another effect of idealism. Throughout the nineteenth and twentieth centuries a few prophets warned that human actions were undercutting the natural base for human life. To say that they were ignored because of the subtle but widespread influence of idealism would be a very partial explanation. But it would not be wrong. The intellectual life of the time and the academic disciplines it spawned did not attend to the natural world in its concrete givenness. In economics, "land" ceased to be a factor of production and became a commodity, represented in the all-determinative mathematical formulas by monetary values. Even in physics, mathematics came to dominate over observation of nature. Only here and there in the natural sciences was there resistance to the shift from observation of the natural world to laboratory experimentation and mathematical calculation. One group among the ecologists did resist, and their warnings of disaster finally broke through the massive resistance of modern habits of thought. For this reason we speak of the "ecological" crisis to refer in general to any of the disasters that the degradation of the natural world inflicts upon us.

The tension between the idealistically determined mentality of the academic disciplines and serious attention to what happens in the natural world did not end when the threat of disaster finally made its way into newspaper headlines. If one attends a meeting of almost any academic guild, one may hear occasional references to environmental threats, but business goes on as ususal. And for business to go on as usual is for it to proceed as if there were no physical world at all. Thought refers to thought, mathematical symbol to mathematical symbol, and language to language.

Even at these meetings one observes that other things take place. Discussion is interrupted for meals. Some people go jogging. Around the edges there are romantic interludes. A speaker may be taken ill. The acoustical system fails. Thus the physical world intrudes upon the deliberations. The fact of such intrusion, however, does not affect what is said and thought. The academic disciplines seem to float free, to have a life of their own. Within these disciplines, it is as if the only reality of the physical world were its reality in thought, in mathematics, or in language.

Everyone lives, of course, as if the physical world had a quite objective reality. We would not stay alive if we did not. We know that the car coming down the highway would kill us if we got in its way too late for it to stop; there is a reality about that fact not exhausted by thought, mathematics, or language. But it is considered naive or in bad taste to bring up this commonsense knowledge in the context of academic discussion or intellectual debate. It is thought of as "naive realism." And since Kant, educated people know that naive realism is out.

I agree that naive realism is out. By "naive realism" I understand the belief that the world apart from our sense experience is much like what is given to us, phenomenally, in sense experience. Philosophy and science have both discredited this idea. My complaint is that the discrediting of naive realism has not led to an intense effort to achieve a "sophisticated realism." On the contrary, the discrediting of naive realism has been taken to rule out realism in general.

The nineteenth and twentieth centuries have not been exhaustively idealist. They have been inhabited by many materialists. In some of the sciences materialism is the regulative orthodoxy. For example, in physiological psychology the aim is to show how all mental or subjective phenomena are explained by physical events in the brain. It is often implied that they are "nothing but" these physical events.

Although a few of the greatest physiological psychologists have insisted that this project cannot be realized because the mind is more than the by-product of the brain, the science as science is not affected and most of its devotees take for granted the materialistic vision.

More generally, the continuing dominance of mechanistic models in chemistry and biology expresses the materialistic bias that underlies them. The programs of research that follow are overwhelmingly reductionistic. Many still draw traditional deterministic consequences, denying all freedom and all contingency. Materialism is far from dead.

I am as concerned to oppose materialism as I am to oppose idealism. One of the attractions of idealism has been that it undercuts the power of materialism. As long as materialism is understood to be the outcome of realism, it is understandable that it will be hard to get a hearing for realism.

I have found in the thought of Alfred North Whitehead a realism very different from both the naive and the materialistic forms, one that by no means denies the true insight of idealism. This is one of the main attractions of his philosophy for me. I find the resultant vision so much more adequate to my experience that I am often puzzled by the deep resistance that it encounters from others. Part of the explanation may be that when one has made one's choice of positions within what one thought was the total range of alternatives, one is not enthusiastic about the introduction of a quite different option. One prefers to view it as another form of one of the options one has already found good reason to reject. Nevertheless, it seems worthwhile to try again to introduce a Whiteheadian realism as a fresh challenge to idealism, at least requiring different arguments, if it too is to be rejected, than the ones used against naive realism and materialism.

II

From a Whiteheadian point of view, human experience is situated in a vast field of events, interacting with other events in complex ways. To explain human experience, thinking, imaging, and using language require an account of this larger field and its influence upon the specifically human events. Hence ontology and cosmology are required to account for epistemology. Whitehead's own discussions of how we know are located in this wider context of reflection, and most Whiteheadians have followed suit.

This accounts in part for the neglect of Whitehead's epistemology. For modern philosophy, and intensified by idealism, epistemology is primary. We cannot talk about a world beyond our experience unless we can justify doing so through an analysis of that experience. The analysis of that experience, however, seems to most epistemologists since Kant to offer only its own contents, contents that do not witness to the reality of anything beyond themselves. Hence any claim that elements in that experience refer to, or correspond with, elements outside it is rejected. Whereas most earlier philosophers supposed that our thought or language corresponded more or less well with a real, objective world, since Kant's work a large majority agree in the rejection of the correspondence theory of truth.

The consequences that would follow if this rejection were thought through to the end are so drastic that no one actually adopts them. They are, indeed, solipsistic. If one did not hope that when one spoke there would be some correspondence between what the hearer understands and what one intends, one would not long continue to speak. The hearer may misunderstand, and, indeed, perfect correspondence between what is heard and what is intended may never occur. But that is not the issue.

Often one hears, among persons who claim to reject the correspondence theory of truth, serious discussions about a past thinker's ideas. One person may criticize another for interpreting those ideas badly. For example, someone might say that I am misrepresenting what was intended by those who rejected the correspondence theory of truth. That means, however, that there is some latent concern about the correspondence of what I say about other thinkers with their actual intentions.

In an important sense I am misrepresenting what most of those who have rejected the correspondence theory of truth have meant. They have been talking about the correspondence between our ideas, images, or language, on the one hand, and something other than ideas, images, or language, on the other. They do not intend, in most cases, to deny that ideas may correspond with ideas. Nevertheless, because this limitation of their criticism is rarely made explicit, as the argument often seems to be that the contents of my experience cannot correspond with anything outside my experience, their rejection of the correspondence theory is less complete than their rhetoric suggests. The concessions involved are more important than is often realized.

Sometimes it turns out that the rejection of correspondence is the denial of the possibility of displaying the two corresponding elements together. Some acknowledge that they do believe that their thought or language corresponds to something, but they point out that when they want to justify their claim, they cannot offer the two items for comparison. Instead, they must appeal to other considerations, such as coherence or pragmatic effectiveness. Some may acknowledge that when they claim a statement to be true, they mean that it corresponds with some state of affairs but still reject the correspondence theory of truth because it implies that correspondence can be directly known or shown. Others argue that because the only test of truth is pragmatic or in terms of coherence, nothing more can be meant by truth than that one predicts that these tests will succeed.

Whitehead defends the correspondence theory of truth in the context of these considerations. For him the affirmation that a statement is true is the claim that it corresponds to some state of affairs, usually beyond the immediate experience of the one making the claim. He also affirms that the test of truth includes an immediate experience of correspondence. In the context of his philosophy, however, these affirmations have a plausibility that is lacking when one approaches matters with a different ontology and cosmology. Although I accept the challenge to explain the epistemological justification of Whitehead's realism in recognizably epistemological terms, I know that I cannot do so apart from such basic Whiteheadian convictions as that we live in a world of interrelated events and that human experiences are to be counted among these, not dualistically distinguished from them. I cannot explain how we know without some assumptions about the nature of the knowing event. The effort to find in epistemology a neutral foundation from which to proceed to other things is illusory.

In epistemological analysis it makes a great deal of difference what examples one takes. The most common procedure has been to begin with sense experience. The result has been idealism. Whitehead proposes beginning with vaguer aspects of experience: for example, the "knowledge" that there has been a past, that the experience that is now taking place did not arise ex nihilo. Bertrand Russell once argued that there is nothing in present experience to count against the hypothesis that the world has just come into being—that there is no past. Whitehead believes there is much in experience that counts against this hypothesis.

The appeal here is what is now called phenomenological. Each reader must ask whether she or he does believe that the present moment may be the first to have occurred. If the answer is negative, then the question is, Why? From Russell's point of view it is sheer chance that no one seems to believe this. But chance is a poor explanation of something that occurs all the time without exception. It seems more plausible to think that there is something about the present experience that testifies to there having been a past.

Those who concentrate on sense experience may not be able to detect this testimony there. Especially if they concentrate on the colors and sounds that constitute the most vivid content of this experience, they are likely to find that these tell no tales about whence they come. This suggests, however, that there is more to experience than sense experience and that concentration of attention on sense experience alone, as if all else in experience arose from it, has been misleading.

When one looks in experience for evidence that there has been a past, the first thing that presents itself for consideration is memory. One may say that she knows there has been a past because she remembers some of it. But how strong is this evidence? David Hume argued that the content of memory is like the content of present sense experience, only less vivid. The presence of a less vivid sense-like experience does not seem strong evidence for a past. Furthermore, we know that we are sometimes simply mistaken, thinking that something is a memory that, in fact, is not. We should not dismiss this kind of memory from relevance to the question, but particular memories of particular past events seem less certain than that there has been a past. We can reluctantly concede that we are mistaken about the past without doubting that there has been a past. Indeed, the recognition that we may be mistaken presupposes that there is a past to be mistaken about.

I shall call the kind of memory considered above "recall" or recollection and contrast with that "immediate memory." As one hears the completion of a musical phrase, one does not recall the beginning of the phrase. The experience of the end of the phrase is just that; it is not the experience of an isolated sound, which one then interprets as connected to sounds that one recalls. If the latter were the case, then there would be no music. The hearing of the beginning of the phrase is still operative in the experience of the end of the phrase. This recent experience is functioning within the present experience.

The same is true when we hear a word. While hearing the end of a word, we do not recall the hearing of the beginning of the word and then engage in a complex process of connecting the two. If we did, there would be no language. The experience of hearing the beginning of the word is still alive when we are hearing the end of the word. Indeed, this is true for phrases, clauses, and whole sentences, but the single word will do to make the argument. As we hear the end of the word we know there has been a past because that past is still functioning, and functioning as past, in the present.

This functioning of the immediate past in the present is so foundational to experience that no one does or can genuinely doubt that there has been a past. I am sure that Russell did not doubt it, even when he could find no reason for rejecting the denial of the past.

I have focused on immediate past experience and the way it continues to be present in the present. My argument against Hume is that past experience is not present as a fainter sense experience; it is present as past. I will add one other feature of experience generally: the experience of the body.

By experience of the body I do not mean the visual or tactile experience of the body. That exists and is important, but the body as experienced through the senses can be treated in the same way as other data of sense experience. I mean, instead, a much more immediate sense of embodiment and of having one's experience informed by that embodiment. In visual experience instead of concentrating on the seen objects, it is better for these purposes to concentrate on the role of the eye. I find that I can hardly doubt that my enjoyment of vision depends on the functioning of the eye. I have introduced "hardly" here because I can imagine hallucinations in which the eye is not functioning when I might suppose it was. Similarly, there can be imaginary toothaches. One could generalize from these possibilities to the possibility that my experience is not dependent on the body at all; yet it is doubtful that anyone can really believe this. Even though there are possibilities of error at every point, the overwhelming sense that our experience derives from the body, just as it derives from past experience, remains. We know we have bodies, not primarily because we discover them through sense experience but because they are the agents of sense experience and of much other experience besides. Our bodies are present in our experience in much the same way as is our past experience.

What does this mean for epistemology? It means that deep-seated assumptions of much epistemological reflection should be rejected. These assumptions, in general, depict the knowing agent as self-enclosed. They picture a clear distinction between what is within the experience and what is external to it. This distinction leads to many baneful conclusions, inevitably pressing toward solipsism. A more accurate account of experience, in Whitehead's view and mine, presents it as inclusive of events other than itself. For Whitehead an experience is an event, and every unit event is an instance of the many becoming one. The many are not external to the one. If they were, then they would remain forever unknown to the one. The many events, past personal experiences and bodily events primarily, participate in making the experience what it is.

The issue of correspondence appears very different in this context from how it is usually presented. The past by its presence imposes some conformity with it. The experience of the beginning of the word when I hear the end of it must conform in some measure to what I heard a moment ago. The conformity is not perfect, but the basic order of the world and of human experience is a function of some considerable measure of correspondence. There is a truth relation between the way a past moment functions in the present and what it was when it was the present.

III

I have emphasized that a great deal in philosophy depends on what features of experience are selected for analysis and what examples one considers. In the development of theories of truth, the example of the relation of an element in one moment of experience to immediately past experiences has not, in general, been in view. Hence when Whiteheadians discuss epistemology they seem to others to be changing the subject. If we are to engage others where they are, then we must also discuss their examples. These examples, such as statements about green grass, however, are from a Whiteheadian point of view immensely complex, so that the question of there being any correspondence between the statement and something existing objectively cannot be easily answered. To say either "Yes" or "No" would be misleading. Still, we must move toward relevance to the more usual discussion.

Consider a situation in which there is miscommunication between two people. Suppose a woman says, "You told me to turn right." A man replies, "No! I told you to turn at the light." The woman might then reply,"Oh! I heard you say 'right.'" Is truth as correspondence relevant here?

When the woman first spoke, she believed her statement corresponded to what had actually been said. When the man replied, she accepted the likelihood that she was mistaken. She then made a statement about her own past experience. This statement very likely corresponds to the experience she recalls.

This simple example brings up a very central question: What can it mean to say that a statement corresponds to an experience? A statement is one kind of thing, and experience another. This problem does not always arise; for example, the man may be correct or incorrect in what he now says he then said. Two sentences or statements can correspond without raising the question now before us. For there to be correspondence between a sentence and an experience, however, there must be some mediation between a linguistic entity and the auditory aspect of an event. The mediating element in Whitehead's thinking is what he calls "propositions."

A proposition is not itself a linguistic entity. It is the actual or possible relation between some event and some form that event may or may not have embodied. In the preceding example there is a relation between a past event in the woman's life and hearing a particular pattern of sounds, namely, "turn right." She is at present entertaining the proposition that in her past experience she heard "turn right." Much of any human experience can be analyzed in terms of the propositions it entertains.

The example above is of a proposition that is verbally expressed. Only a few, however, of the many propositions that are entertained in any moment come to expression in language. For example, at the same time that the woman is articulating a proposition about her earlier experience, she may be feeling that the man is being abrupt or rude. She says nothing about this, even to herself. This proposition, like the one she articulates, is either true or false.

Whether a proposition is true or false is not the most important thing about it. In this case even if the man is not really being abrupt or rude, the fact that she believes he is has consequences for her feelings and behavior. One of Whitehead's oft-quoted statements is that it is more important that a proposition be interesting than that it be true. If a proposition does not hold some interest, then it is not likely to come to expression in language.

One major function of language is to express propositions and to direct the attention of others to them. The word "I" indicates a particular past occasion of the woman's experience. "Heard you say 'right'" identifies a pattern that may or may not have been illustrated in that occasion. The statement as a whole evokes attention to the possibility that the event in question had the character specified. This possibility may or may not correspond to the character actually possessed by the event. The claim is that it does.

Ordinarily, the conversation would end there. That the proposition about the woman's past experience that was evoked in the man's mind corresponded to the actual hearing would probably be accepted. But this might not be so. Perhaps the question of whether the woman had made an honest mistake was important for legal reasons, or the woman's ability to remember simple instructions was at issue. It would become important to decide whether the proposition evoked by the woman's statement was true or false. The question then arises as to whether correspondence plays any role in testing the claim to correspond.

Correspondence cannot identify the only method of testing, although if the woman herself is unsure, then its role may be considerable. She may have ways of reliving the original experience. As she heightens its vividness in recollection she can compare it with the proposition. This may lead to growing doubt or increasing confidence about the correspondence in question. Even if others are suspicious of the woman's account, it would be wrong to exclude something close to correspondence in the checking. She might be hypnotized and invited to relive the experience in that condition.

Even in these cases that provide some comparison of the proposition and the event, other factors are present. The woman's belief that through certain disciplines or psychological techniques she can bring back the past event with greater fullness and reliability is connected with other experiences she has had and, in a very sketchy way, with her entire worldview. That the event as now more vividly recalled corresponds with the event as it initially took place cannot itself be checked by correspondence. It must be accepted because of its coherence with other beliefs and experiences and, perhaps, through pragmatic success in other instances. The evidence from hypnosis would be even more clearly bound up with pragmatic and coherence considerations.

If the issue were being considered by a jury and hypnosis were not allowed, then what kind of testing would be possible? Here correspondence would fade to the background. Nevertheless, it is likely that the major question in the jurors' minds would be the honesty of the woman and her clarity of recall. How will they decide such questions? They will want to learn all they can about the woman's character and memory as reflected in other situations. They will be interested in her mental condition at the time of the incident and in any possible motives for deception. They will finally reach their decision in terms of the coherence of the woman's account with everything else they know about her, and they will judge this coherence in the context of their total life experience. Coherence dominates. But does that exclude correspondence? I think not. In complex ways correspondence pervades the entire proceedings. Perhaps it comes out most clearly in the final decision. In judging whether the woman's correctness in her story is more or less coherent with all the other evidence, one crucial element is a decision as to which pattern of assumptions corresponds better with the way human beings have come to be understood through one's own life experience.

The above discussion illustrates how inextricably intertwined are coherence and correspondence in the process of judging correspondence. The example is one-sided, however, in that it has failed to lift pragmatic considerations to prominence. Actually, Whitehead treats such considerations as primary, although not ultimate or exclusive.

As I glance around the room I entertain many propositions, most of which I do not articulate even silently. I judge one object to be a chair, another, a refrigerator, another, a table, another, a glass, and yet another, an apple. I am not testing any of these judgments. I have inherited them from the past. Basically, I accept them now because similar judgments have oriented me to my environment and led me to actions that accomplished their purposes. The pragmatic success of these judgments has led me to appropriate them and is the main reason I hold them to be true. This is so pervasive that Whitehead says his theory of truth could almost be taken to be a pragmatic one.

Nevertheless, "almost" means "not quite," and that is because pragmatic considerations cannot finally be divorced from coherence and correspondence. Particular judgments would not work well if they did not cohere with the others. Furthermore, the pragmatic test involves correspondence. Consider my judgment that a particular object I see is a table. That judgment results from the fact that judging certain visual patterns to represent or express tables has worked for me in the past. Right now I am not testing my judgment by its correspondence to anything. But at times in the past I have tested the expectations aroused by judging an object to be a table in relation to the experience I have had with it. Often there has been correspondence between expectation and outcome.

I will go at last to the immensely complex example, "The grass is green." What can that mean, and how can it be tested?

The questions must be asked in that order. We cannot discuss how to test a proposition until we know what the proposition is. Any linguistic expression can express and evoke a variety of propositions. It did not seem important to point out this added complexity in the previous examples, but here it is inescapable.

To say that the grass is green may mean that when persons who are not color-blind look in a certain place, under favorable lighting conditions, they will see green. This proposition can be tested fairly easily for its correspondence to actual experience. Such a test will involve the kind of mixture of coherence and correspondence discussed in relation to the previous example. But let us suppose that the propositions intended and evoked are not about observers but about the entities denominated "grass." Are there any such propositions, or is the speaker simply confused?

If the speaker intends that the grass is visually enjoying the color green, then an intelligible but absurd proposition is available for consideration. Whitehead contemplates another possible meaning sympathetically. He thinks the proposition might mean that the grass "feels greenly." Such a proposal has many assumptions that are worked out in detail by Whitehead. For one thing, it entails that the events, constituting what we call grass, consist in relations with other events that fundamentally resemble the relations of human experiences to other experiences. These relations can be called feelings, and feelings have both objective data and subjective forms. "Greenly" would then designate the subjective form of some of the feelings making up these events.

What can be meant by "greenly" when it cannot have reference to the objectified color given to human beings through vision? White-head believes that these objectified colors are products of human creativity that give expression through the mode of vision to sub-jective forms of human feelings. More foundational in human ex-perience than objectified colors, although far less clearly conscious, are emotional tones expressed in them. Whitehead thinks it possi-ble that there is some conformation of the emotional tone in human experience, as derived from the physical impact of the grass upon it, and the subjective form of feeling in the grass cells. If so, then the state-ment that the grass is green may be evoking a true proposition about the grass.

How could the truth of such a proposition be determined? The answer is, In no way, if by "determined" one means settled in a definitive manner. For Whitehead that does not prevent the proposi-tion from being either true or false, because the meaning of truth and falsity is not a function of how propositions are tested. It does mean, however, that it would not be wise to rely upon the statement's truth and draw conclusions from it. Such statements lie at the extreme limit of speculation. This one can be shown to be consistent with the rest of Whitehead's speculation, but its falsehood would also be consistent with it. Whitehead favors it out of deep aesthetic and religious feeling shared with some of the Romantic poets and, less vividly, with the rest of us. To trust such intuitions provisionally is consistent with Whitehead's general understanding of the world and of human experience.

I have taken up this example, which stands at the extreme periph-ery of Whitehead's thought, to show how far the relevance of corre-spondence thinking can go. Much more natural to Whitehead would be emphasis on correspondence between personal experience and that of the cells in one's own body. In a toothache, for example, there is some conformation of personal feelings to those of the cells in the tooth and, therefore, some correspondence between them. One would expect this correspondence to be much greater than that with the cells in the grass, where the influence on us is so much more complexly mediated.

IV

To defend realism in the context of idealistic skepticism, I have focused on the correspondence theory of truth. In the process of defending this theory I have presupposed a particular form of realism. I acknowledged this circularity at the outset. I am convinced that the situation is the same for all epistemological arguments and I rejoice in the current critique of epistemological foundationalism. I only regret that it is often pictured as one more nail in the coffin of realism, rather than as reopening the way to realistic thinking.

As a final defense of the Whiteheadian form of realism, I return to the point I made earlier. This form of realism provides large scope for the positive insight of idealism, that is, the creative activity of history, culture, thought, and language in shaping our worlds.

The real events that make up the world are all di-polar, physical and mental. In human beings, mentality is of very great importance. Thus far I have emphasized the physical pole because this is where conformation takes place, where the body and our own past experiences jointly constitute us as what we are. Although they are inexorable and extremely important constituents of our being in every moment, we are always more than simply the resultant of the causal efficacy of the past. This "more" is our mental pole, which dominates our conscious life so fully that it has hidden from many philosophers the very reality of our physicality. Most of the positive contributions of idealistic thinkers can be appreciated and appropriated as clarifying how human mentality has shaped the human world. What I so strongly oppose is the idea that, in that shaping process, human mentality has created that world ex nihilo or out of itself alone, that there is no physical reality utterly requisite to human experience and formative of the human world. When the physical is denied or neglected, the nature of the mental is profoundly misunderstood.

One danger is that when the physical is acknowledged at all it is viewed as mere matter. The ancient dualism is alive and well among many who in theory reject it. For Whitehead what is mental in one moment becomes physical in the next, inextricably intertwined with what is always physical. There are no merely physical events and no merely mental ones. To treat mentality apart from physicality or physicality apart from mentality is always to abstract. Abstractions are legitimate, but when one forgets the degree of abstraction involved, the results are destructive.

To some idealists, realists seem to claim that their thought escapes the historical conditionedness that contemporary idealists rightly emphasize. They are correct that realists point to features of experience that do not seem to be historically conditioned—features that people share with other animals, for example. The realist, however, should not claim that the conviction that these exist arose anywhere other than in the specific historical situation in which they find themselves. Every word we use and every attitude we express is historically conditioned. The question is, What does that mean? If the worlds we create are created ex nihilo, then it means that our ideas are not about anything at all, except other ideas. If the worlds we create are created out of physical reality, including but not exhausted by the reality of past thinking, then there are common elements underlying and referred to in all our worlds, even though any effort to identify them is caught up in the historical conditionedness of language. As a realist I believe that all people are embodied; that all bodies are composed of cells, many of which are alive; and that these cells require food. I believe that any cultural-linguistic system that discourages attention to these matters or directs human activity away from the procuring of food will self-destruct. I am, however, sure that many cultural-linguistic systems are very different from one another but equally encourage the necessary physical activities that sustain life. Even my belief that human beings need food to live is culturally learned. Still, I believe that some of what is learned culturally and is, in this sense, relative is learned in all cultures and, in another sense, is not significantly determined by cultural particularity. These beliefs also are culturally learned, and so on and so on.

More important, I think, is the recognition that the adoption of realistic thinking places one in one circle of thinking and the adoption of idealistic thinking places one in another. The understanding of everything, including relativism and historicism, is affected. Individual realists or idealists may affirm the rightness of their basic choice more or less dogmatically or with more or less humility and recognition of the ultimate relativity of this choice. Perhaps realists are more guilty of arrogance than idealists. In a scholarly world, however, in which our numbers are so few, we cannot but recognize the possibility that we are wrong and the majority correct. Perhaps that adds to the fervor of our arguments. That fervor does not mean that we deny the relativity of our thinking.

V

For theologians such as Kaufman and myself, the issue of idealism and realism comes to a particularly important focus on the doctrine of God. In contemporary theology, many develop their anthropologies and even their doctrines of history and nature in ways that appear realistic, even when one expects them to abjure on principle any claim to correspondence. It often turns out that the arguments for idealism are really applied with rigor only to certain doctrines, of which the doctrine of God is most central and decisive.

Although some of those who work in this way are not consistent, the distinction is also one that can be made consistently. It can be argued that we have the possibility, in relation to history and nature, of formulating descriptions that do, in some measure, correspond to the reality of the things described, but that this is impossible with respect to God. This may be either because God is pure mystery or because God is only a human projection or construct.

Until this point, my argument about realism is open to either of these directions in relation to God. I have been talking about the reality of past experience, the body, other people, and the natural world in general. It is quite possible to believe all that and to believe that is all, or to believe that whatever else there may be is wholly unknowable. Among realists influenced by Whitehead, there are diverse opinions on this point. Nevertheless, Whitehead and the majority of his theological followers extended his realism to the affirmation of a real God. There can be no question but that this cuts against the grain of modern sensibility, whether idealist, materialist, or relativist, and that it has put off many who might otherwise have been attracted to Whitehead. For those like myself, however, who believe that vital Christian faith will not long survive the death of belief in a reality that can be trusted and is worthy of worship, this move by Whitehead adds greatly to his theological interest.

With what degree of confidence should one make affirmations about God? The choice of realism in general cannot involve certainty, and even given that starting point, there are many other uncertain choices to be made. I follow Whitehead in having considerable confidence in the judgment that the past is effectively present in my present experience. At the other extreme, I gave the example of

Whitehead's belief, acknowledged by him as an act of faith, that there is some conformation of our feeling derived from the grass to the way the grass feels. The degree of confidence that I can attach to God's reality falls somewhere between these extremes.

Despite sustained efforts, no one has yet been able to develop a coherent exposition of Whitehead's cosmology that excises altogether something that renders possibility effective and directive in the world. Whitehead initially called this persistent presence of possibility the Principle of Limitation or the Principle of Concretion. Convinced as I am that Whitehead's conceptuality has extraordinary explanatory power, as well as correspondence at relevant points to my own experience, I believe that Whitehead was correct in concluding that this doctrine was needed.

If Whitehead had stopped there, I doubt that he would have aroused much hostility. Metaphysicians are allowed a few principles! Whitehead, however, judged that what he called the Principle of Limitation was what had been called God by some and other names by other religious people. This claim led to the complex development of the doctrine of God by Whitehead and some of his followers. Whitehead stated that what more was to be said of God must be learned from religious experience, and although philosophical and religious considerations are intertwined throughout his development of the doctrine, this point should be kept in mind. In Whitehead's view, religious experience has not been pure projection but is highly conditioned by cultural and historical factors. His own interpretation of the evidence of this religious experience and his formulation of what God is in light of this evidence are also highly conditioned. Hence much of what he said about God is analogous more to his faith that the complex mediation of the influence of the grass to our experience does not entirely disconnect the two qualitatively than to a woman's memory of what she heard a few minutes earlier. As in the case of the greenness of the grass, he appeals to exceptional experience and develops an argument for what may be. He understands much of this process as more like poetry than hard philosophy, if there really is any such thing as the latter. There is no reason for anyone to follow him unless her experience and religious sensibility correspond somewhat to his.

By contrast, there is no reason to reject Whitehead's speculations simply because they go so far beyond what most moderns are willing to acknowledge. We should be skeptical of making skepticism into a primary virtue. For me, in general if not in every detail, Whitehead provides the most powerful and convincing vision of God I have found. Hence I am a Whiteheadian theist. I am sure, however, that others with different temperaments and different life experiences could agree to the metaphysical Principle of Limitation and then honestly assert that this has nothing to do with what they understand God to be. I am sure that none of our affirmations will be true, if by true one means in perfect conformity to what is; but I also doubt that many of us will be totally wrong, if that means holding beliefs that have no correspondence at all with the way reality is. I also believe in gaining as much correspondence as possible between our thought about God and the way reality is.

How can one possibly formulate responsible judgments of what ideas correspond better or worse to divine reality? In the same way, I think, as one makes other such judgments. Whitehead began with considerations of coherence, but his conclusions from the requirements of coherence can in some measure be tested both pragmatically and in terms of correspondence. One is led to expect that, because a human experience is one of those events within which the Principle of Limitation is working, this principle will have discernible effects in such an event. Whitehead finds these effects in the emergence of novel order and ordered novelty and, in particular, in the sense of a rightness in things that is partly realized and partly missed. This sense has often been connected with religious experience; it is connected with my own.

I have found another confirmatory fact to which Whitehead did not point me. For Whitehead it was important to distinguish the Principle of Limitation from creativity. He did not note that creativity has also played an important role in human religious experience and life. As I have interacted with Buddhists, however, I have found that much of what they say about what is for them ultimate reality (or nonreality), namely, dependent origination, depicts this ultimate in the same way Whitehead depicted his ultimate, creativity. Most Buddhists, like Whitehead, are sure that this is not God. They either deny that there is anything like a Principle of Limitation or discourage attention to such matters. As a result, they do not thematically consider ordered novelty or novel order or a rightness in things that is partly realized and partly missed. The sense of history and the type of ethical reflection related to these dimensions of human experience are poorly developed in Buddhism, in comparison with the biblical faiths that focus on God. By contrast, the implications of realizing that we are instances of creativity are developed with great richness in a way hardly imagined in the biblical faiths and quite unanticipated by Whitehead. As I reflect on these matters, I find pragmatic value in his conceptuality, elements of correspondence with my experience, and growth toward coherence. I am disinclined to give up realistic thinking about God.

10

Communities
of Collaboration:
Shared Commitments/Common Tasks

GEORGE RUPP

Gordon Kaufman is a Mennonite and a woodworker. No doubt other features of his identity figure more prominently in the usual characterizations of his career. But his background in Anabaptism and his avocation as a carpenter epitomize what I take to be central preoccupations of his life and thought.

Those preoccupations revolve around the themes of community and work. That work is central to his identity no one who knows Kaufman would deny—whether the work is the construction of a theological argument or the fashioning of a piece of furniture. Similarly, notwithstanding the abundance of his individual energy and productivity, the crucial role of participation in communities of shared commitment is evident throughout his personal and professional involvements.

In view of that twofold set of preoccupations, in this essay in honor of Kaufman I will examine the themes of community and work. First, I will sketch how a sense of community has emerged as a challenge to be addressed and a goal to be achieved, rather than as simply a state of affairs to be celebrated not only in the modern West but also in, for example, China, Africa, and India. Second, I will note the complex interconnections between our situation today and those religious and secular movements that have developed an ideal of community as in principle universal, rather than one based on particular ethnic or geographical qualifications. Third, I will turn to a domain of experience that has traditionally provided solid grounding for community, namely, work; I will argue that this grounding has been undermined in modern secular societies as acceptance of employment in an occupation has displaced a sense of vocation. Fourth and finally, I will explore how the shared commitment expressed through participation in common tasks may still help to capture a sense of community that is viable in contemporary pluralistic societies.

BEYOND BLOOD AND SOIL

The prominence of the theme of community in contemporary literature and social commentary testifies to the deep sense of its lack, at least in the consciousness of cultural elites in the modern West. This sense of absence or loss all too often indulges in not only nostalgia for an idealized past but also inattention to the continuing power of traditional communities. Both forms of indulgence should be resisted; but such resistance must not be allowed to obscure the contrast between large-scale, mobile, urban, and pluralistic societies, on the one hand, and small, settled, rural, and religiously and ethnically homogeneous communities, on the other hand.

This contrast is so frequently evoked that it is difficult to avoid a barrage of platitudes and stereotypes. The bedrock virtues of the small town and country are corrupted in the big city. Mutual support and respect among individuals are supplanted by anonymous bureaucratic programs. Personal trust, shared responsibility, and cooperative effort surrender to impersonal market forces, and so forth.

To deflect such popular stereotypes, academic discussion has adopted a not infrequently used stratagem: dress up the distinction in the garb of jargon, perhaps using foreign words, preferably German ones—in this instance, *Gemeinschaft* and *Gesellschaft*. This distinction has become a fixture of social theory since its elaborate treatment in Ferdinand Tönnies's 1887 book, titled *Gemeinschaft und Gesellschaft*.[1] The terms themselves, however, also have a rich prior history in philosophical discussions and a continuing currency as ordinary German words. To claim that all those uses—in late nineteenth- and twentieth-century social theory, in prior philosophical discussions, and in ordi-

1. Ferdinand Tönnies, *Community and Society* (*Gemeinschaft und Gesellschaft*), ed. and trans. Charles P. Loomis (East Lansing: Michigan State University Press, 1957).

nary German—are the same would no doubt be to oversimplify egregiously. Nevertheless, each use of the distinction identifies features of the contrast also expressed in the platitudes and stereotypes of small town versus city, intimate community versus bureaucratic society, personal bond versus impersonal market. In this overall sense intellectual reflection and popular wisdom agree in stressing a fundamental divide between traditional communities and modern bureaucratic societies.

To pose the contrast in those terms identifies both ends of a spectrum, which means that many communities, both in the past and today, illustrate points between the two extremes. But the bonds of community certainly assume different forms depending on where on the spectrum a society falls. Furthermore, because "community" is so often construed, consciously or unconsciously, as small, settled, rural, and homogeneous, it is sensed as lacking insofar as a society is large in scale, mobile, urban, and pluralistic.

This sense of deficiency correctly identifies the fact that, for modern pluralistic societies, common bonds cannot simply be taken for granted. The implied contrast is also defensible: in more traditional communities there are such taken-for-granted bonds because of close proximity over long periods of time. Mobility and anonymity first loosen and then often break ties that depend on genealogy and geography, on blood and soil. That such common bonds cannot be taken for granted does not in itself justify the conclusion that there is no sense of community in modern pluralistic societies, but it does focus attention on the extent to which a sense of participation in community is an achievement, not a given.

In modern Western societies, the loosening of natural bonds need not be belabored. When more and more people move frequently from one urban area to another, they do not have the investment, either personal or financial, in one particular place. When work and leisure alike are widely dispersed, elaborate networks of acquaintances often replace direct contact with close friends and immediate neighbors. Similarly, impersonal bureaucracies and markets displace personal relationships as the media through which information is transmitted and products and services are distributed. Connections among members of even a nuclear family are strained because distance in both geography and culture is more the rule than the exception and members of extended families rarely remain in close proximity to each other over multiple generations. In short, in the modern West the ties of blood are severely attenuated and the common ground of soil is seriously eroded.

Outside the modern West, the bonds of blood and soil may continue to hold communities together effectively, but the challenge to traditional ties is evident there as well. The threat to the traditional power of the extended family in postrevolutionary China—regardless of whether the threat is associated with state-sponsored social planning or with private enterprise—is a graphic example. Another is the tension between tribal affiliation and citizenship in postindependence African countries. Those issues are in significant part the result of intrusions from the West—for example, the impact of and resistance to communism in China and the imposition on Africa of geographical divisions from the colonial era. Nevertheless, the result remains a challenge to traditional patterns of small, stable, and homogeneous community.

India offers an especially arresting instance of such crosscurrents. In traditional India the bonds of village and caste are strong indeed. But those bonds have been under sustained pressure in India from the colonial era on. The intellectual traditions, legal patterns, and commercial practices of the British Empire have provided an alternative framework that does not depend directly on intra-Indian ethnic, linguistic, religious, or caste distinctions.

More crucial for postindependence India is that indigenous leaders in turn have also resisted the centrifugal forces of ethnic, linguistic, religious, and caste differences. Even Gandhi, with his commitment to village life and simple technologies and his criticism of urbanization and industrialization, insisted on a nation united under a secular constitution that precludes discrimination on the basis of religion, language, or caste. This insistence became integral to the policies of postindependence India as Nehru led the country toward democratic socialism and a secularism that grounds legal rights on universal appeals to the human as such, rather than on membership in one or another particular community.

As Leroy Rouner argues in *To Be at Home: Civil Religion, Human Community and the Christian Hope*, Gandhi, Nehru, and their colleagues in the Indian independence movement drew on both Western and indigenous traditions to develop what became a new and unified sense of identity for India, an identity that consciously attempts to incorporate traditional communities yet also moves beyond their mutually exclusive and antagonistic claims.[2] This movement emphatically imbued its adherents with a sense of participation in a vital community. Like Western societies, however, India today faces the continuing challenge of sustaining the power of such inclusive senses of community in a modern secular state that may have weakened, although it has not entirely displaced, traditional loyalties.

THE IDEAL OF UNIVERSAL COMMUNITY

The example of India is instructive in a double sense. It illustrates the tensions between the claims of traditional communities and the requirements of large-scale societies, but it demonstrates as well that a movement convinced of its own historical significance may generate a powerful sense of shared identity among its participants.

This development is evident not only in the forging of national identities but also in transnational or universalizing movements that have shaped the modern world. The most striking instances of such movements are the great missionary religions, Buddhism, Christianity, and Islam, and their secular counterpart, Marxism. In each case the goal of the movement is a finally universal community, based on commitment, allegiance, or solidarity rather than exclusively on natural bonds.

No doubt a crucial source of their power is that such religious or secular movements may themselves be expressed or embodied in compelling and, at least initially, intimate communities. Although such a movement may have a goal that is universal in scope, it offers its members a sense of belonging to a community set over against the larger society, the vanguard of what is destined to be a new order. Indeed, the attraction of membership in a community that is in principle inclusive can be crucial for the capacity of missionary religious movements to draw adherents from established alternative traditions, as for example, John Gager in his *Kingdom and Community*[3] has argued in the case of early Christianity.

Although universalizing religious and secular movements may generate their own sense of community, they are nevertheless wit-

2. Leroy Rouner, *To Be at Home: Civil Religion, Human Community and the Christian Hope* (Boston: Beacon Press, 1991), 75–95.
3. John G. Gager, *Kingdom and Community: The Social World of Early Christianity* (Englewood Cliffs, N.J.: Prentice-Hall, 1975).

tingly or unwittingly implicated in the fate of the traditional communities they encounter. In some cases missionary movements in effect become assimilated by the ties of blood and soil. The result is that missionary impulses become enmeshed in traditional mores, as can be seen in the role of caste in predominantly Buddhist villages of Sri Lanka or the role of so-called animism in African Christianity. This result may be applauded as the legitimate and even unavoidable indigenization of a global tradition in a particular location or attacked as uncritical acquiescence to established practices. Either way there is recognition of an assimilation of the missionary movement by the patterns of traditional communities.

In contrast to this tacit support of traditional communities are cases in which religious or secular movements are so intertwined with the origins and structures of large-scale modern societies that they contribute, at least indirectly, to the undermining of traditional communities. The relationship of the Christian missionary movement to Western colonial rule in Asia, Africa, and Latin America not infrequently, perhaps even characteristically, illustrates this tendency, as does the development of Marxism from a revolutionary movement to the officially established political credo of powerful modern states.

Thus universalizing religious and secular movements have multiple complex and even conflicting relations to both terms of the distinction between traditional communities and modern societies. There certainly are cases of both unconscious assimilation and intentional indigenization in the relations of such movements to traditional communities. Similarly, their interlocked histories preclude any clear separation between modern societies on the one hand and movements like Christianity and Marxism on the other hand. Still, in and through the complex and even conflicting interconnections, universalizing religious and secular movements have aspired to embody an ideal of community different in principle from both the given bonds of blood and soil and the taken-for-granted relationships of modern societies.

This conception of a community that is open and, in intention, inclusive has fundamentally shaped human sensibilities worldwide. It is affirmed and then presupposed, not only in missionary religions like Buddhism, Christianity, and Islam and in secular movements like Marxism but also in a host of other voluntary associations and international organizations. This ideal of inclusive community provides critical leverage over against both the provincialism of traditional communities and the complacency of established social order. As such, it is a crucial resource for all who recognize that a return to the intimacy, homogeneity, and stability of traditional communities is not feasible but who also cannot wholeheartedly celebrate the domination of modern pluralistic societies by the impersonal processes of markets and bureaucracies.

Yet despite its power in shaping human sensibilities worldwide, universal community frequently remains little more than an attractive abstraction. It may on occasion be embodied in intimate religious communities or politically vital groups, usually for a brief period and on a small scale. The ideal of universal community may also become institutionalized in more established and longer-term forms. In those forms, however, it all too often fails to generate a sense of intimate and vital belonging, even among those who affirm it ardently. Here international organizations promoting human welfare or voluntary associations dedicated to human rights face the same dilemma that confronts Christianity and Marxism. Pursuit of the ideal of universal community becomes so entangled with the market mechanisms and bureaucratic processes of large-scale modern societies that a sense of lively participation in a shared community is all but lost.

This complex set of historical relationships is the pervasively influential, if seldom recognized, background for contemporary participation in particular institutional expressions of the ideal of universal community, whether those institutional embodiments are small and cohesive groups, such as a house church or a neighborhood housing co-op, or broader-based organizations, such as Amnesty International or UNICEF. Such groups and organizations are a crucial arena in which the struggle to realize community in modern societies is waged. Especially in view of the odds against that struggle, we should no doubt participate vigorously in the efforts of bodies or associations committed to representing the ideal of universal community. Important as it is, however, this participation cannot by itself bear the full burden of our response to the challenge of realizing a sense of community in modern pluralistic societies.

Instead of placing the full burden on groups or organizations that are almost unavoidably marginal in the lives of most participants other than their full-time employees, we must assign a substantial share of the load to our central activities. For us, as for our forebears, that means our love and our work. Few would question that our intimate personal relationships fundamentally shape our sense of participation in shared community—even if, or all the more because, those relationships are under great stress. In contrast, the centrality of work may be more disputable. The frustrations of often routinized jobs together with shorter work weeks and substantial discretionary income mean that leisure activities play a significant role for increasing numbers of people. But important as love and leisure may be, they offer a precarious base for community if there is no sense of satisfaction from work.

FROM VOCATION TO OCCUPATION

The centrality of work to our sense of participation in community is evident across an impressive range of times and places. Bands of hunters in tribal Africa join together in pursuing their common task. In traditional India caste and occupation reflect and reinforce each other. In revolutionary China work groups provide an important basis for collective identity. In contemporary Japan a sense of belonging and mutual responsibility is imbued at various levels of corporate activity, from quite small quality circles to entire large firms.

This centrality of work to individual and corporate identity has a complex history in modern Western societies. Secular developments that often serve to undermine the foundations of traditional communities are themselves grounded in religious conceptions of vocation. We may not accept every point that Max Weber argues in *The Protestant Ethic and the Spirit of Capitalism*, but we can scarcely gainsay the impact of first the Lutheran and then, even more, the Calvinist insistence that worldly work no less than religious vocation is a divine calling.[4]

Modern Western societies have moved far from the position of the Protestant Reformers, albeit in the direction that the Reformers indicated. In its Reformation expressions, the dignifying of ordinary labor pointed to a way of uniting worship and work, of imbuing work with such significance that it contributed to the sanctification of the world and the glorification of God. Celebration of the priesthood of all believers and the interpretation of worldly work as a response to divine calling engendered disciplined activity and careful calibration of

4. Max Weber, *The Protestant Ethic and the Spirit of Capitalism*, trans. Talcott Parsons (New York: Charles Scribner's Sons, 1958), esp. 79–128.

achievements as signs of God's grace. Over time, however, this inner-worldly asceticism, to use Weber's term, was increasingly severed from its religious roots. Disciplined activity and careful calibration of achievements continued, in some cases still construed consciously or assumed unconsciously to be expressions of divine favor; but the long-term effect was the advancement and legitimation of the thorough secularization of economic life.

This economic secularization is at the core of the development of those institutional forms that distinguish modern societies from traditional communities. Transactions mediated through impersonal mechanisms—markets and bureaucracies—replace direct personal contact; *Gesellschaft* displaces *Gemeinschaft*. In such simplified polar contrasts there undeniably lurks the danger of nostalgia for an idealized and irretrievable sense of intimate community, a nostalgia expressed in both reactionary and utopian forms. Despite that danger, however, the contrasts do register an accurate measure of critical deficiencies in the understanding of work in modern secular societies.

The total reduction of ends to means, or at least the complete domination of ends by means, extracts human action from contexts of meaning that afford a sense of accomplishment and satisfaction larger than the one entailed in the discrete acts themselves. To testify with the Protestant Reformers that work contributes to the sanctification of the world and the glorification of God may sound archaic or quaint. But the sense of connection to which this testimony bears witness is sorely needed when work no longer points beyond itself to more inclusive purposes that it participates in realizing—when, in short, work is reduced from vocation to occupation.

Not only in *The Protestant Ethic and the Spirit of Capitalism* but also in his influential writings on bureaucracy and other characteristic features of modern secular societies, Weber reflected on—not to say, brooded over—this set of issues. That Weber's thought provides a point of orientation for continuing discussions is evident, for example, in the way Jürgen Habermas summarizes the transition from traditional communities to modern societies. In his sketch Habermas also refers to more recent thinkers. Nevertheless, he develops his own position ultimately by reformulating the central Weberian concept of rationalization.

Habermas notes that in traditional communities economic activities presuppose a normative sociocultural framework and are conducted within the limits of the framework. This framework is grounded in unquestioned mythical, religious, or metaphysical interpretations of reality, which provide legitimation for economic and other subsystems of action. In short, a community is defined as traditional insofar as a normative sociocultural framework is superordinate to instrumental action in its various forms. In contrast, societies are more modern than traditional insofar as instrumental action extends its reach beyond previously established limits, calls into question traditional forms of authority, and, in effect, provides legitimation through its own productive power. The logical extreme of the modern society is "a fundamental reversal" in that a normative sociocultural framework no longer sets limits for all forms of instrumental action but is, instead, completely absorbed into them.[5]

Habermas affirms the reorganization of social institutions through the extension of subsystems of instrumental action and the attendant questioning of traditional authorities. To describe this process he adopts Weber's term, "rationalization." He also uses this concept in a second sense, namely, what he calls "rationalization at the level of the institutional framework." At this level, he urges a repoliticizing of decision-making, a renewed insistence on the distinction between the technical and the practical. Even as Habermas acknowledges and affirms the extension of subsystems of instrumental action, he calls for the reestablishment of a public context or framework for that action.[6]

As is evident in his adoption of the concept of rationalization, Habermas develops this line of reasoning in direct continuity with Weber's thought. He explicitly refers to Weber's analysis of *zweckrationale Aktion*, which I have rendered simply as instrumental action (rather than using a more literal but also cumbersome translation— "purposive-rational action," for example). Although Habermas presents his reformulation as going beyond what he characterizes as Weber's subjective approach, as attending more centrally to systems of action than to the meaning actors attribute to their actions, his description of the extension of subsystems of instrumental action is clearly an adaption of Weber's concept of rationalization.

Less explicitly continuous with Weber's thought is the second sense in which Habermas uses the concept of rationalization, namely, at the

---

5. See Jürgen Habermas, *Toward a Rational Society: Student Protest, Science, and Politics*, trans. Jeremy J. Shapiro (Boston: Beacon Press, 1970), esp. 94–107.
6. Ibid., 118–20.

sociocultural or normative level; but here, too, Weber is not far in the background. Such continuity is significant because it reinforces the shared resistance of Habermas and Weber to nostalgic idealizations of *Gemeinschaft* over against *Gesellschaft*. Weber's distinction between *Zweckrationalität* (purposive or instrumental rationality) and *Wertrationalität* (value or normative rationality) is well-known and often invoked. Less well known is his correlation of this distinction with the contrast between *Gemeinschaft* and *Gesellschaft*—or, to use Weber's preferred terms, *Vergemeinschaftung* and *Vergesellschaftung* (verbal nouns perhaps less susceptible to reification than Tönnies's simpler substantives). The concept of *Wertrationalität* may all too easily be invoked to represent the traditional framework that the *Zweckrationalität* of modernity undermines. Such an appeal would contrast with Habermas's focus on the need to reestablish a normative context or framework, albeit one that does not repudiate the extension of subsystems of instrumental action that characterizes modernity. Any appeal to *Wertrationalität* that aligns it simply with traditional communities over against modern society is, however, also at odds with Weber's own analysis.

In the opening sections of *Economy and Society*, the magnum opus left uncompleted at his death, Weber outlines a taxonomy of types of social action. He specifies four such types: instrumentally rational (*zweckrational*), value-rational (*wertrational*), affectual, and traditional.[7] This typology in turn structures the categorical scheme he develops to systematize such other issues as types of order or bases of legitimacy. Significant in regard to the question of a normative framework for posttraditional societies is the fact that he identifies not only instrumentally rational but also value-rational action with *Vergesellschaftung* rather than *Vergemeinschaftung*.[8]

Weber notes that his terminology draws a contrast similar to that which Tönnies draws. He develops the distinction, however, so as to emphasize more clearly than Tönnies did that communality (*Vergemeinschaftung*) and association (*Vergesellschaftung*) refer to ideal types—types that are evident in differing ratios in a diverse range of

7. Max Weber, *Economy and Society: An Outline of Interpretive Sociology*, ed. Guenther Roth and Claus Wittich, vol. 1 (New York: Bedminster Press, 1968), 24–26. Because much of the interpretation turns on verbal distinctions with no common English counterparts, cf. *Wirtschaft und Gesellschaft: Grundriss der verstehenden Soziologie*, ed. Johannes Winckelmann (Tübingen: J.C.B. Mohr [Paul Siebeck], 1956), 12–13.
8. Ibid., 1:40–43 (*Wirtschaft und Gesellschaft*, 21–23).

relationships. He also observes that, from the point of view of instrumentally rational action, value-rational action always appears to be irrational. Yet he nonetheless insists that value-rational action is a type of orientation that continues to be crucial in modern secular society—indeed, so much so that "orientation of action wholly to the rational achievement of ends without relation to fundamental values is . . . essentially only a limiting case."[9]

This excursus into the formulations of Habermas and Weber serves to sharpen the question confronting any reflection on work in modern secular societies. Work is virtually by definition instrumental action. Indeed, in distinguishing purposive-rational action from the normative institutional framework that he argues it presupposes and requires, Habermas uses the shorthand contrast of "work" and "interaction."[10] Although this reduction of work to instrumental action oversimplifies and is therefore regrettable, it nonetheless indicates how far secular attitudes toward work are from the conception of vocation, even among those who emphasize the need to reestablish a normative framework for publicly engaging policy alternatives in their practical as well as technical dimensions. Beyond this confirmation that for most members of modern secular societies the transition from vocation to occupation has long since been completed, the fact that work so clearly and centrally exemplifies instrumental action makes it an especially apt test case of whether and how such action may point beyond itself to more inclusive purposes that it participates in realizing.

SHARED COMMITMENTS/COMMON TASKS

Although work exemplifies virtually unalloyed instrumental action, it also offers distinctive strengths for addressing the question of community in contemporary pluralistic societies. Shared commitment that may be expressed through participation in common tasks does not unavoidably depend on particular ethnic or geographical qualifications. The sense of community that may eventuate from such shared commitments hence is not restricted to the bonds of traditional

9. Ibid., 1:26 (*Wirtschaft und Gesellschaft*, 13). A less expansive rendering of Weber's terse statement is "Absolute instrumental rationality of action is, however, also only in essence a heuristic (*konstuktiver*) limiting case."
10. Habermas, *Toward a Rational Society*, esp. 91–94.

communities. At the same time, the sense of community resulting from involvement in common tasks may be central to particular, concrete, mundane actualities in ways that movements devoted to the ideal of universal community often are not. Thus the sense of community associated with work may be especially well suited to modern pluralistic societies because it is particular or concrete, central to secular life, and yet also, in principle, nonexclusive.

Habermas rightly calls for a repoliticized decision-making as an antidote to the complete absorption of all normative considerations into subsystems of instrumental action. His appeal to unrestricted discussion, to undistorted communication is, however, in danger of being disconnected from those subsystems of instrumental action. Here Weber's sober insistence on integral relations between abstract ideals and concrete patterns of action is salutary. This emphasis is sharply expressed in his two late lectures on vocation. In "Politics as a Vocation" he dismisses those who indulge in "mystic flight from reality" because "they have not measured up to the world as it really is in its everyday routine." Similarly, in "Science [*Wissenschaft*] as a Vocation" he insists that even the most exalted work must meet "the demands of the day." In perhaps his most vivid image, he describes politics and allows it to exemplify every vocation: it is "a strong and slow boring of hard boards."[11]

In considering not only politics but especially work in its various expressions, I intentionally include subsystems of instrumental action that may not typically have a salient normative dimension. In the case of political deliberation, the connections between instrumental action and larger goals are integral to at least the rhetoric accompanying the process of decision-making. In contrast, in the case of much work that is executed within an established framework of markets and bureaucracies, even talk about more inclusive purposes may never occur.

It is easy to conjure up examples that register this point, albeit in ways that trade in stereotypes perhaps more characteristic of the past than the future: the utterly routinized labor of bored assembly-line workers in a manufacturing plant, of immigrant seamstresses in a sweatshop, of salesclerks meeting their quotas in a discount store, or of brokers pushing their investments over the phone. This routinization of labor is also evident in institutional settings that have explicit

11. Max Weber, *From Max Weber: Essays in Sociology,* trans. H. H. Gerth and C. Wright Mills (New York: Oxford University Press), 128, 156.

larger purposes. Hospitals may have many workers who execute routinized tasks that they deem to be only remotely connected to medical care or healing. These workers may be clerical staff who process forms, custodians who keep floors clean, or technicians who repair equipment; but they also may be health professionals whose assignments have become so specialized, so focused on technical proficiency, or so preoccupied with efficiency that they sense little connection to medical care or healing. So, too, in schools or in law offices the work not only of clerical, custodial, and technical staff but also of professionals may have become so absorbed into bureaucratic and market-oriented subsystems of action that any larger purposes recede to the periphery of awareness. An institution may have exalted general goals, but the pressing need to execute specific tasks is measured against very mundane standards that do not take those larger goals into direct account.

This situation, which we cannot but recognize as characteristic of virtually all large-scale institutions in our society, demands responses on at least two levels. First, we must ask whether and how in such large-scale institutional settings we may still attain a sense of community through an awareness of shared commitment to common tasks. Second, we must confront the need to assess the relative adequacy of the commitments and tasks that may foster this sense of community. In each case I will sketch an approach that I find promising, and in doing so, I will at the same time attempt to draw together the several lines of argument I have developed.

In his *Tales of a New America* Robert Reich formulates a concept that provides a helpful point of reference for this drawing together of the lines of argument I have developed. Reich calls this concept "collective entrepreneurialism" and elaborates it against the background of what he terms "the myth of the Triumphant Individual." This myth recounts the tale of twentieth-century American economic life as a drama that sets entrepreneurial heroes over against drone workers.

> Much of the political debate over economic policy tacitly or otherwise presupposed the existence of these two categories of activity: entrepreneurial and drone. In the popular mind, people were not fated for one or the other category; the distinction had nothing to do with class. Almost anyone could become an entrepreneur, with enough drive and daring. The economy needed both, of course—creative entrepreneurs to formulate the Big Ideas that would find their way into

new products and production techniques, and drones to undertake the routine chores involved in realizing these ideas. But for the economy to grow and prosper, it was presumed necessary to reward people who opted to become entrepreneurs and discipline those who remained drones.[12]

Against this characterization, Reich presents an orientation that he argues is more adequate for meeting the demands of the new global economy in which we unavoidably participate: "instead of a handful of lone entrepreneurs producing a few industry-making Big Ideas, innovation must be more continuous and collective."[13] Enterprises designed to reduce costs through mass production are organized in a series of hierarchical tiers, so that each superior can ensure that subordinates are working according to plan. In contrast, "collective entrepreneurialism" requires a relatively flat structure in which incremental advances are continuously discovered and applied so as to improve products and processes. Furthermore, because tasks are often so intertwined, success can be measured only in reference to the collective results of work groups or teams.[14]

Reich draws many of his analogies and illustrations from the achievements of Japanese firms in the ongoing process of elaboration and refinement of technical breakthroughs. He is aware, however, that there are many other instances of collective entrepreneurialism. In recent American experience examples include both "professional partnerships" and "small firms producing service-intensive goods." Professional partnerships include associations of lawyers, doctors, accountants, management consultants, architects, or even investment bankers, in which the value of the enterprise is almost exclusively a function of the knowledge and experience of its members. Similarly, in small firms producing service-intensive goods, experts in design, fabrication, and marketing form coalitions that involve few established routines and little hierarchy because all participants contribute to a common enterprise.[15]

Reich's conception of collective entrepreneurialism indicates an approach to attaining a sense of community even in contexts dominated by the impersonal processes of markets and bureaucracies. In

12. Robert B. Reich, *Tales of a New America: The Anxious Liberal's Guide to the Future* (New York: Random House, 1987), 109.
13. Ibid., 121.
14. Ibid., 125–26.
15. Ibid., 126–27.

large-scale institutions, groups or teams of colleagues may express shared commitments and identify with each other in executing common tasks. Members of such groups or teams need not and typically will not be related by family ties or geographical origins. Instead, they will collaborate on the basis of competencies that complement one another and are required for the task at hand. An example is what optimally would be the collaboration of doctors, nurses, technicians, clerical staff, the patient, and the patient's family in the setting of the hospital operating room and its supporting facilities. Other instances include: a research team in a university laboratory, a product development group in a corporation, a rescue squad responding to emergency calls, a construction team specializing in building rehabilitation, an investment banking group dealing in mergers and acquisitions, a sabotage strike force operating in hostile territory, and an organizing committee for a series of protest demonstrations.

Each such team, group, squad, force, or committee focuses on a common task and orders often very complex subsystems of instrumental action to realize the larger purpose that expresses the shared commitment of its members. All who have participated in such task forces know that collaboration in the work required can and does generate a sense of community. When shared commitment to an overall goal is explicit and strongly affirmed, the sense of community is especially intense. Even work that is very demanding or, alternatively, extremely tedious is then executed energetically and to high standards.

The challenge we face is to extend the contexts in which this sense of community through collaboration is attained. In this respect, less hierarchical organizational structures that value initiative and shared responsibility at all levels are a step in the right direction, as is the sustained effort to include a range of competencies and orientations in the group of collaborators. In the case of medical care, for example, the team will be more effective if and insofar as it includes not only doctors and nurses of diverse specialties but also medical technicians, clerical and other staff, and, very importantly, the patient and his or her family. Similarly, in colleges and universities the relatively flat organizational structure that we dignify as shared governance offers one model for more hierarchical organizations in our society. Accordingly, this commitment to collegiality and shared responsibility must be preserved and strengthened. At the same time, however, members of college and university communities as well as faculty must be incorporated with greater sensitivity and recognition into the team of collaborators.

Insofar as our work exemplifies such collaboration it may provide a sense not only of individual identity but also of participation in community, which is all the more crucial when a society is dominated by impersonal markets and bureaucracies. This sense of participation in community through one's work does not replace or render superfluous memberships in voluntary associations of all kinds, including those committed to an ideal of universal community. It does, however, offer the prospect, even within large-scale contemporary institutions, of expressing shared commitments in and through common tasks that are central to daily activities.

This prospect, in turn, calls for a response to the second question it is necessary to address in drawing together the lines of argument I have developed, namely, the question of the relative adequacy of the commitments and tasks that may indeed foster such a sense of community. This question derives unavoidably from the fact that not every shared commitment or common task is to be affirmed simply because it contributes to realizing a sense of community. The esprit de corps of Nazi storm troopers or the potent bonds of solidarity in crime families register this point sharply. Less melodramatic illustrations of the issue also demand attention: the task force formed to defeat a hostile corporate takeover bid, whose members become so engrossed in the intensity of the competition and the scale of the stakes that they bend legal restraints or ignore the legitimate interests of shareholders or other company employees; the investigative unit that becomes so preoccupied with convicting criminals that it overrides the rights of defendants or ignores safeguards for witnesses; the research group so intent not only on discovery but also on recognition that it cooks laboratory data, fails to acknowledge contributions of other researchers, or expends funds without authorization; and the collegiate football team that conspires to circumvent regulations on academic requirements or drug use.

That not every shared commitment or common task is to be affirmed just because it contributes to a sense of community invites and perhaps even requires a renewed appreciation of the critical power of the ideal of universal community. Even as we celebrate the sense of community that shared commitment may foster, we must affirm the ideal of community that is respectful toward the whole of reality and therefore also to all members of the human community, because it is in principle universal rather than limited by ethnic or geo-graphical qualification. In short, while we seek to counter the patterns of modern secular *Gesellschaft* that inhibit a sense of community, we must also resist the provincial exclusivism of *Gemeinschaft*. Only this double vigilance will allow a celebration of community that does not risk degenerating into collective self-glorification. Put positively, this double vigilance allows affirmation of a sense of community that is viable in contemporary pluralistic societies.

PART V

THEOLOGY AND THE
PROSPECTS FOR GOD-TALK

11

Can Theology Still Be about God?

MAURICE F. WILES

Believing in God, like believing the Earth to be flat, was once a basic belief but is so no longer. That is not to say that both are equally clearly false; the belief that the world is round is now both a basic belief and one with decisive evidence in its support, but atheism is not. So it is rather to say that belief in God is not today a part of the commonly accepted stock of beliefs, taken for granted within the community. It is something for which we can be expected to give reasons if we want to draw upon it in contemporary conversation or discussion.

The so-called arguments for the existence of God flourished with particular vigor when belief in God was a strongly held, basic belief. That fact gave rise to their ambiguous character, on which philosophers of religion have loved to fasten. Are they really arguments for the existence of God, or are they more properly described as reflections from within faith on what is involved in believing in God? The answer would seem to be that they are both. They arise from within a context of faith; how could they not, if belief in God was at the time a genuinely basic belief? That fact affects their form and structure but does not necessarily invalidate their status as arguments altogether. With the erosion of belief in God as a basic belief, more weight

I am grateful to David Brown and Arthur Peacocke for helpful comments on an earlier draft of this paper.

came to be placed on such arguments; and it was more weight than they were able to sustain.

One strand—or, better, a family of very diverse strands—in contemporary philosophy of religion and theology has welcomed unreservedly the collapse of arguments for God's existence. On the philosophical side, antifoundationalists have argued that any such grounding of faith is inappropriate and unnecessary, because we can never get behind our basic postulates to some neutral ground from which their validity could be demonstrated. Basic axioms are something we have to choose rather than justify. Belief in God is as "reasonable" an axiom as any other. We may come to recognize its rightness from inside; we cannot ground it in anything external to itself. To try to do so is a sign of philosophical confusion. On the theological side, it is argued (usually with more or less direct inspiration from Karl Barth) that any such attempted grounding of faith is religiously inappropriate to a true understanding of God. God is not an object for our investigation; God is a subject who makes Godself known in God's own way—specifically, in Jesus Christ. "Theism" for these theologians is a boo-word, indicative of a religious insensitivity that is little better than atheism. The reality of God can only be known from within obedient response to God's chosen form of self-revelation. It is sacrilegious to try to ground belief in God any other way.

Before we dismiss these responses as leading to an arbitrary irrationalism—as I believe, in the end, we are right to do—it is important to recognize the elements of truth and the attractiveness inherent in them. It is true that there is no neutral starting point. Arguments concerning the existence of God for the most part arise from within an already existing, broadly based commitment to or rejection of belief in God, and the form an argument takes is ineluctably influenced by those prior commitments. Moreover, the attractiveness of positions of the kind I have sketched is not only the force of their philosophical and religious insights but also the acute difficulty involved in developing any other strategy for upholding belief in God in an age where it is no longer a basic belief. Those difficulties are unlikely to diminish. It is already being claimed that the incoming currents of postmodern thought show the essential rightness of Barth's theological approach in even sharper relief than was evident in his own time.[1] Is there any path

1. See Robert W. Jenson, "Karl Barth," in *The Modern Theologians*, ed. D. F. Ford (Oxford: Basil Blackwell, 1989), 25.

to be followed that will not take the form of a forlorn attempt to prop up the apparently discredited lines of argument embodied in the old proofs for the existence of God? A central feature of Gordon Kaufman's theological agenda has been to look for a third way that involves neither an "attempt to argue the existence of God on theoretical grounds," on the one hand, nor "moving in a purely fideistic direction and simply proclaiming our belief that God exists despite all difficulties inherent in the situation," on the other hand.[2]

I have acknowledged that the old arguments were unable to carry the strain required of them by the transition to the modern world and are still less likely to be able to do so in any emerging postmodern world. Perhaps, however, we should think of them as having buckled, rather than broken, under that increased strain. Not everyone has responded to their collapse in the way that I have described. For some the old arguments have continued to be of significance, but in a much revised form. The ontological argument, always unique in its fundamental conception, has had a correspondingly special place of its own in the recent history of philosophical discussion; but I do not propose to pursue that in this essay. The cosmological and teleological arguments have been seen by many as raising genuine questions about the existence and intelligibility of the physical universe that ought not be dismissed out of hand as pseudo-questions. Nevertheless, they are not generally seen as pointing to the existence of God in the clear-cut way that has often been claimed for them in the past. In Paul Tillich's phrase, they raise rather than answer the question of God.[3]

Furthermore, if one surveys the work of twentieth-century theologians who have felt the need of supplying some grounding for the belief in God that they seek to expound, one finds it is not to those arguments that they have primarily turned. Instead, they have sought to establish an anthropological basis for their fundamental belief in God. Some aspect of what it is to be a human being has supplied their need for a reasoned grounding for the affirmation of God. There is nothing new in the fact of such appeals. One need only recall the inward turn so characteristic of Augustine's thought. Nevertheless, the fundamental role ascribed to such a move in recent theology is a significant development and prompts the question whether it

2. Gordon D. Kaufman, "God as Symbol," in *God the Problem* (Cambridge: Harvard University Press, 1972), 107.
3. Paul Tillich, *Systematic Theology*, vol. 1 (London: James Nisbet, 1953), 228.

constitutes a way particularly appropriate to the needs of our present situation. With that question in mind, I will look briefly at the way in which this approach has been worked out by three major theologians of recent years.

Karl Rahner's starting point is to ask, What is involved in our historical existence as human selves? Any answer we might give to that question must inevitably be based on the particular human experiences that have come our way. Rahner's goal, however, is to use those experiences to lay bare something that is to be distinguished from the particular, contingent experiences themselves—namely, the underlying realities or structures of existence that make any distinctively human experiences possible. How can this be done? Suppose we put to ourselves the question, What constitutes us the particular persons that we are? We can call on a variety of factors to provide information toward an answer: for example, knowledge of our genetic inheritance and of the environment in which we have been brought up and now live. Nevertheless, any answers of this kind only serve to pose more questions. The more we recognize the significance of our origins, genetic and environmental, the more puzzling become our apparent freedom and our sense of responsibility for what we make or fail to make of that inheritance. To deny that we have any such freedom or responsibility is not merely to go against a fundamental aspect of our experience; it is to deny what is most distinctively human about us. We cannot get away from the question of how we are able to contribute to shaping what is apparently given to us in our origins. How is it that we can "make something of ourselves"? Reflection on these questions is likely to lead to the conclusion that, inescapable as they are, they are incapable of being answered, because any answer arising from within the system of acquiring knowledge with which we have to work is bound to generate yet further questions. Thus we are forced on into an awareness of the "infinite question which encompasses us,"[4] a question that can be described either as unanswerable or as its own answer.

This inescapable road of "self-transcendence" shows us that human life has an ineluctable "orientation towards mystery," and that God is the name for that "absolute mystery" toward which this distinctively human style of reflection inevitably points. Rahner's appeal is not just

4. Karl Rahner, *Foundations of Christian Faith* (London: Darton, Longman & Todd, 1978), 192.

to occasions of profound solitary introspection. It is to something that underlies the whole range of human and, therefore, social life: for example, to that which is implicit in such experiences as the unconditional character of love given or love received and the sense of responsibility for one's actions in what is apprehended as an absolute moral imperative. At the heart of all these distinctively human experiences are indications of an all-embracing and inconceivable mystery. I have described the process of reflection that can give rise to awareness of that mystery in highly intellectual terms (even if not in as sophisticated intellectual terms as Rahner employs), but Rahner insists that the experience itself is not dependent for its reality on such intellectual formulation. He argues that it should be recognized as present, as a form of "unthematic awareness," even in the most rudimentary forms of genuinely human experience. Primitive burial customs, for example, are evidence of the presence of such awareness long before it was ever spelled out in any reasoned form.

The writings of Wolfhart Pannenberg reveal many emphases closely parallel to those we have outlined from Rahner's work. Pannenberg finds the distinctive difference between humans and the rest of the animal creation in the anthropological concept of "openness to the world." He sees it as "the condition for man's experience of the world," and insists (in terms closely akin to Rahner's account of the never-ending quest of self-transcendence) that it is an openness "beyond every experience and beyond every given situation . . . beyond a man's picture of the world at any given time . . . beyond every possible picture of the world and beyond the search for pictures of the world as such, as essential as this search may be."[5] Again like Rahner, he lays great stress on the significance of freedom. Atheist critics of the notion of God have often argued that any concept of God the lawgiver is unacceptable precisely because of the implicit restriction of human freedom involved in it. For Pannenberg, however, that argument relies on a superficial understanding both of God and of human freedom. Moreover, he is not content simply to refute it; he stands it on its head. Only a transfinite reality, namely, God, makes real freedom possible.[6] Important as both these themes are in Pannenberg's

5. Wolfhart Pannenberg, *What Is Man?* (Philadelphia: Fortress Press, 1970), chap. 1, esp. 3, 8.
6. See Wolfhart Pannenberg, "Eschatology and the Experience of Meaning," in *Basic Questions in Theology*, vol. 3 (London: SCM Press, 1972), 192–210.

thought, however, neither of them is its most characteristic feature. Pannenberg's particular emphasis falls on another aspect of what it is to be human, namely, hope. It seems, at first hearing, a most unlikely aspect of human living on which to focus attention in this context; particular hopes, as Pannenberg is well aware, may be mere delusions. Recalling once more the historical nature of our existence as human beings, however, he claims that hope as such is fundamental to human existence. It plays a decisive role in the distinctively human function of giving meaning to our lives.

Hope takes many forms. Hope for the future is an essential aspect of what gives purpose to our present work or to the upbringing of a family. Its range can extend much further in time and in scope, taking in both individual hopes for life after death and the Marxist hope for the social revolution that ushers in utopia. Our individual and social lives, however, are set in the context of a universal history. There are no cutoff points at which the search for meaning can rest content. A hope for universal fulfillment cannot, therefore, be dismissed as delusive in principle because it is postulated by the crucial role hope already plays in our lives now. Because that hope cannot be eliminated from life without destroying the distinctively human function of the search for meaning, we are motivated to postulate a goal for human history; in other words, we are motivated to postulate the reality of God and of the eschatological kingdom of God.

My third example is the work of Schubert Ogden. In his analysis of our existence as human selves, Ogden's emphasis is laid on the role of morality. Implicit in our behavior as moral beings, he argues, is a basic confidence in the worthwhileness of existence. Ultimately, he claims, the only alternative to the assumption that existence is worthwhile is the "Absurd Hero" of Albert Camus; and Camus's own insistent call for heroic resistance against the essential absurdity of human life is evidence of the self-contradictory character of the claim of life's meaninglessness. Ogden is well aware that there are happy and moral atheists, free of angst and keen to deny the conclusion he asserts. Nevertheless, that is not in itself argument against that conclusion; we often fail to recognize the implications of things that we take for granted and that are also fundamental to our lives. It is evidence, rather, of the need for careful philosophical reflection. Such reflection on our moral experience (as, indeed, on other aspects of human life) leads us to see, Ogden claims, that a sense of the worthwhileness of things and a confidence in life's ultimate meaning are necessary conditions for specifically human existence. It is, as he puts it, the one really essential "proof of God's existence."[7] The quotation marks around "proof of God's existence" are, however, original and crucial. Ogden's conclusion is no return to the discredited understanding of theistic proofs. It is not a claim that there is, after all, a way of demonstrating the reality of God by some form of external or abstract reasoning. It is rather the claim that the reality of God is something that can, by a process of deep and careful reflection, come to be seen to be genuinely entailed in our practical existence as human selves.

I have taken these three as representative of many twentieth-century theologians who have followed a similar line of reasoning. Does that approach constitute that third way for which Kaufman asks? Before trying to answer that question, some preparatory comments are called for. The three theologians come from very different philosophical traditions. Behind Rahner stands a particular form of neo-Kantianism, specifically, that of Joseph Marechal. Pannenberg draws extensively on the complex patterns of Hegelian thought. Ogden works with a carefully articulated form of process metaphysics, deriving from the work of Charles Hartshorne. Is it possible to reflect in any useful way on all three together, without first examining each individually in the context of his own chosen metaphysic? Such analyses would certainly add to our illumination, and the thought of all three has indeed been subjected to such scrutiny. It would still be important, however, not to miss the forest for the trees. It is my contention that, for all their diversity, there is an agreement in fundamental strategy at the point on which I am concentrating attention. The measure of validity that can properly be allowed to that strategy is the issue at stake. It is true that the three emphasize different aspects of our humanity—Rahner knowledge, Pannenberg hope, Ogden morality. One might say that among them they develop the significances of the three theological virtues—faith, hope, and love. Those differences are, however, primarily a matter of emphasis. In each case, the overall appeal is to a broader range of human characteristics than the particular one on which I have concentrated attention. What all three have in common is that they find a grounding for their belief in God in what it is to be a human self.

7. Schubert M. Ogden, *The Reality of God* (London: SCM Press, 1967), esp. 43.

In seeking to assess the validity of this general line of reasoning, we have first to ask what its role is. None of the theologians whose approach I have summarized attempts to reestablish the kind of argument for the existence of God that came under the hammer of David Hume's and Immanuel Kant's criticisms. And although each is a fully convinced Christian, none simply asserts the truth of Christian belief in God from within the sphere of his explicit Christian commitment. They do not fit within either the "theoretical" or the "fideistic" category, against both of which Kaufman warns us. The starting point from which they seek to develop their reflections is not what it is that makes possible specifically Christian experience but what it is that makes possible human experience as such. We have to ask if it is possible to speak of human existence in such universal terms, and, if it is, whether such universality points as firmly as they suggest in a theistic direction.

The emergence of historical consciousness has led us to emphasize the differences between ourselves and peoples of other cultures and of other ages. We are aware that there are many points at which there are deep differences in how we and they experience the world, because the world that we experience is a world of inherited meanings, which change over time in decisive ways. All this has made us highly suspicious of claims to speak in terms of a universal human nature, claims that were a common feature of much earlier philosophical and religious thought. This is something of which Rahner is acutely conscious. Our present forms of experience are not at the root of his argument, for these necessarily have a contingent and conditioned character about them, which makes it illegitimate to treat them as if of universal significance. His concern is with what he calls "existentials," that which makes any form of human experience possible. That which is common to humankind is, for Rahner, precisely our historical existence as human selves. Nevertheless, although this may reassure us that he is unlikely to succumb to the danger of universalizing what is only a specific contemporary form of human experience, it is no guarantee that he will succeed in delineating what necessarily underlies human experience. The danger is not merely the risk of universalizing one's own form of experience; disputes between anthropologists suggest that it is also possible falsely to universalize what is apprehended of a culture very different from one's own. There is, indeed, no guarantee that we can rightly discern what is essential to human existence. It seems clear that we can, however, by a process of empathy, achieve some genuine understanding of cultures other than our own, and we cannot prescribe in advance any limit to how far that process may take us. It is not unreasonable, therefore, to attempt to clarify what is to be regarded as fundamental to human existence, provided we acknowledge the inevitably uncertain character of any particular account we may give.

If we accept the propriety of that first stage in the line of reasoning we are reviewing—namely, offering some delineation of what it is to be human—we have then to consider what kind of an argument can be built on it. It may help to begin with a nontheistic example. A traditional theme of philosophical discussion has been the grounds for the rejection of solipsism, traditionally spoken of as the problem concerning the existence of other minds. Belief in the existence of other minds is, indeed, a basic belief that we do not normally feel ourselves called upon to justify. If we do try to give reasons for that belief in the form of an inductive inference from the behavior responses of others toward us, philosophers then delight in exposing the formal weaknesses in the arguments propounded. It would be equally absurd, however, to suggest that our belief was some kind of arbitrary decision on our part. A more appropriate account would be to claim that the belief is already implicit in the formulation of the question, because the formulation of the question requires language and language is an essentially communal activity; it can only develop in a communal setting. The communal nature of language means that the existence of other persons is already demonstrated by our ability to raise the question of their existence at all. Indeed, the argument can be taken a stage further. Not only the existence of the other person but also the basic trustworthiness of the other are already given, because the possibility of communication presumes not only the existence of an other but also that other's overall trustworthiness. Deceit and lying exist, but they are parasitic on trustworthiness. If they, not trustworthiness, were the norm, language would have been unable to develop as the form of communication that it is.

Ogden's formulation of the enterprise on which he sees himself engaged makes absolutely clear not only that it is not to be understood as basing itself on specific Christian insights but also that it is of the form that I have illustrated by the example of the argument against solipsism. In seeking to counter secularist negations, his appeal is not to any kind of supernaturalism but to "a secularity which has become fully self-conscious and which therefore makes explicit the faith in God already implied in what it affirms."[8] If the fact of language implies the general trustworthiness of humankind, because it could not have emerged or continue to function on any other basis, then the fact of morality, it is claimed, could not have arisen or continued to be practiced without a confidence in the ultimate worth of life. God is a name for that which calls forth this all-embracing confidence.

Two questions need to be asked of this argument and of the parallel affirmations of God as the answer to the infinite question that encompasses us or as the ground of a universal goal to human history. The first question is if that is the only way of reading our human experience. Granted that the experience to which the argument appeals is human experience as such, not special Christian experience, may not the way of reading the experience nonetheless have been decisively, if unconsciously, influenced by a person's specifically Christian experience? There is no conclusive way of answering that question. Undoubtedly, for those who argue in these terms, their particular understanding of what is involved in being human is an integral element in their Christian faith. Insofar as it is appopriate to speak of a causal connection between the two at all, however, it seems just as reasonable to claim that it is the sense of such an underlying confidence (not necessarily clearly articulated at first) that has led to their adoption of Christian beliefs as to see the connection the other way round. There is certainly no more circularity in this argument than is inescapably present in all reflections of so foundational a character.

The second question is whether the line of reflection we have been following requires us to assert that the infinite question is also an answer or to speak of that which calls forth an all-embracing confidence. Might it not instead be that, in the course of evolution, we have simply devised such conceptions for practical purposes? Kaufman has emphasized very strongly how it is our practical needs as "active-choosing-creative beings," who "must judge what confronts them and attempt to transform it in accordance with visions of what now is not," that have called forth our varied human conceptions of God.[9] The crucial role of human construction in Christian belief in God

8. Ibid., 20.
9. Gordon D. Kaufman, "Christian Theology and the Scientific Study of Religion," in *God the Problem*, 34.

(as in the beliefs of other religions), on which Kaufman lays such stress, seems to me inescapable. Nevertheless, that by itself is, as he insists, neutral in relation to the question of the reality of the "real" God, as contrasted with the "available" God or gods of the particular religions.[10]

Does the issue, then, have to be left in that entirely undecided and undecidable state? It is worth considering the parallel debate between instrumentalists and critical realists in science. The naive realist's claim that the physical scientist can describe for us just what the external world is like is as untenable as the claim that our theological accounts are direct descriptions of the nature of God. The growing realization of the impossibility of a naive realist view of science prompted a swing by reaction toward an instrumentalist view. Could any objective reality be allowed to the concepts with which the scientist works? Was not their "truth" simply a matter of their practical usefulness in helping us achieve our experimental and technical goals? There can be no question of any formal disproof of such a claim. Nevertheless, it would, indeed, be an odd and surely implausible position to maintain that our theoretical understanding of the world could then be so reliable in practical terms, if it bears no relation to how the world actually is. It is an argument that has found a good deal of support among philosophers of science in recent years. The fact that it has been dubbed the "no miracles" argument should not discourage the theologian from adapting it to his or her purpose.[11] The same line of reasoning can be used to suggest that, if the concept of God is of such crucial practical significance as Kaufman claims, then it would be strange if it were nothing more than a useful instrument toward human living and corresponded in no way to the ultimate reality of how our world is.

Not all conceptions of God have had the positive pragmatic value that Kaufman ascribes to the underlying conception of a transcendent divine reality. If an argument of the kind that I have been pursuing lends any support to the validity of belief in God as such, then by the same token it calls for continuing and thoroughgoing criticism of the particular constructions through which that basic belief in God finds its expression. There can be little doubt that such criticisms will be

---

10. See Kaufman, "God as Symbol," 97–100.
11. See Michael C. Banner, *The Justification of Science and the Rationality of Religious Belief* (Oxford: Clarendon Press, 1990), 35.

intensified by those trends of thought that are said to be taking us out of the "modern" into an uncharted "postmodern" age. Theology will need to be attentive and responsive to those trends. Nevertheless, it should not be afraid that all the old landmarks are about to be swept away. What I have been trying to suggest is that, whatever form the discussion of such problems may take, as long as it remains a structured human discussion it will not fail to carry within itself (whatever the substance of the discussion) a seed with the potential of coming to flower as a well-rooted belief in God.

12

The End(s) of Theology

MARK C. TAYLOR

It is an illusion that we were ever alive,
Lived in the houses of mothers, arranged ourselves
By our own motions in a freedom of air.

Regard the freedom of seventy years ago.
It is no longer air. The houses still stand,
Though they are rigid in rigid emptiness.

Even our shadows, their shadows, no longer remain.
The lives these lived in the mind are at an end.
They never were . . . The sound of the guitar

Were not and are not. Absurd. The words spoken
Were not and are not. It is not to be believed.
The meeting at noon at edge of the field seems like

An invention, an embrace between one desperate clod
And another in a fantastic consciousness,
In a queer assertion of humanity:

A theorem proposed between the two—
Two figures in a nature of the sun,
In the sun's design of its own happiness,

As if nothingness contained a métier,
A vital assumption, an impermanence
                    (Wallace Stevens, "The Rock")

   Now I'm going to tell you how I went into that inexpressiveness that
was always my blind, secret quest. How I went into what exists between
the number one and the number two, how I saw the mysterious, fiery,
line, how it is a surreptitious line. Between two musical notes there

exists another note, between two facts there exists another fact, between two grains of sand, no matter how close together they are, there exists an interval of space, there exists a sensing between sensing—in the interstices of primordial matter there is the mysterious, fiery line that is the world's breathing, and the world's continual breathing is what we hear and call silence.

(Clarice Lispector, *The Passion According to G. H.*)

A theorem proposed between the two . . . what exists between the number one and the number two . . . between two notes . . . between two facts . . . between two grains of sand . . . an interval . . . nothingness . . . impermanence . . . the world's breathing . . . the world's continual breathing. . . .

The end of theology is approaching . . . has always been approaching . . . approaching from the beginning . . . even "before" the beginning . . . approaching without ever arriving . . . approaching "before" the beginning and without end. The endless approach of the end of theology might, however, harbor an end that is not merely an end of theology but another end . . . a different end that is not the end of difference. This alternative end implies the irreducible opening of the a/theological imagination. The task of thinking at the end of theology is to think beyond theology's end by thinking the "beyond" of an end that is not theological. This "beyond," which is neither simply immanent or transcendent, has been left unthought throughout the Western theological tradition. Indeed, theologies traditionally have been constructed in order not to think this strange end. It is precisely the unthought of theology that today beckons our thought.

These reflections might seem to be something like what Friedrich Nietzsche labeled "untimely meditations." More precisely, the declaration of the end of theology might have been more timely a quarter of a century ago. For a brief period in the sixties it seemed as if Nietzsche's declaration of the death of God were being realized in Western history and culture. In his widely acclaimed book *The Secular City*, Harvey Cox argued: "The age of the secular city, the epoch whose ethos is quickly spreading into every corner of the globe, *is* an age of 'no religion at all.' It no longer looks to religious rules and rituals for its morality or its meanings."[1] Twenty years later, events forced Cox to revise his assessment of the religious situation in our age. The result was a new book, *Religion in the Secular City*, in which Cox examined

1. Harvey Cox, *The Secular City* (New York: Macmillan, 1966), 3.

"the dramatic reappearance of traditional religion throughout the world, from the grassroots fervor of Christian communities in Latin America to the rise of fundamentalism on network television."[2]

One of the most surprising developments of the past several decades has been the widespread return of traditional religious belief and practice. For many years social scientists have been arguing that modernization and secularization go hand in hand. As the forces of modernization wax, the influence of religion wanes. Max Weber long ago observed that modernity brings in its wake the disenchantment of the natural world and human life. With the rise of modern science and technology, what once had seemed to be the kingdom of God becomes the province of humanity. When the principles of scientific investigation are turned toward human beings, religious belief is demystified through what Paul Ricoeur labels "the hermeneutics of suspicion." Rather than disclosing the truth about the cosmos and human existence, masters of suspicion, such as Karl Marx, Sigmund Freud, and Nietzsche, interpret religion as a problematic expression of primordial economic, psychological, and biological laws and forces. The hermeneutics of suspicion extends the project of enlightenment, which Immanuel Kant accurately describes as humanity's struggle to emerge from "self-incurred tutelage." Sounding more like an Enlightenment philosopher than the founder of psychoanalysis, Freud writes: "The voice of the intellect is a soft one, but it does not rest till it has gained a hearing. Finally, after a countless succession of rebuffs, it succeeds."[3]

Although sophisticated analyses of the secularization process and the imaginative elaborations of the hermeneutics of suspicion have done much to illuminate our understanding of religious thought and conduct, it is becoming increasingly clear that they do not tell the whole story of our era. Religion has proved more persistent than its critics anticipated. The last three decades have given increasing evidence of what might be described as the disenchantment with disenchantment. For many the world and life in it are more mysterious than secularists allow. Moreover, the rigorous analyses growing out of the hermeneutics of suspicion suggest that the obsession with demystification must itself be demystified. Critics of religion often

2. Harvey Cox, *Religion in the Secular City: Toward a Postmodern Theology* (New York: Simon & Schuster, 1984), introduction.
3. Sigmund Freud, *The Future of an Illusion*, trans. W. D. Robson-Scott (New York: Doubleday, 1964), 158.

approach their task with a fervor that borders on the religious. Religion, it seems, is more complex and multifaceted than reductionistic critiques acknowledge.

Nowhere is the disenchantment with disenchantment more evident than in the recent rise of religious fundamentalism. The term "fundamentalism" comes from a series of booklets entitled *The Fundamentals*, published between 1910 and 1915. In these tracts different writers asserted what they took to be the basic beliefs of Christianity that were being eroded by "modern" theology's effort to reach an accommodation with the "modern" world. Fundamentalism, in all varieties, grows out of the deep sense that something is wrong with modernity. The revival of religious fundamentalism is one of the most significant social, cultural, and political phenomena of our time.

It is important to appreciate the complexity and diversity of today's fundamentalism. The revival of religious fundamentalism is not limited to the United States. Fundamentalism is an international phenomenon of considerable significance. From Western and Eastern Europe to the Middle and Far East; from North to Central and South America; from Christianity, Protestant as well as Catholic, to Judaism, Islam, Buddhism, and Hinduism, to say nothing of countless esoteric cults, fundamentalism is exercising enormous attraction and power. In years to come I suspect this religious revival will be regarded as more important than either the first or the second Great Awakening. One of the reasons for the overwhelming significance of this religious revival is its political dimension. Although religion and politics are always closely related, this alliance can be more or less explicit. In the last several decades religion has directly entered into a not-so-holy alliance with a variety of political programs. We need only consider the interplay of religion and politics in the United States, Nicaragua, Brazil, Poland, Israel, Iran, Pakistan, Tibet, Afghanistan, Sri Lanka, and elsewhere to recognize that labels such as conservative, liberal, and radical are not interchangeable in the religious and political domains.

Given the extraordinary diversity of these traditions and cultures, is it possible to identify a common thread uniting various forms of fundamentalism? Fundamentalism, in all of its guises, I would suggest, involves the search for secure foundations to ground thought and action. Fundamentalism, in other words, is foundationalism. From this point of view, religious belief can be used to legitimize social and political actions as different as civil rights marches, abortion clinic sit-ins, opposition to right- or left-wing regimes, nonviolent protests, and violent resistance.

Those of us in the academy should not think that we are immune to these developments. Although less obvious, our struggle with foundationalism is no less important. The so-called crisis in the humanities underscores the currency of academic issues related to the question of foundationalism. The heated debates triggered by Allan Bloom's outrageous book, *The Closing of the American Mind*, as well as former Secretary of Education William Bennett's attacks on higher education and the criticisms of the humanities registered by Lynne Cheney, of the National Endowment for the Humanities, reflect the "back to basics" attitude that pervades much of our culture. This attitude is, in my judgment, pernicious and should be vigorously resisted. Fundamentalism or foundationalism is essentially reactionary. In the wake of the confusion and uncertainty brought by the pluralism and relativity of modern culture, there is a pervasive nostalgic longing to return to the peace and security of a world in which truth seemed knowable and morality doable. But there is no going back. As Wallace Stevens tells us, these simpler times never really existed. Like the houses of our mothers, "they never were. . . . Were not and are not." The question we now face is not how to fashion an antimodern reaction to modernism but how to develop an effective postmodern response to modernity. Something has gone wrong—terribly wrong—in modernity. In this the fundamentalists or foundationalists are right. Nevertheless, their solution compounds the problem. We are not called to reestablish foundations but to think their fault.

In an effort to think this fault, I would like to rethink certain developments in modern theology. The trends we have been considering notwithstanding, the most significant turn in modern theology is what Nietzsche labeled "the death of God." The death of God marks the end of theology. In this context, "end" obviously does not mean the cessation of theology as such. Theology continues, even though it might already have reached its conclusion or achieved its fulfillment. The question that lingers in the wake of the death of God is how to think "beyond" the end of theology.

Twentieth-century theology is, in large part, an elaboration and extension of questions asked and problems posed in the nineteenth century. The most important theological thinking in the last century takes as its point of departure the seminal debate between

G.W.F. Hegel and Søren Kierkegaard. Hegel attempts to develop an all-inclusive System in which human beings achieve Absolute Knowledge. This System is supposed to present the philosophical articulation of the truth represented by the Christian religious imagination. Absolute Knowledge is total self-consciousness, in which God and self are perfectly united. In this union each comes to completion in and through the other. Kierkegaard, however, remains suspicious of Hegelianism's totalizing propensities. Kierkegaard's relentlessly non-systematic critique of the System is a concerted effort to recover the difference and return the otherness that philosophy and philosophical theology repress. To think beyond the end of theology is to unthink repression in a way that allows the return of the repressed. This unthinking admittedly poses certain dangers, intellectual as well as social.

Twentieth-century theology begins with a resounding "No!" proclaimed in 1918 by Karl Barth in his book titled *The Epistle to the Romans*. Barth's "No" grows out of his effort to recover what Kierkegaard described as "the infinite and qualitative difference" between God and humanity that post-Hegelian theology had erased. Having begun with this *"Nein,"* contemporary theology has remained implicitly or explicitly preoccupied with the related problems of transcendence, difference, and otherness. It would be correct to insist that, for most of this century (and not only for this century), theological reflection has been suspended, perhaps even hung up, between immanence and transcendence. Barth's "No" represents a rejection of every form of theological liberalism and all variations of cultural Protestantism in which divine presence is regarded as immanent in historical, social, and cultural processes. Barth argues:

> Religion compels us to the perception that God is not to be found in religion. Religion makes us to know that we are competent to advance no single step. Religion, as the final human possibility, commands us to halt. Religion brings us to the place where we must wait, in order that God may confront us—on the other side of the frontier of religion. The transformation of the 'No' of religion into the divine 'Yes' occurs in the dissolution of this last observable human thing.[4]

As this text suggests, Barth presents a thoroughgoing critique of culture. He views all human constructions—social, political, moral, and

---

4. Karl Barth, *The Epistle to the Romans*, trans. E. C. Hoskyns (London: Oxford University Press, 1968), 242.

religious—with suspicion. Barth's neo-orthodox theology does not, however, involve a return to fundamentalism but is, instead, a radical attack on all foundationalism. The historical situation in which Barth formulated his critique makes his suspicion of humankind's cultural constructs not only understandable but even persuasive. By saying "Yes" to a radically transcendent God, Barth says "No" to the culture that left Western Europe in ruins.

The force of the neo-orthodox critique of culture and society has decreased as the distance from world wars has increased. The most significant index of this development is the death-of-God theology that emerged in the 1960s. The death-of-God theology remains one of the most significant theological movements of this century. I would even go so far as to argue that modern theology reaches a certain end in the death-of-God theology. Any postmodern theological reflection that does not fall into antimodernism will have to pass through the "fiery brook" of the death of God. In this country the most influential proponent of the death-of-God theology is Thomas J. J. Altizer. Altizer's program must be understood in the context of the neo-orthodoxy that dominated theological discourse during the first half of this century. When Altizer declares the death of God, it is really the death of the Barthian God he proclaims. Altizer's "No" to Barth's "No" is at the same time a "Yes" to a radical immanence in which all vestiges of transcendence are erased. In the Hegelian terms Altizer repeatedly invokes, the negation of negation (that is, the negation of radical transcendence) issues in a total affirmation that overcomes every trace of unreconciled otherness. Within Altizer's apocalyptic vision, the death of God is the condition of the possibility of the arrival of the Parousia. When the kingdom of God is at hand, authentic presence is totally realized here and now.

If we are to understand where Altizer departs from and remains bound to the presuppositions and conclusions of classical theology, then it is necessary to reformulate several crucial points in his position. By declaring the death of God, Altizer does not call into question the traditional understanding of Being in terms of presence. On the contrary, he insists that to be is to be present and to be fully is to be present totally. Although never stated in these terms, Altizer's argument implies that the mistake of traditional theism, of which Barthianism is but the most problematic variation, is not that it misunderstands Being as such but that it identifies the locus of true Being as transcendent to, rather than immanent in, the world of space and time. From Altizer's perspective, the total presence of God in the incarnation marks the death of the otherness that inhibits the very possibility of enjoying presence in the present. To cling to the belief that the divine is in any way other or transcendent is to suffer the disappointment brought by the delay or deferral of the Parousia. Precisely this delay or deferral, Altizer argues, ends with the life and death of Jesus.

Following Hegel, Altizer maintains that what is implicit in Jesus becomes explicit in the course of the historical process. With the death of God, transcendent presence becomes totally present in space (that is, here) and time (now). When the identity of the divine comes to completion in the identity of the human, difference and unreconciled otherness are overcome.

> Distance disappears in total presence, and so likewise does all actual otherness which is not the otherness of that presence itself. Difference can now be present only insofar as it is fully embodied in speech. When difference speaks, and fully speaks, it becomes present in speech, and wholly present in that speech. That speech is not simply the presence of difference, or the voice of difference. It is far rather the self-identity of difference, and its fully actualized self-identity, a self-identity in which difference embodies its otherness in the immediacy of a real and actual presence.[5]

With the incorporation of difference in identity, Altizer reinscribes the identity of identity and difference, which, as the Alpha and Omega of reflection, constitutes the very foundation of Hegel's System.

The question that remains after Hegel and after the theological reappropriation of his System is how to think otherwise than being by thinking a difference that is not reducible to identity. As I have suggested elsewhere, this is precisely the task that Kierkegaard sets for himself in his philosophical fragments and unscientific postscripts. In our day the question of difference has been taken up again by, among others, Jacques Derrida. Situating his own interrogation in relation to Hegel's System, Derrida maintains:

> As for what "begins" then—"beyond" absolute knowledge—*unheard-of* thoughts are required, sought for across the memory of old signs. . . . In the openness of this question *we no longer know*. This does not mean that we know nothing but that we are beyond absolute knowledge (and its

5. Thomas J. J. Altizer, *The Self-Embodiment of God* (New York: Harper & Row, 1977), 81.

ethical, aesthetic, or religious system), approaching that on the basis of which its closure is announced and decided. Such a question will legitimately be understood as *meaning* nothing, as no longer belonging to the system of meaning.[6]

To think beyond absolute knowledge (or, perhaps, to think the beyond "of" absolute knowledge) is to think after the end of Western theology and metaphysics by thinking what that tradition has not thought. In his influential essay "The End of Philosophy and the Task of Thinking" Martin Heidegger explains, "What characterizes metaphysical thinking that grounds the ground for beings is the fact that metaphysical thinking departs from what is present in its presence, and thus represents it in terms of its ground as something grounded."[7] Heidegger insists that metaphysics and what he identifies as the ontotheological tradition "does not ask about Being as Being, that is, does not raise the question of how there can be presence as such."[8] The task of thinking, in the strict sense of the term, is to think the unthought of ontotheology, which answers the question of how there can be presence as such. One of the ways Heidegger characterizes this unthought is as "the *difference* between Being and beings" or, more concisely, "difference *as* difference." This difference should not be confused with the presence of any specific difference. Heideggerian *Differenz*, which is the condition of the possibility of all presence and every present, is not a presence and hence can never be properly present; yet neither is it simply absent. What neither philosophy nor theology has thought (because neither can think such an "unheard-of" thought without ceasing to be itself) is that which lies between presence and absence, identity and difference, being and nonbeing. Neither representable in nor masterable by traditional philosophical and theological categories, this margin is the trace of a different difference and another other. Is this other other Stevens's "theorem proposed between the two"? Perhaps.

No one has questioned this strange difference with greater rigor than Derrida. In Derrida's texts Heidegger's *Differenz* returns with a difference as *différance*. The neologism *différance*, which Derrida admits

6. Jacques Derrida, "Différance," in *Speech and Phenomena and Other Essays on Husserl's Theory of Signs*, trans. D. Allison (Evanston, Ill.: Northwestern University Press, 1973), 87.
7. Martin Heidegger, "The End of Philosophy and the Task of Thinking," in idem, *On Time and Being*, trans. J. Stambaugh (New York: Harper & Row, 1972), 56.
8. Ibid., 70.

"is neither a word nor a concept," trades on the duplicity of the French word *différer*, which can mean both "to differ" and "to defer." Suspended between differing and deferring, *différance* involves the becoming-time of space and the becoming-space of time. The time of this difference and the difference of this time open unheard-of spaces in which the a/theological imagination can err. To glimpse the time–space of such erring, it might be helpful to return to my all too schematic outline of twentieth-century theology.

I have suggested that, since at least 1918, theologians have wavered between emphasizing divine transcendence and stressing divine immanence. Whereas Barth attempts to reassert divine transcendence, which calls into question all human achievement, Altizer is concerned to reestablish divine immanence, which is supposed to overcome every form of alienated consciousness. When situated historically, Altizer's critique of Barth can be read as a reversal of Kierkegaard's critique of Hegel. From this point of view, Altizer's "No" to Barth's "No" supplants Kierkegaard's dialectic of either/or with Hegel's dialectic of both/and. After this reversal of reversal, we must ask, What have Barth and Altizer not thought? What does the alternative of transcendence and immanence leave out? Is there a nondialectical third that lies between the dialectic of either/or and both/and? Might this third be neither transcendent nor immanent? Does this neither/nor open the time–space of a different difference and another other—a difference and an other that do not merely invert but actually subvert the polarities of Western philosophical and theological reflection?

To begin to respond to such questions, we must try to think the unthought and perhaps unthinkable difference, which I name with the improper name "altarity," by rethinking the death of God. Instead of leading to the total presence constitutive of the complete realization of both God and humanity, the death of God calls into question the very possibility of fulfillment by forever deferring the realization of presence. The infinite deferral of the end harbors an end that is not the end of theology. An end that is not the end of theology would be an end that is never present—an end that does not, indeed, cannot arrive. Such an endless end is what Maurice Blanchot describes as "the disaster."

The disaster is not an apocalypse. It is not a matter of vision, sight, or insight. The nonsite of the disaster is not a scene of knowledge or self-consciousness. No veils are stripped, no curtains raised. The disaster "reveals" nothing. This nothing is not, however, the nothing of Western philosophy and theology. The nothing of the disaster is neither the no thing that is the fullness of being nor the absence of things that is the emptiness of nonbeing. The nothing that both philosophy and theology leave unthought is "between being and nonbeing." It neither is nor is not; it is not present without being absent. Nothing approaches by withdrawing and withdraws by approaching. Through its approach, nothing ends ending by insuring that nothing ends.

The disaster, then, is the nonevent in which nothing happens. The eventuality of nothing ruins all presence by interminably delaying the arrival of every present. In one of his most provocative accounts of the disaster, Blanchot writes:

> The disaster ruins everything, all the while leaving everything intact. It does not touch anyone in particular; "I" am not threatened by it, but spared, left aside. It is in this way that I am threatened; it is in this way that the disaster threatens in me that which is exterior to me—an other than I who passively become other. There is no reaching the disaster. Out of reach is he whom it threatens, whether from afar or close up, it is impossible to say: the infiniteness of the threat has in some way broken every limit. We are on the edge of disaster without being able to situate it in the future: it is rather always already past, and yet we are on the edge or under the threat, all formulations that imply the future—that which is yet to come—if the disaster were not that which does not come, that which has put a stop to every arrival.[9]

The nonarrival or absence of the end has a retroactive effect on the beginning, even as the inaccessibility of the beginning harbors an aftereffect for the end. If God is the Alpha and the Omega, then the death of God marks the end of the beginning as well as the end. In the presence of this twofold absence, religion itself must be refigured.

Religion is a binding (*ligare*) back (*re*) that is supposed to bind together. The return to the origin that constitutes the end holds out the promise of unifying human life by reconciling opposites and overcoming strife. But what if, as the poet Stevens avers,

> It is an illusion that we were ever alive,
> Lived in the houses of mothers, arranged ourselves
> By our own motions in a freedom of air[?][10]

9. Maurice Blanchot, *The Writing of the Disaster*, trans. A. Smock (Lincoln: University of Nebraska Press, 1986), 1.

10. Wallace Stevens, "The Rock," in *The Collected Poems of Wallace Stevens* (New York: Alfred A. Knopf, 1981), 525.

If the origin is always missing. . . . If the end never arrives. . . . If God is dead, then religion binds back to nothing. When *re-ligare* fails by returning all to nothing, it must be repeated. Through repetition, binding back is transformed into a re-binding that creates a double bind. This double bind is the trace of the nothing that is betrayed by the death of God. To be bound to and by nothing is not to be free but to be entangled in a double bind from which there is no escape. In the aftermath of the death of God, religion no longer heals wounds by binding together the opposites that tear apart. On the contrary, religion exposes wounds that can never be cured. The "re-" of religion marks a repetition (compulsion) that neither solves nor heals but re-marks the devastating space that is the dead time of the nonapocalyptic disaster.

A/theology struggles to inscribe the failure of religion in what Edmond Jabès describes as "wounded words." As Jabès points out,

> One crack and the building crumbles and initiates the endless reading of ruins.[11]

Lispector captures the drift of Jabès's wounded words:

> I return with the unsayable. The unsayable can be given to me only through the failure of my language. Only when the construct falters do I reach what I cannot accomplish.[12]

Faltering constructions—linguistic and otherwise—expose the fault of foundations and the error of every fundamentalism. This crack, this fault, lies "beyond" the end of theology. To write this "beyond" is to write the lack of language that is a nothing other than the nothing of silence. Neither speech nor silence, this lack of language remains in and as the failure of words. The wound of words is a tear that cannot be mended—a tear that can never be wiped away. This tear or tear, which interrupts the system of exchange, is neither exactly inside nor outside the text. As such, it eludes the economy of representation. That which is neither outside nor inside cannot be represented either referentially or self-reflexively. To write the "beyond" that is not the end of theology, it is necessary to write in a way that is nonreferential without being self-reflexive.

In an effort to describe the distinguishing features of this alternative a/theological writing, I have borrowed a term from Freud: parapraxis.

11. Edmond Jabès, *The Book of Questions: El, or The Last Book,* trans. R. Waldrop (Middletown, Conn.: Wesleyan University Press, 1984), 104.
12. Clarice Lispector, *The Passion According to G.H.,* trans. R. W. Sousa (Minneapolis: University of Minnesota Press, 1988), 90.

A psychical parapraxis, Freud explains, "must be in the nature of a momentary and temporary disturbance. The same function must have been performed by us more correctly before, or we must at all times believe ourselves capable of carrying it out more correctly. If we are corrected by someone else, we must at once recognize the rightness of the correction and the wrongness of our own psychical process."[13] A parapraxis, then, involves a failure, slip, error, or mistake. The slip of the tongue or pen underscores the irreducible errancy of parapraxis. In this case, error betrays. Such betrayal always takes place along a border—at the limits of language. "Para," J. Hillis Miller points out, "is a double antithetical prefix signifying at once proximity and distance, similarity and difference, interiority and exteriority, something inside a domestic economy and at the same time outside it, something simultaneously this side of a boundary line, threshold, or margin, and also beyond it."[14] Parapraxical writing is the praxis of the "para." This praxis involves the inscription of the boundary, threshold, margin, or limit. To write parapraxically is to write the limit rather than to write about the limit. The "para" inscribed in parapraxis is "inside" the written text as a certain "outside" that cannot be internalized. Thus parapraxical writing falls between referential and self-referential discourse. There is an inescapably performative dimension to parapraxis. In contrast to performative utterance, however, which always does *something* with words, parapraxis struggles to do nothing with words. It succeeds by failing. By doing nothing with words, parapraxical writing stages the withdrawal of that which no text can contain, express, or re-present.

It is important to stress that parapraxis is not simply a latter-day version of classical negative theology. The nothing toward which parapraxis is drawn is not the nothing of negative theology. Whereas negative theologians tend to regard nothing as the binary or dialectical opposite of being, the a/theologian interprets nothing as neither being nor nonbeing. Parapraxis, therefore, is no more positive than negative. Instead of employing a strategy of simple negation, parapraxis engages in what Kierkegaard labels "indirect communication." That which is unrepresentable cannot be approached directly but must be approached indirectly through linguistic twistings and turnings that

13. Sigmund Freud, *The Standard Edition of the Complete Psychological Works of Sigmund Freud* (1960), vol. 6, 239.

14. J. Hillis Miller, "The Critic as Host," in Harold Bloom et al., *Deconstruction and Criticism* (New York: Seabury Press, 1979), 219.

can never be straightened out. As Michel de Certeau explains, this indirection "denatures language: it removes it from the function that intends an imitation of things. It also undoes the coherence of signification . . . it torments words in order to make them say that which literally they do not say."[15]

To undo the coherence of signification, it is necessary to think beyond representation by thinking after the "theological" age of the sign. Words are wounded when language goes astray. The nonsynthetic imagination employs aberrant syntax to create a text that lacks semantic plenitude. Errant language entails linguistic abuse through which the writer attempts to say the unsayable by allowing language to undo itself. The unsaying of language is not the same as mere silence. By simultaneously inscribing and erasing, parapraxis allows the withdrawal of language to approach in and through the tangled lines of the text. "That which must be said," de Certeau insists, "can only be said in the fissure of the word."[16] The fissure of the word is the fault that remains to be thought—the fault that theology has left unthought or the theology has been constructed not to think.

When language falters nothing happens. This nothing, which is neither the presence of the no thing that is the ground of everything nor the absence of all things, is forever elusive and thus can never be experienced. It is the limit of experience. To approach this limit of experience is to undergo the irreducible experience of the limit. This experience of limit is a liminal experience in which an other that is, in effect, sacred is glimpsed. It is important to realize that this sacred is not God but is that which remains and approaches when gods fail . . . fail to arrive, to be present, or to be present again in our representations. The failure of God betrays the sacred. The site of this betrayal is the text inscribed in parapraxis. The a/theological writer strives to re-stage the sacrifice of the Word. This sacrifice is radical; it is an expenditure without return in which negation is not negated. The sacrifice of the Word in writing is the betrayal of language that mourns the death of God. In the wake of this mourning, nothing is left . . . nothing remains . . . always remains. To write after the death of God . . . to write beyond the end of theology is to betray nothing.

In his posthumously published collection of fragments, *The Will to Power*, Nietzsche writes:

15. Michel de Certeau, *La fable mystique: XVIe–XVII* (Paris: Gallimard, 1982), 195.
16. Ibid., 200.

Nihilism stands at the door: whence comes this uncanniest of all guests? Point of departure: it is an error to consider "social distress" or "physiological degeneration" or, worse, corruption, as the *cause* of nihilism. Ours is the most decent and compassionate age. Distress, whether of the soul, body, or intellect, cannot itself give birth to nihilism (i.e., the radical repudiation of value, meaning, and desirability). Such distress always permits a variety of interpretations. Rather: it is in one particular interpretation, the Christian-moral one, that nihilism is rooted.[17]

Nietzsche's claim is startling. Nihilism, he argues, is not the result of the decline of religion and morality but actually grows out of religious and moral beliefs. By establishing an opposition between good and evil, true and false, here and beyond, what is and what ought to be, religion and morality effectively alienate the self from itself, divide people from each other, and separate self and world. So understood, the affirmation of the foundational principles of religion and morality involves a nay-saying that is profoundly nihilistic. Such nihilism lurks in the midst of contemporary religious and political fundamentalism. History teaches us that such nay-saying, which disguises itself as religious affirmation, often becomes violent. The forms of such violence are not always obvious but frequently are very subtle. This tendency toward violence increases when one is convinced that his or her cause is just, vision is true, and way is divinely sanctioned. Certainty harbors repression. As repression spreads, violence grows. This violence inevitably is directed toward the other who is regarded as a threat. Security—be it national or personal—seems to require the mastery, if not the elimination, of the other. This struggle for mastery is nihilistic.

The nihilism that Nietzsche detects at the heart of morality and of certain forms of religion cannot be overcome by a simple reversal of nay-saying in a yea-saying that affirms what is and denies what ought to be. Such a reversal is characteristic of the death-of-God theology. The death of God issues in the divinization of humanity and the sanctification of the world. When what is, is what ought to be, one must embrace reality rather than seek ideality. This radical affirmation approaches what Hegel describes as Absolute Knowledge and Nietzsche labels Gay Science. All too often, however, there is a curious similarity between the nay-saying of the religious and moral struggle for mastery and the yea-saying of Absolute Knowledge and Gay Sci-

17. Friedrich Nietzsche, *The Will to Power*, trans. W. Kaufman (New York: Random House, 1968), 7.

ence. In each case, otherness and difference seem to be intolerable. The death of the transcendent God is the disappearance of the absolute difference which establishes every difference that cannot be reduced to the same and every other that cannot be made my own.

In the postmodern world, nihilism is, in a certain sense, unavoidable. It cannot be overcome by returning to a premodern search for foundations or the modern affirmation of presence. By thinking beyond the end of theology, by thinking the "beyond" of an end that is not theological, we approach the possibility of thinking otherness otherwise and thinking difference differently. One of the most pressing problems we face—indeed, have always faced—is the difficulty of remaining open to a difference we cannot control and an other we can never master. It is, perhaps, naive to believe that a/theological thinking can contribute to our psychological, social, and political struggles with difference and otherness. I would hope, however, that this naivete is, in Ricoeur's terms, a "second naivete," a naivete that has been tempered by reflection and its inevitable failure.

The sacrifice of the Word inscribed "in" the text as an exteriority that cannot be internalized creates a wound that never heals. This wound marks the opening of opening itself. The wound of the Word implies another space in which difference can approach differently. The task confronting us is to affirm difference without negating it—to accept otherness without denying it.

The end is approaching . . . has always been approaching . . . approaching from the beginning. Still, it seems closer today than ever before. We are on the edge of disaster, under its threat. That threat is real, and we delude ourselves by trying to deny or repress it. Can disaster be delayed? Will it be deferred? We cannot be sure. If there is hope, then it lies not in certainty but in uncertainty, not in security but in insecurity, not in foundations but in their faults, not in cures but in wounds—wounds that sometimes are inflicted on and by the Word. In "the twilight of the idols," we linger—linger with the wound that is not precisely ours. That wound might be our hope. Small hope. Fragile hope. Nothing more. *Nothing* more. Wound of the Word . . . a theorem proposed between the two . . . between the number one and the number two . . . between two notes . . . between two facts . . . between two grains of sand . . . interstices of primordial matter . . . nothingness . . . impermanence . . . the world's continual breathing. . . .

13

Feuerbach on Religion
as Construction

VAN AUSTIN HARVEY

I

The originality of Gordon Kaufman's theological work lies in his proposal that theology be considered an imaginative projection. Rejecting most of the traditional strategies that Protestant theologians since Schleiermacher have used to establish the reasons for believing in a transcendent, divine being standing over against the world, Kaufman has argued that God is not revealed in unique historical events, given in religious experience, or inferred as a "ground of being." Instead, God is an imaginative construct that functions to provide human beings and their world with human significance.[1] Consequently, the aim of theology is not to explore the various avenues for the knowledge of God but to provide reasons why one should construct the concept in one way rather than another. The issue is not whether the concept of God is true to Scripture, revelation, and religious experience, but whether it facilitates or inhibits humane forms of life. The question is not which concept of God is true but "What possibilities does it open up for men and women?"[2]

In his earlier sketches of this radical program, Kaufman's "major act of construction" yielded a deity not unlike that of some previous forms of religious liberalism: a moral agent for which the traditional

---

1. See Gordon D. Kaufman, *An Essay on Theological Method* (Missoula, Mont.: Scholars Press, 1975), 29.
2. Ibid., 30.

language about loving and caring like a parent was appropriate if hedged about by the de rigueur appeals to metaphorical and symbolic language. Although Kaufman, like his (our) mentor H. Richard Niebuhr, saw God as the great relativizer of all things finite, a void into which all things tumbled, this same void was believed to be a friend.[3] God is still "that which fulfills and completes our humanity . . . that in which we can put our full confidence and trust."[4] In short, although the statements about God are set within the brackets of "construction," they do not read much differently from those liberal theologies that operated on the assumption that God was a "given."

In his more recent work, however, Kaufman seems to have retreated from this liberalism. The symbols associated with personal theism are now explicitly rejected in favor of symbols of God that point to

> an ultimate tendency or power, which is working itself out in an evolutionary process that has produced not only myriads of living species but also at least one living form able to shape itself and transform itself, through a cumulating history, into spirit, i.e., into a being in some measure self-conscious and free, living in a symbolic or cultural world which it has itself created.[5]

In this new mode Kaufman reads like a less speculative version of Hegel. As in Hegel's work, here, too, there seems to be a teleological conception at work—God is a power "working itself out in the evolutionary process"—albeit a much vaguer teleology than that of Hegel, where the World Spirit was progressively revealed in art, religion, and philosophy.

It is doubtful that this religious baptism of the evolutionary process will have any more religious appeal to the contemporary believer, who may have learned that the evolutionary process seems genuinely random, than the short-lived religious naturalisms in the early part of this century. And for the same reason. There is little in this version of Christianity that justifies the traditional symbols of personal providence (not to mention general providence), incarnation, and the resurrection of the dead. It does not offer the solace of a superhuman helper who loves each individual and to whom each can pray.

---

3. See H. Richard Niebuhr, *Radical Monotheism and Western Culture* (New York: Harper, 1970), 122ff.

4. Kaufman, *An Essay on Theological Method*, 54.

5. Gordon D. Kaufman, *Theology for a Nuclear Age* (Philadelphia: Westminster Press, 1985), 43.

That this should prove to be the case would not have surprised an earlier but more radical constructionist, German philosopher of religion Ludwig Feuerbach. He understood that what human beings most desperately want is to invest the world with "profound human significance," that is, to discern a world that undergirds our deepest moral insights. Human beings wish, above all, to believe in a deity for whom the individual's well-being is its highest anxiety. God is by definition, he argued with Martin Luther, the being concerned with human welfare, a god who frees human beings from the oppression of fate and destiny, sin and evil, and, above all, death. God is the one who not only wants but also has the power to make us blessed.[6] Only such a being can fulfill and satisfy the supreme wish to be known and loved forever. Anything less is no god at all.

Unlike Kaufman, however, Feuerbach thought that just because this wish is so fundamental, we ought to be more suspicious than we are about its validity; we should suspect that the wish itself may be the generating cause of the construction. To use the Freudian category, the theological construction is an illusion.[7] If such be the case, Feuerbach argued, then this wishful drive might be the clue to the pattern and logic of the religious doctrines themselves: that is, the premium put on immortality, prayer, miracle, providence, eschatology, and, above all, the incarnation. Moreover, he asked the disturbing question, Has the human community paid a heavy price for indulging in this wishful construction? Perhaps what we most dearly wish for and believe gives the world its significance costs us dearly in terms of other possible human virtues, such as honesty and courage. He entertained the radical thought that the satisfaction of our deepest wishes for a superhuman helper may also be the source of our alienation from ourselves and others.

Feuerbach's projection theory deserves more attention than it has hitherto received from Protestant theologians, the notable exception being Karl Barth, who properly recognized in him "a thorn in the flesh of modern theology."[8] Feuerbach did not just claim, as others have done, that theism is a projection; rather, his projection theory was the

6. See Ludwig Feuerbach, *The Essence of Faith according to Luther*, trans. and ed. Melvin Cherno (New York: Harper & Row, 1967).

7. Freud was careful to distinguish an illusion from a delusion. Illusions need not necessarily be false. See his *The Future of an Illusion* (Garden City: Doubleday, 1964), 48–49.

8. See Barth's introductory preface in Ludwig Feuerbach, *The Essence of Christianity*, trans. George Eliot (New York: Harper, 1957), xxiv. Cited hereafter in the text as *Christianity*.

basis for a systematic, alternative reading of the Christian symbolic structure, what Paul Ricoeur has taught us to call "a hermeneutics of suspicion."[9] We have here a genuinely critical theory of religion: a theory that claims to cast light on the roots of religion in the human psyche, that explains why important Christian doctrines have assumed their particular forms—the doctrines of the Trinity, creation, incarnation, Logos, and resurrection—and why these are at once so emotionally powerful, but conceptually confused when made the object of direct theological inquiry. The question runs like a silver thread through his work: Why is it that ordinary believers desire a god of miracles and divine intervention, but theologians inevitably are forced to demythologize these doctrines and thus create the perennial contradiction between the god of theology and the god of naive belief? Few interpreters of religion have explored this question or its importance for the interpretation of religion as profoundly as Feuerbach, just as there are few passages in the history of atheistic criticism of Christianity as insightful and telling as the chapter titled "The Contradiction between Faith and Love" in *The Essence of Christianity*.[10]

So far, I have written as if there were but a single Feuerbachian theory of religion as projection; but even though his name has been virtually identified with the infamous book published in 1841, he actually continued to modify his position until his death in 1877. His first book, written in 1828 when he was still an idealist, was a passionate critique of the doctrine of personal immortality,[11] and his last, written thirty years later,[12] was still another attempt to reformulate his projection theory. He once noted that all of his books had but one theme: religion and theology and everything connected with it.[13] He continued to worry religion, much like a child worries a loose tooth. Barth called

9. Paul Ricoeur, *Freud and Philosophy: An Essay on Interpretation*, trans. Denis Savage (New Haven: Yale University Press, 1970), 32ff.

10. Feuerbach, *The Essence of Christianity*, chap. 26.

11. See Ludwig Feuerbach, *Thoughts on Death and Immortality, from the Papers of a Thinker, along with an Appendix of Theological-Satirical Epigrams*, edited by *One of His Friends*, trans. and with intro. and notes by James A. Massey (Berkeley: University of California Press, 1980).

12. See Ludwig Feuerbach, *Theogonie nach den Quellen des klassischen, hebräischen und christlichen Altertums* (Berlin: Akademie-Verlag, 1969).

13. See Ludwig Feuerbach, *Lectures on the Essence of Religion*, trans. Ralph Manheim (New York: Harper & Row, 1967), 5. Hereafter referred to in the text as *Lectures*. I have made my own translations of the German text when it seemed warranted. *Vorlesungen über das Wesen der Religion: Nebst Zusätzen und Anmerkungen* (Berlin: Akademie-Verlag, 1967).

him "an unhappy lover of theology," but his own explanation was that it was important to illumine "the obscure essence of religion" with the torch of reason, because religion was nothing less than the foundation of ethics and politics and subject to manipulation by those who used it for oppression.[14] In short, religion was too important a matter to be left to the theologians.

Scholars have paid relatively little attention to Feuerbach's later formulations of his projection theory. Partly because of the important role *Christianity* played in the overthrow of the Hegelian system, and partly because the model upon which it is based—the inversion of the Hegelian notion of Spirit coming to self-consciousness through its objectified expressions—is so ingenious and worked out with such consistency and rhetorical power, his later theory fell under its shadow. He was, in a sense, a victim of his early and sensational success. This neglect of his later work, however, is to be regretted, because it is, I believe, much less vulnerable to the objections many contemporary philosophers and theologians would make to his *Christianity*: that it is too dependent upon a speculative theory of consciousness, that it rests on an essentialist view of human nature (species being), and, therefore, that it is too oriented to theism. Consequently, I shall reconstruct this later theory, contrast it in important respects with the earlier one, and attempt to show that, although less elegant, it is a more interesting and viable theory. By reformulating it in the way he did, Feuerbach may have distanced himself from his left-wing Hegelian friends, but at the same time he made it possible for contemporary historicists to take him more seriously.

II

When *The Essence of Christianity* first exploded on the German cultural scene, it quite naturally provoked sharp and vehement criticism. From the standpoint of religious studies, in contrast to theology, two of these criticisms are noteworthy. First, critics said that he had ignored the "religions of nature." Reformulated in more contemporary terms, his analysis was too closely tied to Christian theism and had little to say about the many diverse religious traditions. Second, although he claimed to engage in what we would now call a phenomenological analysis of the naive believer's consciousness, he had failed to deal

14. Ibid., 22.

with the most obvious feature of that consciousness: namely, the sense of being in contact with a numinous "other" external to the self.

Both criticisms arise because of Feuerbach's heavy reliance on the Hegelian paradigm of self-consciousness. As long as religion is regarded as the objectification of human nature, one will naturally regard theism as the essence of religion and Christianity as the culmination of its basic religious impulse.[15] Moreover, because the religious projection is the projection of consciousness, it will be difficult to account for any believer's sense of being in touch with an external "other." Religion, then, is essentially cosmic narcissism, an "acoustical feedback" that is involuntarily created in the process of achieving self-consciousness.

These criticisms might have bothered Feuerbach more than they did, had he not already been in the process of criticizing and rejecting Hegel in the months following the publication of his book.[16] In three monographs published between 1842 and 1844 he not only made a complete break with Hegel but programmatically formulated the basis for a "new philosophy."[17] He had three closely related objections to Hegel. First, he believed that Hegel's theory of Spirit was unable to deal with matter. Hegel was only able to incorporate matter into the system at all by making it a "moment" in the development of God. Hegel's deity, like the heroes of paganism, had to struggle to attain divinity. Nevertheless, Hegel had no sooner affirmed the truth of materialism, Feuerbach claimed, than he retracted it by arguing that deity can only fully be realized by the "negation" of the matter that had originally been defined as the negation of God. Because for Hegel the "negation of the negation" is the true affirmation, we are, after this convoluted wheel-spinning, back where we started from, "in the bosom of Christian theology."[18]

15. Feuerbach accepted the Hegelian assumption that the Christian religion is the absolute religion. See *The Essence of Christianity*, 145.

16. As Marx Wartofsky has shown, *The Essence of Christianity* is itself one of the last stages in Feuerbach's self-education and liberation from Hegelianism. Some of the conceptual tensions in the book, however, esp. the 2d ed. can be explained by the fact that even though he rejected fundamental elements in the Hegelian model, he was still dependent on it to some degree. See Wartofsky, *Feuerbach* (Cambridge: Cambridge University Press, 1977).

17. *Vorläufige Thesen zur Reformation der Philosophie; Grundsätze der Philosophie der Zukunft; Das Wesen des Glaubens im Sinne Luthers*, all in Ludwig Feuerbach, *Kleinere Schriften II (1839–1846)* (Berlin: Akademie-Verlag, 1970).

18. Ludwig Feuerbach, *Principles of the Philosophy of the Future*, trans. and with intro. by Manfred H. Vogel (Indianapolis: Bobbs-Merrill, 1966), para. 33.

Second, Hegel's philosophy rests on the identity of thought and being. This principle, which qualifies everything in the system, was for Feuerbach but another way of expressing the divinity of reason—that thought or reason is the absolute being.[19] The difficulty with this divinization of reason, however, is that one cannot then do justice to the particularity and concreteness of existence itself. One can only find essences, ideas, and abstractions to be intelligible and hence real. Third, Hegel ignored the role of what Feuerbach calls "sensuousness" (*Sinnlichkeit*) in our knowledge of ourselves and others. Concrete (other) beings are given to us through sense, feeling, and love, as well as reason. "The new philosophy regards and considers being as it is for us, not only as thinking but as really existing beings. . . . [Being as it is for us] is the being of the senses, perception, feeling, and love."[20]

These objections to Hegel naturally raised questions about Feuerbach's own argument in *Christianity*, because it, too, was based on Hegel's notion of self-consciousness. If Hegel could be criticized for excessive abstractionism, then so could Feuerbach. According to his own later testimony, Feuerbach only fully shook off Hegel's influence in his little book on Luther.[21] In writing it he discovered that all of Luther's explicit affirmations concerning the transcendence of God actually made an implicit appeal to human self-love. Although Luther consciously operated within the theological framework of an independent, absolute "other," he interpreted this "other" as by nature concerned with human welfare. In practice, Luther abolished all distinctions between a "God-in-himself" and a "God-for-us." He defined faith as the certainty that the essence of God is love for humanity.

This argument, together with his new emphasis on matter and *Sinnlichkeit*, led Feuerbach to reformulate the argument advanced in *Christianity*, a reformulation that culminated in a short little book, *Das Wesen der Religion* (1845), which, in turn, became the basis in 1848 for a series of *Lectures on the Essence of Religion*, published in 1851. The former book consists of fifty-five brief sections that vary in length from a sentence or two to a few pages. Despite its brevity and unsystematic

19. Ibid., para. 6.
20. Although his epistemological position is not without its problems, they are compounded if one translates Feuerbach's *Sinnlichkeit* as "sense data," in the modern sense of those words. It is clear from the context that he includes feeling and love in the meaning of the term. See *Principles*, para. 33f.
21. See *Kleinere Schriften III* (1846–1850), ed. Werner Schuffenhauer (Berlin: Akademie-Verlag, 1971), 188–89.

nature, it is a gem. The latter book, by contrast, consists of thirty lectures that seem hastily put together and somewhat repetitious. Nevertheless, the arguments that inform both later books are more powerful than the book with which Feuerbach's name is so often identified and less open to the criticisms that book received.

III

In *The Essence of Christianity* the idea of God was not regarded as a response, however mistaken, to some external reality but rather as the reification of the idea of the species latent in self-consciousness. If, for Hegel, Absolute Spirit objectifies itself in creation and comes to self-consciousness through the appropriation of this "otherness," then for Feuerbach human spirit objectifies itself in the idea of God and achieves full self-conscious freedom by appropriating this projection. Thus Feuerbach could write that religion "is identical with self-consciousness—with the consciousness which man has of his own nature."[22] We might characterize this theory, then, as monopolar.

What we have in *Religion* and the *Lectures*, by contrast, is a more complex, multicausal theory that revolves around two poles: the subjective grounds of religion, on the one hand, and the objective factors, on the other hand. Moreover, the subjective pole is no longer described in Hegelian terms—spirit coming to self-consciousness—but in terms of a subjectivity in the grip of a basic self-love and drive-to-happiness (*Glückseligkeitstrieb*).

The essence of the new theory is articulated in the initial paragraphs of *Religion*:

> The basis [*Grund*] of religion is the feeling of dependency; but the object of this dependency—that upon which human beings are fully dependent—is originally, nothing other than Nature. Nature is the first, original object of religion, as is confirmed by the history of all religions and peoples.[23]

The rest of the book is the development and elaboration of this theme. The basic picture is that human beings first emerge into self-consciousness over against nature, upon which they know them-

22. Feuerbach, *The Essence of Christianity*, 2.
23. Ludwig Feuerbach, "Das Wesen der Religion," in *Kleinere Schriften III*, para. 1. Hereafter referred to in the text as *Religion*.

selves to be completely dependent for their existence and well-being. Not originally distinguishing themselves from nature, they naturally believe that the beings upon which they are dependent are sentient and conscious. The reasons for this belief lie not only in ignorance of the laws of nature but in the nature of feeling itself; human beings instinctively believe that the objects and beings that cause beneficent feelings in them are themselves beneficent, just as human beings instinctively attribute malice to beings and events that cause them hurt and pain. Feuerbach argued, as did Ernst Cassirer much later, that human thought goes through a mythological stage in which the way things impinge on human sensibility naturally finds expression in the attribution of subjectivity to them. We transform natural beings (*Naturewesen*) into feeling beings (*Gemütwesen*).

> In affect—and religion is rooted only in affect and feeling—man projects his being outside of himself. He treats the lifeless as living, the involuntary as voluntary, and he ensouls the object with his own sigh for it is impossible for him to appeal in affect to a feelingless being.[24]

This tendency to personify nature is reinforced by the changeableness of nature itself. It is a natural tendency of the mind to reason analogically that just as human actions are the results of human intention and will, so also are changes in nature. Because certain changes in nature affect human well-being more than others, humans naturally seek to modify these changes in their own favor; hence the universal practice of petition, prayer, and, above all, sacrifice. In sacrifice, Feuerbach argued, we see most clearly the essential nature of religion. In it we see the mixture of anxiety, joy, affirmation, and doubt as to whether the gods will look kindly on human undertakings.[25] In it we see that religion is that activity in which human beings seek to make less mysterious the mysterious (*heimlich*) nature in which they live, move, and have their being.[26]

By emphasizing the encounter with a sensuously perceived nature, Feuerbach accomplished several things. First, he was able to fill a gap (what he called *eine grosse Lücke*) in his earlier theory that his critics had seized upon.[27] He could now deal positively with those religions of nature that he had been criticized for ignoring. Second, by making

24. Ibid., para. 32.
25. Ibid., para. 29.
26. Ibid., para. 34.
27. See Feuerbach, *Lectures*, 19.

nature the enduring ground of religion, he could treat Christianity as just one of many religions, rather than as the final or absolute religion. Indeed, he could argue that Christianity is inferior to the degree that it cannot accommodate nature and sensuousness. Third, he was able to make just those features central to his own system—nature and sensuousness (*Sinnlichkeit*)—that he had accused Hegel of ignoring. Flattering as it must have been for him to have been praised for having cleverly inverted Hegel's theory of Spirit, his old position had been, nevertheless, parasitical on his teacher's. His new position, however, was sufficiently different that it could no longer be regarded as an inversion of Hegel's and hence a footnote to idealism.

In the *Lectures*, Feuerbach considerably expanded and developed the themes so economically articulated in *Religion*. With respect to the subjective pole, for example, he first characterized it in terms of the "feeling of dependence" (*Abhängigkeitsgefühl*). The choice of this category must have been deliberate because it clearly served to emphasize the difference between his own philosophy of religion and that of Hegel, for whom religion was a work of reason. By using it, however, he risked identification with Schleiermacher. Therefore, he took some pains to argue that although he agreed with Schleiermacher about the centrality of feeling in religion, he regarded the theologian's formula to be metaphysical and unempirical. Archaic persons have no general feeling of being dependent on a "universal nature system," as Schleiermacher proposed; rather, archaic persons have concrete religious feelings of wonder, joy, and fear, attached to quite specific objects and beings—to trees, astronomical bodies, and animals. To illustrate this, Feuerbach wrote a quite interesting chapter on animal cults.[28]

As the *Lectures* proceed, it becomes evident that the feeling of dependence fails to describe fully the subjective pole of religion. For this reason Feuerbach introduced the notions of egoism (*Egoismus*) and the drive-to-happiness (*Glückseligkeitstrieb*). The choice of the term "egoism" was not entirely a happy one, especially because he had occasionally employed it in *Christianity* as a derogatory term and contrasted it with altruism. In the *Lectures*, however, egoism is no longer used in a narrow psychological sense but has been expanded into a fundamentally anthropological, even ontological, category. He writes,

28. Ibid., lecture 6.

By egoism I mean the necessary, indispensable egoism—not moral but metaphysical, i.e., grounded in man's essence without his knowledge or will—the egoism without which man cannot live . . . the love that spurs him on to satisfy and develop all the impulses and tendencies without whose satisfaction and development he neither is nor can be a true, complete man.[29]

This egoism will include not only the *Glückseligkeitstrieb* but also love and altruism. It refers to the affirmation of life that is the presupposition underlying the unconscious demand that the gods, too, should affirm life.

So far I have discussed three concepts around which Feuerbach organized his analysis of the subjective pole of religion: the feeling of dependency, egoism, and the *Glückseligkeitstrieb*. None of these concepts, however, really explains how the act of projection takes place, how the concepts involuntarily produce the idea of God. One can feel dependent and possess the rage to live but not necessarily personify nature. In *Christianity* that act of projection occurs in the process of spirit coming to self-consciousness about its essential nature. What is comparable to this in the *Lectures*? What is the causal mechanism producing projection?

Surprisingly, Feuerbach did not get around to dealing with this problem until the end of the Nineteenth Lecture, whereas in *Christianity* it is the first issue discussed. When he does treat it in the *Lectures*, the emphasis falls not on self-differentiation but on the role of the imagination—*Einbildungskraft* or *Phantasie*, two terms that he uses interchangeably. Imagination is the organ or power rooted in the emotions that creates its world in abstraction from the reality principle. Unlimited by reason and moved by impressive natural events, persons, and even abstractions, the imagination seizes upon them and hypostatizes them. "But what is it that transforms a natural phenomenon into a human being?" he asked.

> The imagination. It is the imagination that makes an object appear to us differently from which it really is; it is imagination that bathed nature in the enchanting, dazzling light for which human language has coined the term divinity, godhead, god.[30]

The imagination, then, proves to be "the theoretical cause (*die theoretische Ursache*) or source (*Quelle*) of religion and its object, God."[31]

29. Ibid., 50.
30. Ibid., 177. My translation.
31. Ibid., 178.

Although the concept of the imagination is crucial for Feuerbach's later theory—as, indeed, it was for the earlier—it is not always easy to understand precisely what role it plays in his epistemology and, especially, its relation to *Sinnlichkeit* or sensuousness, perhaps the most problematic notion in his later writings.[32] Nevertheless, without going into the technicalities, I believe the main outlines are clear. The imagination, rooted in desire, feeling, egoism, and the *Glückseligkeitstrieb*, personifies and reifies whatever it seizes upon. To use Freudian terminology, the imagination expresses the infantile sense of the "omnipotence of the wish," the setting aside of the reality principle.

This view of the imagination as an instrument of omnipotent wishing enabled Feuerbach to equate imagination with faith, an equation for which he claimed the authority of Luther, "the greatest German hero of faith." It was Luther, he noted, who wrote that "faith brings into being what is not, and makes possible things that are impossible,"[33] who claimed that faith is not bound by the laws of necessity and therefore believed in miracles—the transformation of Communion into the body and blood of Christ, and, above all, the resurrection from the dead. One can then infer from Luther, Feuerbach proposed, that "this power of faith or God, unhampered by the laws of nature, is precisely the power of the imagination, to which nothing is impossible."[34]

Although by necessity the imagination is not restricted by the reality principle, it nevertheless does not create ex nihilo. It requires raw materials, ranging from sense impressions to abstractions. "At first," Feuerbach argued, "the imagination which makes men's gods worked only with nature," that is, those phenomena of nature—earth, fire, animals, astronomical bodies, and the like—upon which humans felt dependent and that make the most forceful impression upon them.[35] But the imagination also took its fire in some cases from historical personages such as Jesus, from the mind or spirit, or, indeed, from abstractions themselves, such as the notion of "the whole" or "Being as such." For example, Feuerbach explains the difference between polytheism and monotheism as a result of the imagination being fascinated by the multiplicity of beings, on the one hand, and the "coherence,

---

32. As sympathetic an interpreter as Wartofsky argues that the relationships between imagination, conceptualization, and sensuousness (*Sinnlichkeit*) are far from clear. See Wartofsky, *Feuerbach*, chap. 11.

33. Feuerbach, *Lectures*, 179.

34. Ibid.

35. Ibid., 190.

the unity of the world, from a world which man, by his thought and imagination, has shaped into a unified whole," on the other hand.[36]

There are even different ways in which an abstraction, such as the coherence and unity of nature, can provide fuel for the imagination. As a result, there are two forms of monotheism: the metaphysical, which is characteristic of Christianity, and the practical-poetic, which is characteristic of the Old Testament and of the Qur'an. In both the Old Testament and the Qur'an, for example, the activity of God is indistinguishable from the activity of nature. It is indifferent whether one says God or nature provides the food of the earth, makes rain fall from the sky, endows creatures with sight, and brings the living from the dead. The workings of God are the workings of nature. Because nature is omnipresent, God is omnipresent; because nature is all-powerful, God is all-powerful. God is nature made subjective by the imagination, which is to say that the imagination regards the workings of nature as the work of an unconditioned and unlimited being for which nothing is impossible.[37]

The major difference between Christian monotheism and Jewish and Islamic monotheisms is that the latter base their conceptions directly on the perception of nature, whereas the Christian imagination closes its eyes, separates the personified essence of nature entirely from sense perception, and so transforms what was originally nature into an abstract metaphysical being.[38] There is something lively and animated about Yahweh and Allah, whereas the God of the Christians is a "withered, dried-out God in whom all traces of His origin in nature is [sic] effaced."[39] The God of the Muslim or the Jew is the union of imagination with nature; the Christian God is the union of imagination with the abstraction of thought. This metaphysical God is nothing but a compendium of the most universal attributes abstracted from nature and made into a personal subject, of which the most abstract attribute is "Being itself." Being is abstracted from all those beings on which it is predicated and is then transformed by the imagination into a personal subject.

This explanation of the role of the imagination in creating personal theism dovetails with Feuerbach's criticism of Hegelian metaphysics, which he also believed to be the reification of abstract predicates. The

36. Ibid., 192.
37. Ibid., 319f.
38. Ibid., 321.
39. Ibid.

question of God, he wrote in a remarkable passage, is whether universals possess an independent existence of their own.

> Theists take class concepts, or at least the totality of class concepts, which they call God, as the ground and source of real things; they hold not that the universal had its source in individuals, but, on the contrary, that individuals sprang from the universal. . . . And from the standpoint of the thinking that disregards the senses, this seems perfectly natural; for the abstract, the spiritual, the purely cogitated, is closer than the sensuous to the intellect that abstracts concepts from sense perceptions.[40]

To sum up, we have in the *Lectures* a different model of projection than in *Christianity*. The imagination, in the grip of the *Glückseligkeitstrieb*, seizes upon various aspects of and abstractions from nature and personifies them. Nature, not the idea of the species-being, is the real underlying object of religion. The secret of religion is this identity of the subjective and the objective.

IV

If in *The Essence of Christianity* we found a theoretically elegant model for the interpretation of religion—the objectification of the idea of essential human nature that is implicit in the self-differentiation of the I from the Thou—then we find a less elegant, more complex multicausal theory in the *Lectures*. Feuerbach, quite naturally, attempted to minimize the difference between the two theories. The reason he had ignored the religions of nature in his earlier version, he rationalized, was that Christians themselves were concerned with God only as a moral and not as a physical being. Insofar as the deity is regarded as a moral being the earlier theory was correct: God is the objectification of the essence of the mind. Insofar as God is regarded as the cause of nature as well as humankind, however, one must add that the deity is to be explained as personified nature. Whereas he earlier argued that "theology was anthropology," now it is only necessary to add that "theology is anthropology *and physiology*."[41]

Some commentators have accepted at face value Feuerbach's attempt to minimalize the differences between the two theories. F. C. Copleston, for example, has argued that the two versions can be reconciled in this way:

40. Ibid., 124–25.
41. Ibid., 21.

Man, conscious of his dependence on external reality, begins by venerating the forces of Nature and particular natural phenomena. But he does not rise to the concept of personal gods without self-projection. In polytheism the qualities which differentiate man from nature are deified in the form of a multiplicity of anthropomorphic deities, each with his or her peculiar characteristics. In monotheism it is that which unifies men, namely the essence of man as such, which is projected into a transcendent sphere and deified.[42]

There are, to be sure, some passages that seem to support this view,[43] but this attempt to fuse the two theories into one consistent theory fails to account for the quite different way self-differentiation is described in the new theory and how this alters other important aspects of Feuerbach's earlier interpretation of religion. In the *Lectures* he has all but discarded the paradigm of self-consciousness that was the foundation of his earlier theory of projection in favor of a more psychological, one might even say, existentialist projection theory. This indicates a different account of the derivation of the divine attributes and of the classification of religions. (Feuerbach's later theory also involves dropping those two notions so dear to the heart of left- and right-wing Hegelians alike: namely, that religion is necessarily a stage in the evolution of consciousness and that objectification necessarily entails alienation. I shall not, however, pursue these topics here.)

Consider, first, the important differences in how self-differentiation is conceived and described in the two theories. In *Christianity* the religious projection is explained as an unconscious but necessary objectification of the latent idea of an essential human nature or species-being. In the *Lectures*, by contrast, self-differentiation is still the core of religion but is conceived in a quite different manner. Oddly enough, this altered conception receives its most powerful expression in a passage that appears not in the body of the text but in a note to the fifth lecture. In a passage reiterating his idea that the real object of religion is nature, which includes both external and inner nature, Feuerbach writes:

> The ultimate secret of religion is the *relationship* between the *conscious* and the *unconscious*, the *voluntary* and *involuntary in one and the same individual*. Man wills, but often he does so unwillingly. . . . [H]e is conscious

---

42. Frederick Copleston, *A History of Philosophy*, vol. 7, part 2 (Garden City, N.Y.: Doubleday, 1963), 63.
43. E.g., see Feuerbach, *Lectures*, 273ff.

yet achieves consciousness unconsciously. . . . He lives, and yet he is without power over the beginning and end of his life; he is the outcome of a process of development, yet once he exists, it seems to him as though he had come into being through a unique act of creation. . . . [E]very pain is an undeserved punishment; in happy moments he feels that life is a gift. . . .

Man with his ego or consciousness stands at the brink of a bottomless abyss; that abyss is his own unconscious being, which seems alien to him and inspires him with a feeling which expresses itself in words of wonderment such as: What am I? Where have I come from? To what end? And this feeling that I am nothing without a *not*-I which is distinct from me yet intimately related to me, something *other*, which is at the same time my *own* being, is the religious feeling.[44]

This is a remarkable passage and had we not known that it was written in the mid-nineteenth century, we might have easily attributed it to a contemporary. The roots of religion lie in the sense the "I" has—the Heideggerian term *Dasein* does not seem anachronistic here—of being given to itself. Although the I wills, it does so unwillingly; although the I is conscious, it achieves consciousness unconsciously. Pain appears phenomenologically like punishment, happy moments like gifts. Feuerbach, like Nietzsche, even suggested that the inrush of unconscious forces explains why particular disorders, such as epilepsy, states of ecstacy, and madness, "have been looked upon as divine revelations or manifestations."[45] This fusion of the I and the not-I is the foundation of individuality as well as religion. This not-I awakens feelings of wonderment, and the imagination, under the pressure of the rage to live, attempts to reduce the mysteriousness of this other by making "it" into a subject.

The sense of being a part of and dependent upon the not-I (nature) is the religious sense. It is, for example, the source of the "humility with which man recognizes that he did *not* obtain *from himself* what he is and has, that he does not possess life and being but merely holds a lease on them and can therefore be deprived of them at any moment."[46] In contrast, the *Egoismus* that drives the self is the source of the anxiety of finitude. The other not only gives the self to itself but limits it. It can, as it were, slay the self. Therefore, Feuerbach can write

44. Ibid., 311.
45. Ibid.
46. Ibid., 313.

that the religious feeling is the thought of death. "Man's tomb is the sole birthplace of the gods."[47]

Noticeably lacking from this new description of self-differentiation are not only the idealistic language about the infinitude of consciousness but also the concept of an essential human nature implicit in self-consciousness, both of which played important roles in *Christianity*. This absence, in turn, has important implications for the derivation of the attributes of deity. In *Christianity* these attributes are said to be the absolutization and reification of the three essential human "faculties" or perfections: the understanding, the moral will, and the affections. The metaphysical attributes—first cause, necessary being, unity, infinitude, eternality, incorporeality, and the like—are all derived from the objectified "understanding." The moral predicates are the result of the objectivizing of the will, and the attribute of love is a reification of the affections. In the *Lectures*, by contrast, we have a far more complicated attribution of predicates to the deity. Many of the metaphysical attributes earlier derived from the absolutization of the "understanding" are now said to be derived from nature. Furthermore, in at least one passage the attributes of justice and even the goodness of God are declared to be abstractions not from the species-being but from nature. "God's goodness," he writes, "is merely abstracted from those beings and phenomena in nature which are useful, good, and helpful to man, which give him the feeling or consciousness that life, existence, is a good thing, a blessing."[48] Even though Feuerbach still occasionally argues that Christians personify the human mind, he now regards the idea of God as a composite figure and not solipsistically derived from self-consciousness alone.

The quiet elimination of the appeal to an essential human nature is also reflected in Feuerbach's more complex classification of the religions. Although in *Christianity* he did not seriously attempt to classify them, he did claim that Christianity should be regarded as the "absolute religion" because "only in Christ is the last wish of religion realised, the mystery of religious feeling solved."[49] Christianity, in other words, is superior to the religions of nature, as Hegel also had argued.

---

47. Ibid., 33.
48. Ibid., 111.
49. Feuerbach, *The Essence of Christianity*, 145. Feuerbach, like Hegel, assumed that Judaism was an inferior religion. His treatment is somewhat cruder than Hegel's, however. He accuses Judaism of egoism, etc.

In the *Lectures*, however, Feuerbach shockingly proposes that nature religions are superior to Christianity, because they, at least, are sensuously in touch with the earth and nature, whereas Christianity abstracts from nature and makes God a separate, sexless, spiritual being. Christianity puts God and nature in contradiction. One can, he argued, at least sympathize with nature worship and appreciate the sensuous impressions it makes upon the imagination, but Christianity inevitably leads to a morass of contradictions because of its projection of God as a spiritual being apart from nature. In Christianity "we see how God and nature, the love of God and the love of man, are in contradiction, how the activity of God on the one hand and that of man and nature on the other cannot be reconciled except by sophistry. Either God or Nature! There is no third, middle term combining the two."[50]

Apart from the overstatement, unfortunately abundant in Feuerbach's rhetoric, his view that nature is the real object of religion occasionally seduced him into concluding that science must succeed religion; consequently, this view tended to block him from exploring as fully as he should have the implications of the idea that religion arises from the confrontation of the I with the not-I. He occasionally concluded, unfortunately, that because personification serves to make nature less uncanny, its aim must be prediction and control. Hence he argued that any interference with and control of nature necessarily diminishes the role of the gods. Philosophy, poetry, medicine, astronomy, and law, he noted, were once religiously grounded but have since become independent spheres. Religion and civilization, he concluded, are contraries.[51]

This rather crude conclusion does not, however, necessarily follow from his own position, nor is it characteristic of Feuerbach's own deepest insights. As he earlier argued, religion is the response of an embodied self-differentiated being in the grip of desire and confronted by the mysterious not-I that impinges on it. Given to itself, conscious that it is not the cause of its own being, helpless before the forces that impinge on it from within and without, and terrified of death, the self, to use the language of Ernest Becker, engages in a kind of cosmic transference, an attempt to symbolize the Other.[52] No amount of con-

50. Ibid., 161.
51. Ibid., 215.
52. See Ernest Becker, *The Denial of Death* (New York: Free Press, 1973), chap. 7.

trol of external nature, as Freud also came to understand, can diminish the problem of finitude and death. The control of nature may be closely related to this confrontation with the not-I in certain respects, as the history of the relation of magic to religion makes clear, but it is a confusion to equate the control of nature with the sense of absolute dependence, the awareness of contingency, the sense of the gift of the self, and the fear of the extinction of the I.

Furthermore, the substitution of science for religion is not consistent with Feuerbach's own deepest insight that religion arises out of the rage of the I to live, confronted with the implacable and unyielding limit of the not-I. Again and again he noted that just this desire to live forever had generated the need for an omnipotent deity.

> Thus the belief that the world originated in a free, transcendent, supernatural being is closely related to the belief in an eternal, heavenly life. For a Christian's only guarantee that his supernatural desires will be fulfilled lies in his conviction that nature itself is dependent on a supernatural being and owes its existence solely to the arbitrary exercise of this being's will.[53]

This theme—the desire to live forever and the type of narcissistic universe required to sustain that wish—was explored by Feuerbach in his earliest work, *Thoughts on Death and Immortality*, which he had written as an idealist. Nevertheless, if he had there emphasized the comfort in the thought of surrendering one's isolated ego to become a part of an infinite spirit, then in the *Lectures* he emphasized accepting oneself as a part of nature. If at one time Feuerbach argued that the deleterious effects of Christianity consisted in its alienating propensities—the projection of an ideal human nature that could never be realized on earth—then his later criticism is that Christianity abstracts persons completely from nature, that it is so preoccupied with life after death that it must be judged as an expression of a "diseased eros." "It tries to make more of man than he should be, and consequently makes less of him than he could be; it tries to make him into an angel and consequently, given the opportunity, makes him into a true devil."[54] Parts of the *Lectures*, indeed, anticipate some of Nietzsche's criticisms of Christianity: that it treats the body as an illness, that it regards sensuous needs and desires as evil, that it longs for

---

53. *Lectures*, 234.
54. Ibid., 302.

another life rather than this life. Christianity, in short, puts too great a premium on spirit. The virtue of paganism is that at least its desires and wishes do not exceed the sensuous world; its gods are not the unlimited beings who can guarantee immortality. For the pagan the world is still glorious; for Christians, however, it is only a stage to the next life. Consequently, Christians can never really be satisfied with this world; their desires are unearthly, supersensory, and superhuman desires. Their wishes are Promethean wishes: to be perfect and to be free from all the imperfections of life. If in *Christianity* Feuerbach ranked Christianity above the natural religions, because it embodied the spiritual essence of humanity, in the *Lectures* this is just what he deplores. Christianity postulates the immortality of a nonsensuous, disembodied being without sensuous needs.[55] The perfect "species being" of *The Essence of Christianity* is now regarded as a sick and decadent ideal—one of self-mutilation and mortification.[56]

55. Ibid., 257.
56. Ibid.

Contributors

GORDON D. KAUFMAN is the Edward Mallinckrodt, Jr., Professor of Divinity at Harvard Divinity School. He is the author of numerous volumes, including *Theology for a Nuclear Age; The Theological Imagination: Constructing the Concept of God;* and *An Essay on Theological Method.* He is currently completing a volume on theological anthropology, cosmology and the reconception of the doctrines of God and Christ.

LINELL E. CADY is Associate Professor and Chair of the Religious Studies Department at Arizona State University. She is the author of a number of articles and of a recently completed volume on religion, theology, and American public life.

JOHN B. COBB, JR., was for many years the Avery Professor at Claremont Graduate School, Ingraham Professor of Theology at Claremont School of Theology, and Director of the Center for Process Studies. He is the author (with Herman E. Daly) of *For the Common Good: Redirecting the Economy toward Community, the Environment, a Sustainable Future;* and, most recently, *Matters of Life and Death.*

SHEILA GREEVE DAVANEY is Associate Professor of Theology at Iliff School of Theology. She is the author of *Divine Power: A Study of Karl Barth and Charles Hartshorne* and the editor of *Feminism and Process Thought.*

269

WILLIAM DEAN is Professor of Religion at Gustavus Adolphus College and the author of *History Making History: The New Historicism in American Religious Thought* and *American Religious Empiricism.*

FRANCIS SCHÜSSLER FIORENZA is the Charles Chauncy Stillman Professor of Roman Catholic Theological Studies at Harvard Divinity School. He is the author of *Foundational Theology: Jesus and the Church*, and most recently has co-edited *Systematic Theology: Roman Catholic Perspectives.*

JAMES M. GUSTAFSON is Henry R. Luce Professor of Humanities and Comparative Studies at Emory University, and former University Professor of Theological Ethics at the University of Chicago. His most recent works are *Theology and Ethics* and *Ethics from a Theocentric Perspective.*

VAN AUSTIN HARVEY is the George Edwin Burnell Professor of Religious Studies at Stanford University. He is the author of *A Handbook of Theological Terms* and *The Historian and the Believer*. He is currently completing a volume on Feuerbach.

SIMON S. MAIMELA is Professor and Chair of Systematic Theology and Theological Ethics at the University of South Africa. His most recent publications include *Proclaim Freedom to My People* and *Modern Trends in Theology.*

SALLIE McFAGUE is E. Rhodes and Leona B. Carpenter Professor of Theology at Vanderbilt University. She is the author of *Metaphorical Theology: Models of God in Religious Language* and *Models of God: Theology for an Ecological, Nuclear Age.*

WAYNE PROUDFOOT is Professor of Religion at Columbia University. He is the author of *God and the Self: Three Types of Philosophy of Religion* and *Religious Experience.*

GEORGE RUPP is President of Rice University and Professor of Religious Studies. He is former Dean of Harvard Divinity School. He is author of *Beyond Existentialism and Zen: Religion in a Pluralistic World* and *Commitment and Community.*

270

MARK C. TAYLOR is William R. Kenan Professor of Religion at Williams College and Director of the Center for Humanities and Social Sciences. He is author of *Erring: A Postmodern A/Theology; Altarity;* and *Tears.*

M. THOMAS THANGARAJ is Ruth and D. W. Brooks Visiting Professor of World Christianity at Candler School of Theology. He is author of *The Bible in Today's Context; Preaching as Communication;* and *Pudu Peyar Pudu Valyu.*

MAURICE F. WILES is Regius Professor of Divinity at Oxford University. His most recent publications include *Faith and the Mystery of God* and *God's Action in the World.*

Index